Translation and the Rise of Inter-American Literature

UNIVERSITY PRESS OF FLORIDA

Florida A&M University, Tallahassee
Florida Atlantic University, Boca Raton
Florida Gulf Coast University, Ft. Myers
Florida International University, Miami
Florida State University, Tallahassee
New College of Florida, Sarasota
University of Central Florida, Orlando
University of Florida, Gainesville
University of North Florida, Jacksonville
University of South Florida, Tampa
University of West Florida, Pensacola

Translation and the Rise
of Inter-American Literature

Elizabeth Lowe and Earl E. Fitz

Foreword by Ilan Stavans

University Press of Florida
Gainesville/Tallahassee/Tampa/Boca Raton/Pensacola
Orlando/Miami/Jacksonville/Ft. Myers/Sarasota

12 11 10 09 08   6 5 4 3 2

A record of cataloging-in-publication data is available from
the Library of Congress.
ISBN 978-0-8130-3168-2

The University Press of Florida is the scholarly publishing agency
for the State University System of Florida, comprising Florida
A&M University, Florida Atlantic University, Florida Gulf Coast
University, Florida International University, Florida State Univer-
sity, New College of Florida, University of Central Florida, Uni-
versity of Florida, University of North Florida, University of South
Florida, and University of West Florida.

University Press of Florida
15 Northwest 15th Street
Gainesville, FL 32611-2079
www.upf.com

To Gregory Rabassa, to Ezra Fitz,
and to the important work that all translators do

The original is unfaithful to the translation.

Jorge Luis Borges, on Henley's translation of Beckford's *Vathek*, 1943

A book is more than a verbal structure or series of verbal structures; it is the dialogue it establishes with its reader and the intonation it imposes upon his voice and the changing and durable images it leaves in his memory. A book is not an isolated being: it is a relationship, an axis of innumerable relationships.

Jorge Luis Borges, "A Note on (toward) Bernard Shaw," 1951

I found America the friendliest, most forgiving, and most generous nation I had ever visited. We South Americans tend to think of things in terms of convenience, whereas people in the United States approach things ethically. This—amateur Protestant that I am—I admired above all. It even helped me overlook skyscrapers, paper bags, television, plastics, and the unholy jungle of gadgets.

Jorge Luis Borges, autobiographical essay, 1970

Contents

Foreword

Ilan Stavans

In *Don Quixote*, part I, chapter IX, it is stated (in Samuel Putnam's translation):

> I was standing one day in Alcaná, or market place, of Toledo, when a lad came up to sell old notebooks and other papers to a silk weaver who was there. As I am extremely fond of reading everything, even though it be but a scrap of paper in the street, I followed my natural inclination and took one of the books, whereupon I at once perceived that it was written in characters which I recognized as Arabic. I recognized them, but reading them was another thing; and so I began looking around to see if there was any Spanish-speaking Moor near by who would be able to read them for me. It was not very hard to find such an interpreter, nor would it have been even if the tongue in question had been older and a better one. To make a long story short, chance brought a fellow my way; and when I told him what it was I wished and placed the book in his hands, he opened it in the middle and began reading and at once fell to laughing. . . .
>
> I urged him to read me the title, and he proceeded to do so, turning the Arabic into Castilian upon the spot: *History of Don Quixote de la Mancha, Written by Cid Hamete Benengeli, Arabic Historian.* It was all I could do to conceal my satisfaction and, snatching them from the silk weaver, I bought from the lad all the papers and notebooks that he had for a half a real; but if he had known or suspected how very much I wanted them, he might well have had more than six reales for them.
>
> The Moor and I then betook ourselves to the cathedral cloister, where I requested him to translate for me into the Castilian tongue all the books that had to do with Don Quixote, adding nothing and subtracting nothing; and I offered him whatever payment he desired. He was content with two arrobas of raisins and two fanegas of wheat and promised to translate them well and faithfully and with all dispatch. However, in order to facilitate matters, and also because I did not wish to let such a find as this out of my hands, I took the fellow home with me, where in a little more than a month and a half he translated the whole of the work just as you will find it set down here.

Hence, Cervantes's narrative itself is a fake. Unexpectedly, its author isn't the down-and-out soldier and tax collector whose literary misfortunes turned him into an outcast. In fact, the book isn't even fiction. It's history written in a barbaric, second-rate tongue. *Cide*, in Arabic, means señor; *Hamete* is a name; and *Benengeli* is probably an Arabic variation of the Spanish *cervatillo*. In part II, chapter 2, Sancho Panza calls him Cide Hamete Berenjena, eggplant.

The emphasis on replicas, duplicates, and counterfeit traveled across the Atlantic Ocean in the 15th century. To this day it reverberates in the polyglot Americas, where the original is always evasive, a façade, a mask behind which a convoluted identity struggles to define itself. Nothing is what it seems in the continent. Even *One Hundred Years of Solitude*, a response to *Don Quixote* and the other magnum opus of Hispanic letters, wasn't written, as the reader comes to realize at the end, by a Colombian journalist in the vein of William Faulkner. It was drafted in scrolls by an immortal gypsy known as Melquíades.

From the time of the Crusades onward, Hispanic civilization has been built as a Babel-like addition of linguistic layers that include Greek, Latin, Berber, Hebrew, Aramaic, Catalan, Gallego, Castilian, Nahuatl, Mayan, Otomí, Toltec, Quechua, Guaraní, Ivo, Teso, Hausa, and Karamojong. Indeed, every word in the Spanish language is a time capsule, showcasing in its DNA a tumultuous history of incessant invasions, edicts of expulsion, proud missionary urge, fanciful philosophical disquisitions, exercises in miscommunication, secret love affairs, failed military campaigns, and impossible drives toward cultural self-determination.

In its colonial enterprise, Portuguese, too, rebuilt itself as a sequence of forgeries. Elizabeth Lowe and Earl E. Fitz, in *Translation and the Rise of Inter-American Literature*, delve into these intricacies in suitable fashion: from the outside in. What happens, they ask, when a literature defined by ersatz—from Old High German *irsezzan*, replacement—is rendered into yet another imperial language? Their protagonists are the English-language inheritors of Benengeli and Melquíades (Gregory Rabassa, Helen Lane, Margaret Sayers Peden, Edith Grossman, et al.), falsifiers whose task it is to make authentic the inauthentic. Reading their pages, it becomes clear that only through translation, which is nothing but the art of embellished falsification, are the Hispanic and Portuguese Americas best appreciated, as an echoing landscape where imitation becomes truth.

(This foreword is a translation.)

Preface and Acknowledgments

Latin American identity has been formed out of the intimate relationship between agents of cultural change—be they writers or conquistadores—and their translators. Because of the often passionate and conflictive nature of this relationship, the tango seems like an appropriate metaphor to describe the dynamic. Ilan Stavans's essay "Translation and Identity" offers a historical perspective on the pivotal role of translation in the formation of a collective Latin American identity from the early days of the conquest. His thesis is that the "birth of Latin America is also the overshadowing of many aboriginal tongues; in order to enter Western history, the continent has been forced to appropriate a foreign, non-native vehicle of communication."[1] He cites the examples of the Mayan translators Melchorejo and Julianillo, Mayan Indians captured in 1517 and forced to become interpreters for the Spanish. Small acts of mistranslation constituted passive resistance to the Spanish until Melchorejo ultimately fled his captors and was killed when he attempted to rejoin his people—the innocent betrayer, betrayed. Malinche, Cortés's mistress, is held up as a national symbol of betrayal for her role as translator and concubine, an often used metaphor for the translator to this day.

The appearance of the new Latin American literature in translation is due to a combination of events. Some of it had to do with the moment: the writers of the "Boom" all surfaced at the same time. Deborah Cohn, in her report funded by the Rockefeller Archive Center, provides an account of the role of the Rockefeller Foundation in sponsoring the literary and marketing phenomenon of the Boom, and the rise of agents, editors, and translators who formed a close network to ensure the success of this literature ("Tale," 140–64). The Translation Program of the Center for Inter-American Relations in New York and a translation subsidy program administered by the Association of American University Presses were established by Rockefeller philanthropies "to promote cross-cultural understanding and . . . further U.S. foreign policy interests" (141) in the Americas in the context of U.S. concern in the 1960s with the rise of Castro and the Cuban Revolution. Additionally, a few key publishers, agents, professional organizations, and literary journals supported this movement.[2] The translators who were the architects of the phenomenon and often acted as agents for their authors, sometimes without subsidy or guarantee of publication, were led and mentored by Gregory

Rabassa and included Suzanne Jill Levine, Edith Grossman, Barbara Shelby, Helen R. Lane, Margaret Sayers Peden, Alfred Mac Adam, Eliot Weinberger, Jo Anne Engelbert, Ilan Stavans, Asa Zatz, Clifford Landers, and ourselves. Professional organizations grew up around translation, and the American Literary Translators Association (ALTA), founded by Rainer Schulte of the University of Texas at Dallas, became a major player in the advocacy and promotion of the work of literary translators.

In addition to the translators, the cast of champions of Latin American literature in translation from 1960 to 2000 includes publishing magnates Cass Canfield, of Harper and Row, and Alfred A. Knopf. Carmen Balcells, the renowned Barcelona literary agent, and Thomas Colchie, a New York agent who specializes in Brazilian fiction writers, aggressively pursued publishers and insisted on market-price contracts for their authors and translators. Translations of short fiction were commissioned by the editorial staff of *Review*, a publication of the Rockefeller-sponsored Center for Inter-American Relations (now the Americas Society), and a host of literary magazines and journals including *Fiction, Luso-Brazilian Review, Brazil/Brasil, World Literature Today, Translation, Translation Review, New World, City, Hispania*, and the *Literary Review*. The *New York Times Book Review*, the *New Yorker*, the *Times Literary Supplement*, and the *Washington Post* offered occasional reviews of these translations, although the reviewers often lacked sadly in critical skills for the review of translations.[3] Indeed, Rabassa lambastes some of these "critics of translation" using Sara Blackburn's epithet "Professor Horrendo," someone who looks for the wrong things when reviewing a translation and, worse yet, attempts to theorize about it. Rabassa muses, "I guess theory is all right, but the difference is that when I think of theory I think of Einstein's theory that explains something that is already there. Literary theory is often telling you how to do it. The theoretical writing I like is Cortázar's theory of going down stairs. Two translators will do a paragraph very differently. I don't think you can tell why they do it that way. They are two different people. You would have to theorize the whole human race" (interview, 2003).

Since 2000 the rate of publication of Latin American literature in translation has slowed. The 1998 UNESCO World Culture Report states that North America (the U.S. and Canada) published a total of 1,750 translations in 1980 and 1,400 in 1996.[4] According to a 2007 report, only 3 percent of books published in the United States are translations, as compared with 27 percent in Italy.[5] Consequently, the role of publisher-promoter has shifted to smaller presses such as Aliform Publishing, Curbstone, Dalkey Archive Press, and Seven Stories. Some university presses have committed to publishing new Latin American works in translation, although most shy away from literature.

Duke, Florida, Minnesota, Oxford, Texas, and Louisiana have taken on initiatives to bring Latin American literature and scholarship to the United States. Online booksellers such as Amazon.com and Babelguides.com publish reviews and carry out-of-print copies of translations. Literary translation is supported and encouraged by PEN, which offers translation prizes, and by ALTA and the National Endowment for the Arts. The Banff Translation Center offers residencies for translators to work on their projects in the company of other translators. However, the fact remains that there are now only about 200 fiction titles translated into English per year and some 25 of poetry. Eliot Weinberger comments that in the 1960s and 1970s "Latin American poets won an enthusiastic U.S. audience . . . and in the process they influenced U.S. poets. But today very few American poets are translating and very little Latin American poetry is getting published in the United States." Weinberger, a translator of Octavio Paz, attributes the decrease in translations of Latin American literature in the United States to multiculturalism, which he says has led not to internationalism but to a new form of nationalism (see also Rabassa, *Treason*, 44). Instead of promoting foreign writers, the publishing industry promotes "hyphenated" American writers, foreign-born or of foreign parents. "I think publishers feel, 'Oh, well. We have this Latino writer, you know, what do we want a young Mexican or Peruvian writer for?'"

Still, the writers and works discovered by cultural agents like Gregory Rabassa continue to fascinate, intrigue, and seduce. They represent an enigma, a cross-cultural puzzle and wonder. Rabassa describes his first impression of Clarice Lispector at a conference on Brazilian literature in Texas in the early 1960s. "I was flabbergasted to meet that rare person who looked like Marlene Dietrich and wrote like Virginia Woolf" (*Treason*, 70). He comments on the paradox of Lispector, a Russian-Jewish immigrant, writing in Portuguese on subjects that had little to do with the Holocaust or her Jewishness. In spite of the ironies and contradictions of Latin American identity as expressed through its languages, its literatures, and their translations, as long as there are authors and translators seduced by them, the dance will go on. We hope in this volume to illuminate the nature of the dance as it applies to Latin American literature in translation and something of its impact on the inter-American dialogue.

To achieve this end, we approach the issue of translation from two distinct but interconnecting perspectives: the methodological and the textual. By this we mean that the importance of translation to the development of inter-American literature as an emergent new field is best understood as, on the one hand, a problem of comparative analysis, one that involves a vision of translation as both textual interpretation and artistic creativity, and, on the other hand, as a function of the always volatile interplay between reception theory and cultural difference. It is not our intention to deal with translation "theory" per se, but rather with its more practical and aesthetic issues. These issues, moreover, are framed in a very specific context, the rapidly accelerating interaction between North, Central, and South American literature. When American readers pick up *One Hundred Years of Solitude*, for example, they must be aware that the text they are about to read was written not by Gabriel García Márquez but by his English-language translator, Gregory Rabassa, whose efforts on behalf of a host of Brazilian and Spanish American writers have largely made the field of inter-American literature possible. To understand how and why the text known as *One Hundred Years of Solitude* differs from the text known as *Cien años de soledad*, and to comprehend what this means for one's response to it, is to begin to understand the importance of translation and the role of the translator in the dissemination of literature in the Americas.

It is our intention, then, to call attention to the importance translation has had, and continues to have, on the reception of Latin American literature in the United States, where it has made available to English speakers the richness, sophistication, and diversity of writing in Brazil and Spanish America. Although this book will emphasize the role translation has played in the ways Latin American literature is read in the United States, its basic argument also applies to the Canadian situation, which, as we argue, should never be overlooked or minimized when one contemplates the true nature of the inter-American perspective and the centrality of translation to it. Indeed, some of the most sophisticated and innovative thinking currently being done about the nature of translation is by writers and scholars in Québec and Brazil, the two literary cultures most often ignored as the inter-American perspective grows and develops.

As professional translators ourselves, and as longtime advocates and teachers of inter-American literature, we have here chosen to focus both on the innumerable choices that the translator must make at the textual level, where the complex nature of the word-to-word exchange wrought by the translator between two different texts takes place, and on the more conceptual—though egregiously underappreciated—problem of how very different cultures, literary histories, and critical expectations can be brought together for purposes of mutual illumination. To make this argument, we have selected certain texts as being particularly notable or influential in their impact on the North American reading public and its critical establishment. It is our feeling that while the works of some authors—Neruda, Fuentes, Rosa, Cortázar—require close textual analysis to show what the translator has created and why, others such as Lispector, Borges, Machado de Assis, Vallejo, and Fuguet benefit more from a discussion of the reading strategies, interpretational orientations, and cultural prejudices that are inescapably involved in their consumption. Different texts, we feel, call for different exegetical tactics.

The choosing of texts to be discussed in a study like this is always difficult and frustrating. Inevitably, many worthy works of Spanish American and Brazilian literature had to be left out, unfortunate victims of space and focus. Our goal was to select texts that demonstrate in a particularly vivid or exemplary fashion the many decisions that the translator has to make, linguistically, aesthetically, and culturally, in the process of literary re-creation, and that have had some special or significant impact on the reception of Latin American literature in the United States. To accomplish these goals, our process of selection focused on three considerations: (1) translators who participated in the work of the Translation Program at the Center for Inter-American Relations, many mentored by Rabassa, and who played a pioneering role in marketing Latin American literature to publishers and agents in the United States and Canada; (2) translators whose close personal and working relationships with their authors contributed in an usually dynamic and creative way to the accuracy of the translation; and (3) works of Spanish American and Brazilian literature that, in English translation, have achieved international recognition through reviews in influential publications and that, in the process, have became catalysts for the introduction of Latin American literature to audiences around the world. Given these considerations, certain well-known works and authors were not selected. For example, we decided against including discussions of such "blockbuster" authors as Paulo Coelho, Isabel Allende, and Laura Esquivel because we were more concerned with works that have been a "hard sell" with publishers in the United States and whose translations invite artistic creativity on a level with the original. Nor did we elect to engage in commentaries on such "testimonial" writers as Carolina Maria de Jesus and Rigoberta Menchú. Though the value and importance of their work is clear, we felt that it went beyond the scope of the present study, which, again, seeks to focus on the art of translation and the crucial role the translator plays as the agent of cultural exchange between North and South America and in the rise of inter-American literature as a new field.

Overall, then, our concern has been to show how the choices made by the translator ultimately determine how well, or how poorly, a particular text is received by a very different reader from a very different culture and with a very different set of expectations. The revolutionary *Ficciones* of Borges and

Guimarães Rosa's linguistically daunting epic *The Devil to Pay in the Backlands* are two famous, if contrasting, cases in point. The nature of this reception—whether positive or negative—is of course crucial to the development of inter-American literature as a whole, and so the role of the translator must be carefully considered, both at the interpretive and creative level and at the cultural level, where the issue of what it means to claim to know a foreign literature in its original language or in translation comes into play.

The latter issue is central to comparative literature, which, as a discipline that both embraces translation and emphasizes foreign language study as a sine qua non of its basic methodology, counts inter-American literature as one of its fastest-growing new areas of development. The cultural pressures that bear upon the issues of influence and reception in an age of virtually instantaneous electronic communication and border-blurring identities make translation a comparative problem of the most fascinating and fundamental sort. And yet, because of their physical proximity, their historically troubled interactions, and their ever more complex contemporary relationships, the nations of the Americas are aware more than they have ever been that these same patterns of influence and reception, of cultural cross-fertilization, must be confronted and dealt with in new and more honest ways if we in the Americas are ever to understand and appreciate each other's literatures and cultures. It is in this spirit, of improved hemispheric understanding, that our book is written.

Finally, a word must be said about terminology. It is difficult, when writing comparatively about the various literatures of the Americas, to avoid using the terms *America* and *American* to refer both to a single nation and to the hemisphere in its entirety. Although we are fully cognizant of the political complexities involved in this issue, and although we concur with Frederick Philip Grove's statement on this matter,[7] we have nevertheless determined, for reasons of stylistic felicity, to use these terms with reference both to the United States and, alternatively, to the larger New World community. We trust that context will make it clear which meaning is intended.

This is a project that started in the 1970s while we were graduate students at the City University of New York under the tutelage of our mentor Gregory Rabassa. The introduction to Latin American authors and issues of the day that we gained from Professor Rabassa inspired not only our academic careers but also our personal commitment to Latin American letters as translators and observers of the inter-American scene. It seemed to us both appropriate and timely to write this "chronicle" of our experiences as scholars and translators in honor of our mentor. We hope that future generations of scholars, translators, and readers of world literature will find this book useful as they practice and ponder the craft of translation.

We owe special thanks to Gregory's wife, Professor Clementine Rabassa, for her generosity in opening their home to us when we needed to consult with Gregory on this project. We are grateful for access to Gregory Rabassa's personal files and archives and for delightful conversations with both Gregory and Clementine Rabassa about this project and many related topics.

To our spouses we give loving recognition for their support, patience, and good cheer during the course of our labors. Julianne Fitz and Terry McCoy are loyal partners in our domestic and professional endeavors. Ezra Fitz, Earl's oldest son, has followed in his footsteps and carries the baton as a translator of the McOndo generation. For his keen observations and helpful criticism, we thank him. To Elizabeth's colleague Efraín Barradas we express our appreciation for the conversation and encouragement that "seeded" this project. Lourdes Catala was a very helpful and diligent research assistant for this project during her time as a graduate student in Latin American studies and translation studies at the University of Florida. Thanks too to K. David Jackson of Yale University for the opportunity to present our research to the Yale Council of Hispanic and Latin American Studies.

Enduring friendship and uncompetitive collegiality are rare commodities, and we are grateful to have found such special qualities in each other.

An Inter-American Approach to Translation and Its Implications for the Study of Latin American Literature, Reception Theory, and the Development of Comparative Literature as a Discipline

The emergent field of inter-American literature has been able to develop as successfully as it has largely because of the role translation has played in it. We approach the importance of the translator's art to the evolution of inter-American literature both as a function of textual transformation and through the special relationship that translation studies enjoy with the discipline of comparative literature, particularly as to one of its most fundamental concerns, the problem of influence and reception. As a key part of this discussion, we seek to demonstrate why, beginning in the 1960s, the reception of Latin American literature in the United States must be understood through the efforts of a number of skillful translators. Scholars and writers like Gregory Rabassa, James Irby, Edith Grossman, Helen Caldwell, and Margaret Sayers Peden made crucial decisions about which works by which authors from Spanish America and Brazil would be translated. Then they produced English-language versions that would in most cases prove extraordinarily successful, capturing not only the content of the original Spanish and Portuguese texts but their style and tone as well. The invigorating new perspectives that American readers received, then, from Latin America during the tumultuous Boom period, when Latin American writing was finally gaining a beachhead in the United States, were largely a function of what some translators were able to achieve.

As a field, inter-American literature did not really exist before Latin American and Québécois literature began, in the 1960s, to be translated extensively into English. Thanks to the efforts of such gifted translators as Rabassa, Caldwell, Peden, Samuel Putnam, Susanne de Lotbinière-Harwood, and Barbara Godard, the literatures of Spanish America, Brazil, and Québec began to develop readerships outside their original linguistic boundaries. In the process, the works produced by these very different cultures made it evident that the literatures of the New World could profitably be studied not in isolation, as has traditionally been the norm, but as constituting part of an evolving geopolitical whole—the Americas, North, Central, and South—replete with profound political, economic, linguistic, and cultural differences but still linked by a common, if far from identical, historical experience (see Bolton). As we conceive of it today, the rapidly developing field of inter-American literature thus owes its praxis largely to the role translation has played, and continues to play, in its development.

Though too often given short shrift even by professional comparatists, translation—both its theory and its practice—has become more essential than ever to the continuing growth and development of comparative literature as a discipline, where, it must be said, translation has long been regarded as important (see Frenz), though its full cultural significance is rarely studied. As a reaction to this tendency, perhaps, a new field called "translation studies" is coming into its own by integrating a variety of seemingly disparate subjects, including linguistics, history, psychology, politics, and anthropology. In the opinion of Susan Bassnett, one of its leading advocates, translation studies "posits the radical proposition that translation is not a marginal activity but has been and continues to be a major shaping force for change in the history of culture" and that it is "especially significant at moments of great cultural change" (10). Given the importance of translation to its development, the emergence of inter-American literature, which enjoys the endorsement of the International Comparative Literature Association as a new field rich with promise, would seem to affirm Bassnett's argument, especially in the sense that inter-American literature clearly represents a moment of "great cultural change," one in which our orthodox notions of what it means to be "American" are being challenged—most notably in the United States, where the issue is still quite contentious. "Translation," as André Lefevere declares in a comment pregnant with meaning for the entire inter-American project, "is not just a 'window opened on another world,' . . . translation is a channel opened, often not without a certain reluctance, through which foreign influences can penetrate the native culture, challenge it, and even contribute to subverting it" (2).

A crucial ingredient in the growth of inter-American literature, as it is in the development of world literature generally, translation deserves a more prominent position within the methodological apparatus of comparative literature as a discipline (see Damrosch; McClennen, "Comparative"). Although nothing can diminish the importance of being able to read literary texts in their original languages, no one can deny the importance of translation in bridging cultural walls and in rescuing worthy national literatures, authors, and texts from the oblivion that comes from being written in the "wrong" languages. Though never neutral in its operation, translation is the mechanism that allows us to get beyond ourselves and to make contact with literatures and cultures that would otherwise remain forever alien to us. A creative form of "adaptation," in which the "new metaphor" is made to fit the "original metaphor," translation involves the transformation not only of a text but of an aesthetically and culturally distinct consciousness as well (Rabassa, "Snowflakes," 2, 4). As such, translation is of inestimable value to comparative literature, a discipline that by definition takes an international approach to creative writing, the arts, and humanistic study. Within this methodologically traditional context, we will argue in this chapter that inter-American literature—which focuses (in addition to our rich indigenous traditions) on the literatures of Canada, both Anglophone and Francophone, the United States, Spanish America, Brazil, and the Caribbean—has effectively emerged as the twenty-first-century prototype of comparative literature generally. But we will also show that, within the larger context of inter-American literature, the driving forces behind the discipline's current growth and development are coming from Spanish America, Brazil, and Canada, nations that share a long and sometimes troubled history with the United States and that, more recently, are beginning to discover what they themselves have in common as New World cultures. As the tangled issues of globalization inexorably draw us ever nearer, we in the Americas need to know more about each other, and this is precisely the service rendered by the translator, the person most able to overcome cultural prejudices and promote mutual respect and understanding, the person who, as Pushkin felicitously put it long ago, functions as the true courier of the human spirit. The literatures of Brazil, Spanish America, the Caribbean, and Canada are, in effect, powering the growth and development of inter-American literature at the same time that they are reenergizing and revalidating comparative literature as a discipline—one too long defined only, or primarily, in terms of English, French, and German literature (see Fitz, "Comparative Approach"; see also González Echevarría, "Latin American and Comparative Literatures"; McClennen). The European tradition is unquestionably marvelous, but it is not the only such tradition, and, indeed, in practice inter-American literary study deals not only with the sundry ways our New World cultures have related to each other but with the ways they have reacted to both European and African influences and traditions. Happily and not so happily (the conflicts surrounding NAFTA, for example, or issues of immigration), the Americas are more closely bound together today than they have ever been, a development that is manifesting itself in a number of different fields, from law to music and from literature to economics.[1]

Amid the profound social, political, and economic changes that mark the Americas in the early twenty-first century, translation must be understood not only in its traditional context, as an agent of linguistic transformation, but in a larger cultural and historical context, that is, as what many scholars term *cultural translation*, the complex process by which one culture overcomes the prejudices that blind it to another and by which it begins to "see" another culture (and itself) in a truer and more comprehensive light. "When cultures cross and mingle," says Rabassa, "there is a good deal of exchange, especially in language," with words first coming over as exotic importations but eventually finding a home in the receiving language as completely normal terms. As the creative agency charged with facilitating this exchange on a more formal and extensive basis, "The translator must be modest, then, must be careful, cannot impose himself, and, yet, he must be adventurous and original, bound all the while to someone else's thought and words. In this sense translation is a baroque art, one where the structure is foreordained but where the second artist must decorate it according to the lights of his own culture" ("Words," 88, 89). Thus does translation, understood in this larger, more comprehensive context, serve to raise our consciousness of other peoples and their systems of belief and social organization. By adjusting our sense of *mirage*, a term comparatists have long used to refer to the general impression, or impact, one culture makes upon another, translation assumes a political dimension that exceeds, perhaps, even the aesthetic importance it enjoys in its traditional role as a purely literary function. In this sense, it is impossible to exaggerate how important translation has been in transforming the United States, with its huge reading audience and its extensive educational structure, from a culture that was oblivious to, and at times disdainful of, its hemispheric neighbors (except insofar as they represented cheap sources of raw materials and markets to be exploited) into one that is rapidly becoming bilingual, necessarily more attuned to its ever more complex relationships with both Canada and Latin America, cultures whose citizens have long known much more about the United States than Americans have known, or cared, about them. As Robert G. Mead Jr. outlined it in a 1978 *Américas* article, the essential problem throughout the 1960s, and to some extent to the present moment, is the considerable imbalance in how the Americas regard each other, which has made mutual respect difficult if not impossible (2–3, 8). Since North Americans, by all indications, "prefer to think of Spanish Americans as exotic, often charming, generally irresponsible, and never consequential," all too often stereotypes come to dominate, and therefore distort, relations between Latin America and the United States (Brushwood, 14). Working the other side of the equation, John T. Reid, in

Spanish American Images of the United States, 1790–1960, published in 1977, sums up the views, both pro and con, that reflect the ways many Spanish Americans and Brazilians view the United States—this being a perspective of great utility for Americans seeking to know both themselves and how they are seen by others:

> many Latin Americans do like U.S. enterprise, individualism, mass public education, the relative social freedom of their women, their high standard of living, their best writers, and their generally democratic and egalitarian way of life; on the other hand, many Latin Americans do *not* like the predominantly materialistic values of U.S. citizens, their overly technical and overly specialized education, their ethnocentrism and their treatment of ethnic minorities, their exaggerated fear of communism and their support of dictators, their corporate economy and the passive consumerism it generates, their sensationalistic press, the stupefying effect of their mass media, and the breakdown of the family in the United States. (Reid; quote from Mead, 1980, 6)

What is perhaps most striking about Reid's summary is how well Latin Americans know the United States and its culture—a situation that, because it implicitly points up how poorly Americans know Latin America and Canada, also underscores the importance of the entire inter-American project. Speaking from his dual perspective as an American citizen and a highly respected scholar of the Spanish American novel, John Brushwood touches on this same cultural tension, or imbalance, when he writes, of his notoriously self-absorbed compatriots in the United States, "our resistance to foreign literature includes more than Latin America. We are an intensely provincial people, in spite of the lives and money we have scattered around the globe. We resist foreign literature in general, and this basic position is exacerbated with respect to countries that are not financially or militarily powerful" (14). Former *New York Times* columnist Russell Baker made a comment that has since become well known to Latin Americanists: "Americans will do almost anything for Latin America except take it seriously" (qtd. in Mead, "Boom," 2). In a quite literal sense, it is precisely this feeling of American disdain for its fellow New World nations that is the primary obstacle that translators such as Gregory Rabassa have had to overcome. Thanks largely to their efforts, however, the various cultures of the Americas have begun to regard each other in new, less hidebound ways, and it is our hope that this positive trend will lead to even greater levels of mutual respect, trust, and rapport. This is the great promise of inter-American study generally, and it is an eminently worthy undertaking.

Revitalization of North American Letters through the Reception of Latin American Literature in the United States

In its application to inter-American literary study, the issue of "cultural translation" relates directly to the question of reception, specifically why the intelligentsia and reading public of the United States had such a difficult time coming to terms with the literature that was surging forth from Spanish America and Brazil during the 1960s. Widely denigrated at the time in American academia as inferior languages, Spanish and Portuguese were, in contrast to English, French, and German, not regarded as worthy of serious literary scholarship. The prejudice against Spanish and Portuguese was deeply rooted, and those who chose to study them did so knowing that they would not be respected for their efforts, especially if Latin America, closely associated in the minds of many with the rise of Fidel Castro's communist regime in Cuba, was the primary focus. No less a figure than Karl Shapiro could fret about what, for him, was the inescapably pernicious influence of certain "South American Marxists," poets who, by means of what he took to be "garish translations," were polluting the pristine body of U.S. poetry with "large doses of angst, warmed-over surrealism, anti-American hatred, and Latino blood, sweat, and tears" (210).[2] Likely one of the main targets of Shapiro's ire, the 1971 Nobel Prize winner, Pablo Neruda, was forced to wait many years for his prosocialist, pro-Allende, and yet deeply inter-American poetry to be recognized in the United States. Neruda's widely acclaimed poem *Alturas de Macchu Picchu* (1943; tr. Nathaniel Tarn, *The Heights of Macchu Picchu*, 1967), which connects twentieth-century Latin America with its ancient Incan past, took more than two decades to be translated. His masterpiece, *Canto general* (1950; tr. Jack Schmitt, 1991) effectively "Americanizes" Spanish American *vanguardista* poetry but, recalling the best of Whitman, it also ties North, Central, and South America together, though in ways that do not shy away from the divisive historical, political, and economic issues that have long made hemispheric relations difficult. Even the great Borges, to cite an even more revealing example of cultural bias, had to be celebrated first in France for translations done there before his artistry could be accepted in the United States. And more recently, Brazil's Clarice Lispector had to be translated in both Britain and France, and celebrated by Hélène Cixous, before she could be embraced in the United States. Such cultural differences as religion (Protestantism vs. Catholicism), race (miscegenation, biological as well as cultural [Kaup and Rosenthal]), and damaging stereotypes (the Frito Bandito, the Canuck, the wetback) also figure prominently as obstacles to intercultural understanding, as do our misguided ideas about some New

World cultures being inherently "inferior" while others are inevitably "superior." Indeed, the cultural tide did not begin to turn in the United States until the publication in the *Atlantic Monthly* of two very influential essays by John Barth, "The Literature of Exhaustion" (1967) and "The Literature of Replenishment" (1980), praising the Spanish American masters Borges, Cortázar, and García Márquez. But as important as Barth's essays were in opening the door for Latin American literature in the United States, they should be seen in their proper historical context as part of a general discontent with the state of American literature in the late 1950s and 1960s. A bit earlier in 1967, for example, Stephen Koch wrote in the *TriQuarterly Review* that American writing was in need of "another rebirth," and that it was "idling in a period of hiatus," one marked by an "eerie silence" with respect to what he felt was its production of important, imaginative literature. "In the past fifteen years," Koch contended, "writing in English has touched bottom and survived what in my opinion will eventually be regarded as the lowest and most impoverished point in its history since 1870" (5). Silence, in fact, became one of the critical touchstones of the time, as evidenced in much of Beckett's work, in John Cage's 1961 book *Silence*, and then, a few years later, in Susan Sontag's widely read and much debated 1969 essay "The Aesthetics of Silence," in which she suggested that American culture had so exhausted and frustrated itself that a kind of "zero degree" malaise had set in, rendering writers unable to cope with what many people felt to be the outlandish realities of that tumultuous period. "The art of our time," Sontag wrote, "is noisy with appeals for silence. A coquettish, even cheerful nihilism. One recognizes the imperative of silence, but goes on speaking anyway. Discovering that one has nothing to say, one seeks a way to say *that*" (187–88). This disjunction of literature and its sociopolitical context was anathema to most Latin American writers, whose experience with brutally repressive regimes had taught them that the right to speak is an essential one for a healthy society and that it is the obligation of the writer to have something significant to say, to lead a culture toward the kinds of civil freedoms and legal protections that the United States had for so long represented to oppressed people everywhere. For the writers of Brazil and Spanish America, literature could not and would not abdicate its social responsibility. As Mario Vargas Llosa put it, in a 1967 essay titled "Literature Is Fire" that places this essential difference between the cultures of North and South America in sharper perspective,

> it is necessary to remind our societies what awaits them. To warn them that literature is fire, that it signifies non-conformism and rebellion, that the writer's very reason for being is protest, contradiction and

criticism. To explain to them that there are no half-measures, that societies always suppress that human faculty which is artistic creation and eliminate once and for all that social agitator who is the writer, or they admit literature into their midst, and in this case, they have no choice but to accept a perpetual torrent of aggression, irony, satire that will range from the descriptive to the essential, from the temporary to the permanent, from the tip to the base of the social pyramid. (432)

Continuing to examine this glaring difference between the ways North America and Latin America viewed the purpose of literature in their respective societies during the turbulent 1960s, the Peruvian writer, emphasizing the writer's duty to be a social and political activist, also contends that

the American reality offers the writer a virtual orgy of motives for being a rebel and living dissatisfied. Societies where injustice is law, these paradises of ignorance, of exploitation, of blinding inequalities, of poverty, with economic, cultural and moral alienation, our tumultuous countries provide sumptuous material, examples galore to demonstrate in fiction, either directly or indirectly, . . . that life must change. (433)

In a certain sense, then, the Boom literature of Latin America can be said to have rekindled in the writers of the United States a new commitment to their own potency as social commentators and critics and, just as important, to their own validity as intellectuals. In a message that resonated deeply at the time with at least those Americans familiar with Latin American history and politics, Vargas Llosa, along with many other Spanish American and Brazilian writers, was reminding everyone that literature did not have to be frivolous, that it could—and should—claim for itself a serious role in the organization and functioning of its society.

The North American Writer's Task: How to Make the American Experience Credible

North of the Rio Grande, the situation was quite different. As a survey of American critical writing of the late 1950s and early 1960s suggests (see Kazin; Howe; Roth; Bellow; Phillips), before the establishment of Latin American literature in the United States, a great many artists and intellectuals were decrying what seemed to be the rapidly escalating perversion of the American experience, its debased values, its brazen hypocrisy, its crude materialism, and its blatant meretriciousness. To many writers of the time, these stunning developments defied encapsulation in anything but self-indulgent exercises in absurdity, in black humor, and in texts conceived as alienated "antinovels," Joseph Heller's *Catch-22* (1961), Saul Bellow's *Herzog* (1964), Richard Fariña's *Been Down So Long It Looks Like Up to Me* (1966), John Barth's *Giles Goat-Boy* (1966), and Philip Roth's *Portnoy's Complaint* (1969) being a few cases in point.[3] The prevailing view was that while much was being written, very little of significance was being said, and even that seemed to show that the post–World War II grotesqueness of American reality outstripped the ability of language to express it.[4] As Philip Roth put it,

> the American writer in the middle of the 20th century has his hands full in trying to understand, and then describe, and then make *credible* much of the American reality. It stupefies, it sickens, it infuriates, and finally it is even a kind of embarrassment to one's own meager imagination. . . .
>
> The daily newspapers . . . fill one with wonder and awe: it is possible? is it happening? And of course with sickness and despair. The fixes, the scandals, the insanities, the treacheries, the idiocies, the lies, the pieties, the noise. (144–45)

As a defining feature of American culture in the 1960s, observed Benjamin DeMott, there seemed to be a kind of "universal descent into unreality" (quoted in Roth, 145), a situation that would make the embracing of Spanish American "magical realism" by American writers that much easier. The time was ripe for change. In 1965 "The Sound of Silence" was a chart-topping song by Simon and Garfunkel, and the silence was deafening in the United States, a culture suffering from both the "exhaustion" that Barth and Sontag identified and a profound sense of estrangement and anomie. By the mid-to-late 1960s, the United States was a culture waiting, in Koch's view, to be reborn, to rediscover its highest and greatest principles. Latin American literature, and especially the *engagé* poetry and narrative being advocated by Vargas Llosa and others—a heady brew of progressive politics and avant-garde art, the very thing decried by Shapiro—would become the catalyst for this re-generation, a development that would alter the nature and form of American literature and that would awaken it to the possibilities inherent in itself (its rapidly growing Hispanic identity, for example; see Ramos) and in its new relationships with its hemispheric neighbors, north and south.

With the wildly enthusiastic reception in 1970 of *One Hundred Years of Solitude*, Gregory Rabassa's translation of García Márquez's 1967 novel *Cien años de soledad*, two things, both quite apparent even then to Latin Americanists if not to Americans, began to happen simultaneously: first, what was rather carelessly being called "Latin American" literature was quickly discovered by American writers seeking a means to this rebirth, and, second, it was almost immediately subjected to a serious misinterpretation by its enthralled new readers, one that would skew their ability to fully appreciate the richness and diversity of Latin American literature for years to come and one that only now, with the advent of inter-American literature as a distinct discipline, is being ameliorated. The dramatic entrance of the Boom writers on the world stage was greatly aided by their cosmopolitanism and their accessibility to the media, and they very quickly gained a following not only in North America but in the international community generally. For Johnny Payne, the surprisingly warm reception given in the 1960s to writers like Borges, Carlos Fuentes, Mario Vargas Llosa, Julio Cortázar, and of course Márquez in the United States, a powerful nation whose leaders were piqued by the unexpected success of the Cuban Revolution in 1959, was "not the product of simple cultural dilettantism on the part of U.S. readers but rather the result of a complicated attempt to appropriate Latin American fiction as a 'solution' to a particular crisis of confidence in contemporary U.S. society and its fiction" (4). In retrospect, Payne seems to have been correct in asserting that, for perhaps the first time in inter-American literary relations, the United States was influenced by a movement (the *nueva novela hispanoamericana* or "new novel of Spanish America"; see Fuentes) that was gathering force in Spanish America: the critical myths that sprang up in both the popular and scholarly press emphasized the tropicality of Latin American fiction and met U.S. writers' and critics' need to project their own sociocultural anxieties about the impending dissolution of U.S. literature onto another literary tradition. This emphasis ultimately resulted in erroneous rumors of the "death" of Latin American literature (Payne, 8). Noting the special role that Borges was already playing in this process of literary resuscitation, John Updike wondered, in the October 30, 1965, *New Yorker*, whether the Argentine writer's elegant and worldly "fictions" might, in fact, be pointing to a "way out of the dead-end narcissism and downright trashiness of present American fiction" (qtd. by Rostagno, 117; see also Rostagno, 119).

Although there is no doubt that the appearance of texts from Spanish America and Brazil did begin to showcase a new and hitherto ignored culture flourishing close by the United States, it is also true that American readers almost immediately began to characterize what they insisted on referring to, generically, as "Latin American" literature strictly in terms of the exotic, antirealistic yet studiously literary new style they were getting from the Boom writers. To avoid confusion and imprecision, we recommend that the term *Latin American* be used only when the literatures and cultures of both Spanish America and Brazil are being discussed. The phenomenon known in the United States as the Boom was almost entirely a function of Spanish America only. Very few novels from Brazil were involved, and those that were—by Lispector, Amado, and Machado de Assis, for example—were products of a very different literary tradition and had little to do with the kind of writing that was coming out of Spanish America, especially Borges and, somewhat later, the works of García Márquez, whose wonderfully humane and subversively comic novel *One Hundred Years of Solitude* became de rigueur reading for students on college campuses across the nation.[5]

The (Mis)Reading of Magical Realism

What we can now see as a classic problem of influence and reception, this ardent response to Borges and Márquez was both encouraging and dismaying for Latin American writers and scholars, who were only too aware that their literature involved much more than "magical realism," a notoriously imprecise critical term that has led astray as many readers as it has helped. From the perspective of writers and scholars of Spanish American and Brazilian literature, this reception of their literature in the United States was woefully misguided, the conclusion of an audience who knew very little about Latin American literature, history, or culture, and who thus read the Boom novels, naively, as texts that not only represented but defined Latin American letters and in ways that distorted the more complex nature of Brazilian and Spanish American literature. The idea that Latin American literature is somehow defined by magical realism has gained such enduring currency in the United States that it is still being cited as the standard against which all other "Latin American" texts must be judged. It has been at this unexpected encounter of two very different cultures that the inadvertent misinterpretation occurs. As Payne, noting the importance that translation played in the entire process, writes of this historic turn of events:

> It is in this context that the boom of Latin American fiction in English translation, which began in the sixties, and the specific form of reception—and often distortion—it has taken in the minds of U.S. writers and readers can be understood. An equally self-conscious and experimental but more vigorous, fertile, and "organic" Latin American fiction rushed, by most accounts, into the sterile vacuum of impoverished American writing. An infusion of the tropic staved off the entropic. (15)

While it was exciting to see their literature begin to break out of the "solitude" that had long plagued it, no serious student of Spanish American and Brazilian literature would ever fail to see—as American readers, dazzled by the technical virtuosities of a kind of complex writing that was being touted, and oversimplified, as "magical realism" tended to do—the historical, cultural, and political implications of novels like Cortázar's *Rayuela* (1963; tr. Gregory Rabassa, *Hopscotch*, 1966), Fuentes's *La muerte de Artemio Cruz* (1962; tr. Alfred Mac Adam, *The Death of Artemio Cruz*, 1964), Miguel Ángel Asturias's *Mulata de tal* (1963; tr. Gregory Rabassa, *Mulata*, 1967), or *One Hundred Years of Solitude*. As early as 1969, Emir Rodríguez Monegal—an influential figure who, as an expert in both Spanish American and Brazilian literature and as a Latin American intellectual thoroughly familiar with the United States, was instrumental in bringing the two cultures together—pointed out that this problem with how Latin American writers and texts were then being (mis)read in the United States could be solved only by a greater awareness of Latin American literature and culture on the part of Americans. And while it was evident to just a few scholars at the time, a major aspect of this heightened awareness had to be a realization that Latin America was "American" too, that its writers and thinkers spoke to the larger questions of hemispheric identity with as much validity as did commentators from North America, perhaps more so. Since Latin Americans have, historically, had to know much more about the United States than Americans have ever felt obliged to know about Latin America, it is not difficult to see how the people of Brazil and Spanish America could argue quite convincingly that their contributions to what was for them an already ongoing inter-American dialogue—one dominated, historically, by the United States—were actually more revealing of the various truths about "American" identity than those coming from the United States, a culture increasingly trapped, ironically, by its own power and cultural arrogance. As the Mexican poet and intellectual Octavio Paz writes, Latin American literature "is the response of the real reality of Americans to the utopian reality of America" ("Foundations," 4). It was obvious even in the late 1960s, to those writers and artists who wanted to see it, that a release from this entrapment and a return to its highest, noblest principles was precisely what the then nascent inter-American perspective offered the United States, its politics and culture as well as its literature. In the view of Monegal, who from his post at Yale was keenly cognizant of the tremendous change in literary relations between North and South America that was then beginning to take place, the new Latin American fiction of the late 1960s had already transformed itself, gaining strength and vitality as the hybrid product of many different international influences while also renewing a "vision of America and of a concept of what the American language is" as well as a clear awareness that language was "the ultimate 'reality' of the novel" form ("Novelists," 16, 28). Ironically, then, while the Boom novels were wildly successful in awakening American readers to a very different and exciting kind of literature—one, moreover, that was being written right on their doorstep—it is also clear now that these same experimental texts ended up distorting and, eventually, stereotyping Latin American literature in ways that would, in the long run, actually inhibit American readers interested in trying to see Latin American literature and culture as they really were. The American reception of Latin American literature in the late 1960s and early 1970s was thus both positive and negative in its effects and in its implications for improved literary and cultural relations between North and South America, a process of discovery and validation in which translation was playing a vital role.

Translation as Interpretation and Creation

Discussing translation as an act of both "interpretation and creation," Suzanne Jill Levine, herself an accomplished translator of modern Spanish American fiction, also reminds us that it "is an act of choosing where the emphases lie, which meaning is most urgent" (*Scribe*, xiv, 159), a point likewise stressed by Gregory Rabassa as an essential part of the translator's task (see Rabassa, "Snowflakes," 5–7). Then, emphasizing translation's importance in this fledgling process of North-South cultural exchange and understanding, Levine further insists:

> North American readers need to hear the voices of that "other" America alienated from the United States by a torturous political history. But these readers also need to understand *how* Latin American writing is transmitted to them, and *how* differences and similarities between cultures and languages affect *what* is finally transmitted. Knowing the other and how we receive or hear the other is a fundamental step toward knowing ourselves. (*Scribe*, xiv–xv)

Also confronting this crucial and deeply rooted question of why interhemispheric relations were so strained and wracked by bitterness, the writer William Gass, referring to the positive but misunderstood nature of the Boom and its reception in the United States, frames the issue a bit more tartly, and in a way that accurately sums up the rancorous social, political, and economic history that continues to mar the inter-American experience:

And if these South American nations had not been previously despised by a North American commercial culture which had continuously exploited them; and if they weren't so carelessly differentiated and indiscriminately lumped (Brazilians and Bolivians are simply Latins, Central America is the same as South; in fact, in the mind of most Americans, Mexico falls like a full skirt all the way to Patagonia); if they hadn't been thought to be Spaniards gone native, mostly asleep beneath their sombreros, and of slowly mixing blood, although when awake also of mean bandito intentions; then where would the boom have come from—this boom as if from one gun? . . . booms reverberate only from unexpected places, suddenly and sonically, as if from empty air. Nothing was there before, and then BOOM!

. . .

It is because we have not been paying proper attention that everything seems to be going off at once. ("Boom," 34–35)

Gass's words are ironic here, for he understood perfectly well that Latin American literature had a very rich past, though this fact was not known by the vast majority of American readers and critics, who mistakenly thought that the "boom" was somehow the "birth" of Latin American letters. This misperception accounts for a large measure of the frustration felt by Latin American writers and scholars as they watched the readers of the Boom simultaneously praise and misconstrue their texts, authors, and literary history.

The Role of the Reader

In addition to the revivifying effect that, as we have seen, can be attributed to the ecstatic (if slightly skewed) reception of Latin American literature and culture in the United States of the late 1960s, it is also worth considering another, less obvious issue, the impact of American reader-response criticism and most especially the influence of Stanley Fish, whose work was, to a large extent, shaping the debate. Openly opposed to the methods employed by the New Critics, Fish is closely identified with a kind of critical thinking that emphasizes the role of the reader, an issue that, interestingly enough, had characterized Brazilian narrative since the nineteenth century—and nowhere more vividly than in the novels and short stories of Machado de Assis, a writer who, as we have seen, was first translated into English as a novelist in 1952.[7] The development of a new and much more critically engaged reader would, some fifty years later, also rank as one of Borges's most significant contributions as well, one whose participation in the game of fiction would play directly into his vision of what a new, "fantastic" narrative might be like. Over time, Fish would refine his theory in terms of what the process of reading meant to our sense of what literature really was and how its significance would be established and evaluated—a development that had the potential to inspire groundbreaking comparative studies involving any number of Spanish American, Brazilian, and American texts. Eventually, Fish would be led to the conclusion that the role of the reader who is actively involved in the creation of meaning actually redefines not only the nature of literature but of meaning itself, with the latter term coming to be understood as a function of the sundry and evolving ways the reader "consumes" the text. To Latin Americanists familiar with both the Machado de Assis of 1880 and the Borges of the 1930s, this view of reading was not startling news, though its relevance to the reception of Brazilian and Spanish American literature in the United States would quickly reveal itself to be considerably more problematic. Although in his early work Fish tended to place literary texts at the center of his exegetical strategies as carefully wrought structures that would determine the nature of the reader's response, he later assumed a more radical position, one that effectively displaced texts from their privileged position as authoritative organizers and controllers of meaning and regarded them as little more than a particular set of readerly conventions, the expectations of any given "interpretive community," a vague conglomeration whose views, standards, and values would inevitably dictate the interpretive strategies of every reader in it. American reader-response criticism, quickly seen by a variety of interested scholars as necessarily engaging questions of phenomenology, hermeneutics, structuralism, and eventually poststructuralism, also led to the invention of a plethora of different kinds of readers—implied readers, ideal readers, actual readers, super readers, and, for the later Fish, "informed readers." Fish's reader-response criticism also led to a new interest in texts that generated the terms of their own understanding, texts that Fish would eventually describe as "self-consuming" and that could be seen, superficially at least, as having a lot in common with many of the Spanish American "new novels."

The peak years of the reader-response school's influence in the United States are usually thought to fall between the late 1960s, when the Boom began to gain real prominence, and the early 1980s, when it had all but withered away. Three major works by Fish effectively bracket this same period: *Surprised by Sin: The Reader in "Paradise Lost"* (1967), "Literature in the Reader: Affective Stylistics" (1970), and *Self-Consuming Artifacts: The Experience of Seventeenth-Century Literature* (1972). It is interesting, in this respect, to consider the possibility that the growth of reader-response criticism in the

United States of the late 1960s and early 1970s had, on balance, an adverse effect on the ways Latin American literature was being received, on the critical terms under which it was being read and under which its "meaning" was being adduced—by a culture not only alien to it but largely antipathetic as well. Because, for the Fish-oriented reader-response critics, meaning had become a function not of the text itself but of the reader's experience of it, the reader's consciousness began to emerge as the most important factor in the process of reading. While this might be expected to work reasonably well for readers and authors coming out of the same cultural milieu, it seems much less viable as an interpretive strategy when authors and readers come from radically different cultures, different language systems, and different historical contexts. One of the problems of early reader-response criticism, clearly, was that such volatile factors as race, age, gender, sexual preference, and class were not sufficiently taken into account. As reader-response criticism began to erode the objectivity and supremacy of the text and to situate the determination of its meaning in the application of the knowledge that each reader possessed, it became obvious that the quality of the reader's historical awareness would also be a decisive issue, one with serious implications for the reception of Latin American literature in the United States, a culture whose "consciousness" of Latin America could hardly be described as "informed," as Fish's theory required. More to the point, one has to question how accurately the Spanish American and Brazilian authors of a politically engaged "literature of fire" were being interpreted by readers from a culture pervaded by ennui, as Barth, Sontag, Koch, and others described the United States of the late 1960s. If—by means of a handful of discrete texts read in translation—the American "experience" of Latin American literature in the 1960s turned on the linguistic, historical, and cultural competency of the individual American reader, and of that reader's typically middle class "interpretive community," then one can easily understand why most American readers would have missed a great deal of the Latin American novels, poems, and dramas to which they were being introduced. Perhaps a different critical environment, one stressing the *ostranenie*, or defamiliarization, of Russian Formalism as well as an honest consideration of divergent ideological perspectives and a judiciously comparative application of the semiological conventions (to use Jonathan Culler's term) that define the Western tradition, would have proven more productive in terms of the generally positive though too often confused reception that Latin American literature was being afforded in the academic and public press. Even as reader-response criticism "re-politicized" the American literary scene (by demonstrating that one's interpretation of a text depends on one's social, political, and economic status, a development that, unfortunately, did not lead to a reconsideration of literary relations with Brazil and Spanish America), the insularity of American culture effectively blinded even progressive, democratically minded readers to the seriousness and originality of Latin American literature and to the commentary on the larger, inter-American experience that it offers. Given the degree to which the receiving culture was virtually oblivious of the influencing one, how accurate could American interpretations of the Boom writers have been? Could reader-response criticism actually have impeded the American "interpretive community" in its efforts to understand Latin American literature? Although Fish's reception theory easily accommodated open, ironically self-conscious texts like *Hopscotch* or *One Hundred Years of Solitude*—novels that, on one level, clearly, if subversively, lay out for the reader the terms of their own consumption—his ideas would not have done much for the American reader who might have been interested in the social, political, or historical aspects of these same texts. In reviewing the discussions of early reader-response criticism, one concludes that it encouraged a basically ahistorical approach, an interpretive line that would have been very misleading for American readers of most Spanish American and Brazilian literature of the period, since this literature was all but inseparable from its social, political, and historical contexts.[8] In large measure, the theory being promulgated by Fish seems inimical to the ways Latin American writers, readers, and scholars viewed the same issues. Even Borges's *Ficciones* (1944; ed. Anthony Kerrigan, tr. Anthony Bonner 1962), the fictional embodiments of structuralist theory—and perhaps for that reason so celebrated in French intellectual circles of the late 1950s— evinced a very definite political and social context, a fact routinely discussed in classes on Spanish American literature but ignored outside of them. An American adept of early reader-response theory, for example, would have almost certainly missed the profound political dimensions of such seemingly whimsical exemplars of "magical realism" as *One Hundred Years of Solitude*, a text that is still not infrequently dismissed as fluff, as an entertaining read but not "serious" literature.

As Latin Americans have long understood, however, this landmark novel demands to be read as an interlocking parable about Colombia's tragic political history—in particular the *violencia* that has long plagued it—and about Latin and inter-American political and economic history generally, and as a poignant commentary on how the Latin American experience, encapsulated in the mythical town of Macondo (reminiscent of Faulkner's Yoknapatawpha County), serves as a metaphor for the larger human experience, seen to be devastated by its penchant for solitude and isolation, vitiated by selfishness and violence, and tormented by the failure of love. Given the ignorance of its hemispheric neighbors that isolates the United States, or that did so in the late 1960s, it seems highly unlikely that even the most "informed reader" of Fish's American "interpretive community" would have seen a novel like *One Hundred Years of Solitude* in anything near its full historical and cultural significance. With the exception of certain writers, like John Updike, William Styron, William Gass, and John Barth (all of whom saw in the Latin American literature that was being translated in the 1960s exciting new possibilities and creative modes), and of scholars and students who, as specialists in Spanish and Portuguese, were well aware of Latin American literature's excellence, how could mainstream American "interpretive communities," handicapped by their chronic dismissal of Latin America, have possibly "experienced" the politically and aesthetically challenging works of Neruda, Fuentes, Asturias, Machado de Assis, Vallejo, or Lispector except in a historical vacuum, and thus at the most superficial level, as amusing but ultimately inconsequential examples of "exotic" literatures and cultures that seemed to flout conventional Anglo-American norms and standards? The more intriguing question, in fact, is what would such truly "informed readers" as Borges, Fuentes, Donoso, and Lispector, and their various Brazilian and Spanish American "interpretive communities," have been saying about the influence, both real and potential, that their texts were exerting—and (thinking, especially, of García Márquez and his famous July 3, 1984, pronouncement in the *Village Voice* about the eventual "hispanization" of the United States) that they would exert—on American literature, culture, and intellectual life? It seems much more likely that Fish's theories, with their heavy emphasis on the reader's reaction to the text, would have led the uninformed American reader away from seeing these larger social and political ramifications, making them seem, in the process, nothing more than stylistic frills, the fulfillment of preexisting *yanqui* stereotypes about the instability of Latin American politics, about Latin American poverty and backwardness, about strutting machismo, about gringo efficiency and business acumen, and about seductive, sexually precocious Latinas.

Something similar, we suspect, can be said about many of the other politically charged Latin American novels and poems that were being introduced into and misconstrued by the American cultural consciousness during the Boom period. Jorge Amado's very popular *Gabriela, cravo e canela* (1958; tr. James L. Taylor and William L. Grossman, *Gabriela, Clove and Cinnamon*, 1962) can easily be considered a slightly earlier example of a text that suffered a similar fate, its political and, indeed, inter-American implications being for the most part missed in favor of dehistoricizing readings that focused almost entirely on more superficial issues, especially the unabashed sexuality of the novel's *mulata* protagonist. In terms of understanding the debate that raged within the American academy over Fish's theories, it is important to remember that reader-response criticism, along with its ana- logue, reception theory, sought, ostensibly at least, to divorce itself from formalism and formalistic analysis—which, given the sophistication of many of these Latin American texts, might well have rewarded the kinds of careful scrutiny associated with formalism—and to concentrate instead on the mo- ment-to-moment process of reading itself and on the consciousness of the reader.[9] But in terms of the impact Anglo-American reader-response criti- cism had on the reception of Latin American literature in the United States of the late 1960s, it is also possible that this mode of thought, uninterested as it was in questions of politics, history, sociology, or economics, contributed to a serious misunderstanding of a great many complex works coming from some very different Latin American cultures. From Argentina to Mexico and from Guatemala to Brazil, there was an explosion (thanks to the efforts of translators like Gregory Rabassa who acted as cultural agents) of subtle, sophisticated literary texts that required, for their full appreciation, a high level of historical and political awareness on the part of their readers, some- thing Americans tended not to possess.[10] Although texts were being read, the cultures that produced them were not, and for American readers of the wonderful if sometimes seemingly bizarre Spanish American and Brazilian literature that they were devouring so enthusiastically at the time, this failure would produce if not a wholesale disconnect then at least a disruption in the very inter-American dialogue these same texts and readers were in the process of establishing.

Translation and the Establishment of Inter-American Literature as a Field of Comparative Literary Study

Mindful of this experience, it is our belief that "cultural translation," aided and abetted by textual translations and understood in the context of a new and more comprehensive sense of reception theory, can succeed in helping us all to confront our biases and learn to see not only the very real differ- ences that separate us but the similarities that bind us together. Whether performed textually or understood in terms of culture, translation lies at the heart of the entire endeavor. Providing a new context for the study of American literary relations and American literary history, translation has made inter-American literary study possible as a field. But in doing so, it has also rejuvenated comparative literature as a discipline by reminding us all of its singular ability to cross borders, to overcome prejudices, and to promote better cultural understanding. Indeed, as Daniel Balderston and Marcy Schwartz observe, "Translation has become both a mechanism and a metaphor for contemporary transnational cultures in the Americas," an underappreciated art form that is nevertheless "integral not only to the distribution and circulation of printed literature but more fundamentally to the constitution of contemporary culture itself in the Americas" (1, 9).

But if translation is least appreciated and understood in the United States, where translations of foreign works typically do not sell well and where foreign cultures are often viewed with a jaundiced eye, in our larger vision of the Americas it is unquestionably best understood and appreciated in Canada and in Latin America, two cultural regions that have long embraced the theoretical dynamism and the international perspective demanded by comparative literature, including the growing role translation plays in it.

In Portuguese-speaking Brazil, a huge and culturally diverse nation whose population equals that of all the nations of Spanish-speaking America combined, both the theory and the practice of translation have been dominated, in recent years, by Haroldo de Campos, a poet and intellectual closely associated with the growth and development of Brazil's very influential Concretist movement. "De Campos's approach," observe Balderston and Schwartz, "has influenced many scholars of translation in Brazil, especially at the University of Minas Gerais and at the Pontifícia Universidade Católica de São Paulo, largely devoted to explicating his ideas" (4). Along with his brother, Augusto, and others, de Campos has developed an approach to translation that replaces its traditional passive role with a more proactive one—one that, in ways that parallel the synthesizing aesthetic behind Brazil's Anthropophagy movement of the 1920s, is not averse to reconfiguring the relationship between the source text and the translation in the process of re-creating the former's tones, verbal plays, and levels of meaning. This position has much in common with that taken by Levine, who contends: "Far from the traditional view of translators as servile, nameless scribes, the literary translator can be considered a subversive scribe. Something is destroyed—the form of the original—but meaning is reproduced through another form. A translation in this light becomes a continuation of the original, which already always alters the reality it intends to re-create" (*Scribe*, 7–8).

Something similar, though more often inscribed in terms that are feminist and openly sexual, has evolved in Canada in the final decades of the twentieth century. As Bassnett explains, focusing on the importance that Brazilian and Canadian theoreticians have placed on translation studies:

The new work in Brazilian translation studies is characterized by a series of physical metaphors, often violent ones, that stand out in sharp contrast to the gentler metaphors describing translation as a servile activity. Similarly, developments in the field in Canada from the mid-1980s onwards have also stressed the physical, though primarily in terms of redefined sexual relations, perceived from a feminist perspective.

. . . Feminist translation theory . . . reconstructs the space in which the translation takes place as bi-sexual, belonging neither to one nor to the other.

Some of the most exciting work . . . has centred around lesbian or bisexual theorists and translators. The group . . . around Nicole Brossard, for example, reject both writer-oriented criticism and the newer reader-oriented criticism, arguing that neither writer nor reader should be prioritized. (155–56)

Pressing on with her comparison of the Brazilian and Canadian translation schools, Bassnett also points out:

The Brazilian and Canadian groups of translation theorists have in common the aim of celebrating the role of the translator, of making the translator visible in an act of transgression that seeks to reconstruct the old patriarchal/European hierarchies. Translation seen in their terms is indeed a political activity, and one of the utmost importance. Haraldo [sic] and Augusto de Campos use translation as a way of affirming their right as Brazilians to reread and repossess canonical European literature, while the Canadian women see translation as fundamental to their existence as bilinguals and as feminists struggling against phallo/logocentric values. Both groups are concerned to find a translation practice and terminology that will convey the rupture with the dominance of the European heritage even as it is transmitted. (157)

One should not conclude from this, however, that inter-American literature in any way rejects either its European origins or its close relationships with Africa. While it is true that, as a field, inter-American literature seeks to emphasize North-South literary relations and comparisons, and to promote the writers and literatures of the Americas, it does not advocate any kind of rupture with Europe and Africa, many of whose nations still maintain close ties with their New World kin. To do so would be fatuous in the extreme and would serve only to cripple our ability to understand many of our finest poems, novels, and plays, nearly all of which feature extra-American aspects. At the same time, the point being argued here by Bassnett—that in both Canada and Brazil scholars are seeing in translation a mechanism for effecting a particularly acute form of self-affirmation and identity—helps underscore the validity of the entire inter-American project, which seeks to integrate the literatures and cultures of the Americas, but without homogenizing them and without eliding or minimizing the very real differences that separate them. Indeed, for the study of inter-American literature, as for comparative literature generally, the most vital aspects of the proposition reside with the differences, not the similarities, for it is in differences that we can see what is unique about each American culture and text we are considering. And, as Rabassa notes, these important cultural differences may well "lie unnoticed until someone sets out to translate a book," at which time not only the language but the language's cultural moorings must be properly brought over ("Words," 89). Further emphasizing the symbiotic relationship between language and culture, Rabassa also reminds us: "The fact that language is culture and culture is language is brought out most sharply when one tries to replace his language with another. A person can change his country, his citizenship, his religion, his politics, his philosophy, and now even his sex more easily and smoothly than his language. It is the very sound of the language that sings the culture it represents." Finally, after pondering the deep differences between the gauchos of the Argentine pampas and the cowboys of the Wild West, Rabassa declares:

> We translators, then, by our very act of translating are divesting the work of its most essential cultural aspect, which is the sound of the original language. After this it is ever so essential that we preserve whatever slim shards of the culture may be left lying about, and the way to do this is to acculturate our English as if it were his mother tongue, as if England had not lost the "purple land," perhaps, and not to reproduce a cowboy stumbling clumsily about in *bombachas* and *chiripá*, uncertain about defending himself with a *facón*. (91)

Though we have long been neighbors in the Americas, it is only now, at the dawn of the twenty-first century, that we are beginning to look at each other with new eyes, and translation continues to play a vital role in what we see when we do. Beginning in the 1960s, the literatures of Brazil, Spanish America, the United States, and Canada began to cross-pollinate each other at an unprecedented rate. As Latin America engaged more and more with both Canada and the United States, new patterns of influence and reception began to proliferate, with the result that our understanding of what it really means to be "American" became transformed. A new sense of the New World was being birthed by the inter-American project.

It was out of this rapidly changing literary and cultural landscape that inter-American studies began to emerge. Developing rapidly as a new and, for some, very contentious field (see Fitz, "Quest"), it was, from the beginning, driven primarily by Latin America and by American scholars of Latin American literature—that is, by people who had grown up in the United States and read its literature and history but who, by dint of their professional training, were also steeped in the literature, culture, and history of Spanish America and Brazil. For many of these visionaries, the possibilities for inter-American study were both obvious and of tremendous value, though it was also clear that Canada and the Caribbean would have to be actively involved as well. It was clear too that, in its conception as well as its practice, the inter-American vision was profoundly comparative in nature, demanding the full deployment of comparative literature's theoretical and methodological arsenal. For students of Spanish and Portuguese in the 1960s—a decade in which these languages were still regarded as only marginally important, even by some comparatists—this realization was exhilarating, since as inter-American Studies progressed as an academic field, it would eventually reveal its greatest validity and worth as a conspicuously energizing form of comparative literature (see Fitz, "Comparative Approach"). A similar prejudice made it difficult for those who wished to study the French of Québec, known as *joual*, or its vibrant literature and culture.[11] Early pioneers in the field, like Gregory Rabassa, Oscar Fernández, and Robert G. Mead Jr., were perfect advocates for the inter-American project. Articulate in expression and innovative in thought, they were simultaneously Latin Americanists, Americanists, and inter-Americanists, scholars who were reared and trained in the United States and therefore knew it intimately but who, as experts fluent in both Spanish and Portuguese (and typically French as well) and in the literatures of both Spanish America and Brazil, were uniquely situated to read their country of birth as Other, as but one piece—an imposing and very influential piece, to be sure—of a larger inter-American mosaic. This rather dislocating reconceptualization of the United States as Other within a suddenly more comprehensive and decentering reconsideration of what it means to be American would prove to be problematic for several more decades. Indeed, it is only now, in the opening decade of the twenty-first century, that such a vision is slowly gaining acceptance in academic circles, where, it must be said, some still view it as a threat to the status quo. Though it remains a controversial issue for many English departments and their American literature faculty, for example, and for many colleagues holding appointments in such fields as American studies—which, from its inception in the 1950s, has defined itself in terms of the United States alone, though this is now changing—the inter-American initiative is nevertheless steadily gaining strength and new adherents.[12]

Translation and the Liberation of Brazilian and Spanish American Literature from the Solitude of Cultural Ignorance and Prejudice

The Creation of a New World Paradigm

The condition of solitude, as it is elevated to a symbol of hemispheric importance in *One Hundred Years of Solitude,* is a now unifying though previously divisive New World experience. Translation is the mechanism that has allowed the literary cultures of Spanish America and Brazil to overcome the cultural solitude, born of disrespect, that had so long plagued them and inhibited their recognition by their hemispheric neighbors and by the world audience generally. In addition to Márquez, other Latin American authors whose translated work has helped validate this breakthrough include Pablo Neruda, Octavio Paz (whose *Labyrinth of Solitude* can be regarded as a turning point in inter-American literary and cultural relations), Carlos Fuentes, Euclides da Cunha, and Darcy Ribeiro. Many of their texts lead us to a greater appreciation of the Native American presence in New World literature and to a recognition of the degree to which race relations, complicated by the entwined issues of gender and class, pertain to the larger American experience.

While the condition of solitude is unquestionably common to the larger human experience, there is something unique to the role it has played in New World literature. From the beginning of the European discovery and conquest in the late fifteenth century, the New World was seen as an earthly paradise, a strange but alluring place where all things might be possible and where one might, finally, escape the corruption of the Old World.[1] This urge to begin again, to learn from the mistakes of the past and to construct civilizations that might actually achieve some measure of the long-sought utopian state, would animate the European conquerors in greater or lesser degrees throughout the various colonial periods of the Americas. But, as history has shown, this utopian vision has too often proved to be more of an illusion, a cruel hoax, than a lived reality, and it is this discrepancy that continues to color its treatment even today.

It can be argued that the prevalence of solitude as a theme in the literature of the Americas stems from precisely this failure, the failure of the European conquerors to establish societies that were capable of becoming what they wanted them to be. Too many crimes were committed during the periods of conquest, too many injustices were built into the colonial sociopolitical structures, too much emphasis was placed on greed, violence, and exploitation, and too much zealotry was allowed to flourish. While it is relatively easy, for those well versed in Pan-American history, to see the relevance of these problems to the Latin American or Canadian experience, they are less obviously a perceived reality with respect to the United States. Yet even there, these failures obtain. Nevertheless, our obstinate tendency to undervalue the contributions of other cultures, our willful ignorance of the languages, cultures, and histories of other peoples, and our reluctance to consider foreign models as ever being instructive of our own situation all contribute mightily to what commentators have long regarded as our fundamental American provincialism—a condition that, in addition to inhibiting our ability to relate to the rest of the world, is putting us ever more at risk in the arena of global Realpolitik. In the United States, it seems, we are simply not much interested in other cultures and other peoples. In any given year, for example, book translations into English published in the United States tend to hover around 3 percent. It is, history teaches us, entirely possible to become a prisoner of one's own cultural arrogance, isolated, ironically enough, because of one's power and influence. If it is not tempered by a counterbalancing interest in the Other, the cultural hegemony of a dominant nation can, especially when fueled by a tenacious monolingualism, very quickly morph into a vitiating form of isolation. For a variety of reasons, then, in all of the nations and cultures of the Americas, solitude has established itself as one of inter-American literature's most defining themes, coming, finally, to rank as one of its most striking characteristics (see Fitz, *Rediscovering*, chap. 9).

Of all the many works that touch on this issue, García Márquez's epic masterpiece, *One Hundred Years of Solitude*, invites consideration as the prototype, the one text that casts the theme in its most complete New World perspective and that exposes its relevance for a variety of disciplines. Pertinent both to problems of Latin American history and politics and to the larger philosophical issues of human existence, *One Hundred Years of Solitude* demands to be read on several interlocking levels of interpretation. An expanded version of Faulkner's Yoknapatawpha County, Mississippi,

Márquez's fictional town, Macondo, becomes a metaphor for the entire New World experience as well as for the human experience worldwide. No small part of Márquez's genius in *One Hundred Years of Solitude* is that he makes it ring true on a local level (as the story of the people who inhabit it), on the continental level (as an allegory of Latin American political history), and as a statement of the human condition (our struggle to overcome our isolation and connect with other human beings in a nonpredatory way). And though it was not as apparent to American readers as it was to those in Brazil and Spanish America, the novel's commercially seductive yet ultimately ruinous inter-American dimension was established with the arrival in Macondo of the banana company train, an event that, recalling the arrival of the lumber company train in *The Bear*, opens the door for the plundering of Macondo (read Latin America and Canada) by American corporations. To put this in more up-to-date parlance, the people of Macondo were among the first to be on the receiving end of American globalism, and their painful experience of it constitutes the most harrowing and shameful sections of the second half of the novel. To Latin American and Canadian readers of the early 1960s, *One Hundred Years of Solitude* spoke volumes about their frequently unhappy historical experience with the United States. What was too often being read in the United States as a weird story about bizarre people in a bizarre place doing bizarre things was being understood in Latin America and Canada as thinly fictionalized history, as a painfully accurate account of U.S. economic, political, and military intervention in their cultures.

But while Márquez's great novel exemplifies how the theme of solitude resonates throughout the Americas, its unique New World relevance manifests itself in two primary categories, modern America's still unresolved relationship with its ancient indigenous past and its slowness in recognizing the importance of Canada and Brazil, the two nations most often left out when people begin to think about the inter-American paradigm. With respect to the Canadian situation, moreover, it is hard to imagine an American culture that receives less recognition than Québec, whose long struggle to "survive" as a distinct culture has exposed numerous affinities between the historical experience of the Québécois and that of not only Brazil but Macondo as well (see Atwood). Within the context of inter-American scholarship, there exists vast potential in comparative studies involving Brazil, Spanish America, and Canada, all of which, as distinct forms of the Other in both hemispheric and world literature, have a great deal to tell us about perspective. As Arnold Davidson, speaking for the Canadian perspective, puts it, "In essence Canada provides a North American experiment different from the one regarded as definitive ('manifest') by most residents of the United States" (3).

Putting a somewhat sharper point on this same argument, Lorna Irvine and Paula Gilbert Lewis stress that the "marginal status" of Canada and, in particular, Québec "results in representations of the New World quite different from those offered by the United States and the Spanish-dominated Mexico" (328). In short, the varying forms of solitude in which Canada and Latin America have for so long existed in the Americas now offer fascinating alternatives to the dominant vision of what it means to be "American," that of the United States. Seen from this hemispherically comprehensive perspective, the theme of solitude reveals itself to be so endemic to the New World experience that it appears, to a greater or lesser extent, as a defining aspect of its literature, especially from the late nineteenth century on. In Latin America, for example, major works by such figures as Márquez, Neruda, Paz, Fuentes, Vargas Llosa, Machado de Assis, Rosa, and Ribeiro cultivate it as the decisive motif of the American experience. And if *One Hundred Years of Solitude* stands out as the literary prototype of solitude in its New World context, then, as we will demonstrate in this chapter, several other canonical texts come very close to achieving the same status.

At first glance, it might seem odd to include Neruda, the great socialist poet, among those New World writers who cultivate solitude as a primary motif. But it is precisely the isolation of each human being—a condition he expands to include Latin America's historical experience—that Neruda seeks to overcome, whether in personal life or in political consciousness. If human solidarity and connection represent Neruda's highest aspirations as a poet, it is also true that he uses the theme of solitude as a foil, as a mechanism by which he can cast the conflicted human condition into sharper relief. In 1943, after a visit to the ruins of Macchu Picchu,[2] Neruda was inspired to compose his *Alturas de Macchu Picchu*, a poem that many regard as his single greatest achievement. Later incorporated into his *Canto general* (1950), *The Heights of Macchu Picchu*, thoughtfully translated by the English poet Nathaniel Tarn, was one of the most important and influential of the many Spanish American texts that were being rendered into English during the 1960s. Although, as Sandra Hochman points out in a 1967 *Book Week* review, he was still relatively unknown in the United States,

> in Latin America and in Europe Neruda is considered to be one of the two or three greatest living poets. His work has been read all over the world and has been translated into 24 languages, making him, perhaps, one of the most popular living poets. Jean-Paul Sartre, when he recently snubbed the Nobel Prize, gave, as one of his reasons, the fact that the prize should have been offered first to Pablo Neruda. And yet, with all of his fame, Neruda is just beginning to be known in the

United States. Although admired by a group of poets, who are not really a group at all but spread out all over the country, in the United States his influence on younger poets has been minimal. "No writer of world-renown is perhaps so little known to North America as the Chilean poet, Pablo Neruda," Seldon Rodman wrote recently. (Hochman, 19–20)

While this situation was partly due, in the early 1960s, to a relative paucity of translations, it was also a function of American disdain toward Spanish as a language and toward Spanish American literature in general. Commenting on this impediment to positive inter-American relations, Rodríguez Monegal in 1968 felt compelled to write that in a country where influential critics like Edmund Wilson and Lionel Trilling could routinely disparage the literature and culture of Latin America, it was small wonder that the general population had so little regard for the cultures of Spanish America and Brazil. Astonished and dismayed by such untroubled displays of ignorance and bias emanating from Latin America's great neighbor to the north, Monegal, fully cognizant of the importance not only of the Boom literature but of the imaginative and long-gestating literary cultures that lay behind it and had, in fact, generated the Boom authors and texts, went on to say that "the critics and readers who know the astounding content of this boom must continue the fight against blind literary prejudice—no intelligent reader can continue to ignore the literature in the Spanish language unless, of course, he prefers the outlook of the ostrich" ("Literature," 3). Making an obvious point that simultaneously underscores both the cosmopolitanism of Latin American literature and the parochialism of the United States, Monegal further contended:

The painful contrast with what is now happening in Europe makes the situation here all the more noteworthy. In France, Italy, Spain and even England, people are quoting Borges at every turn (sometimes without any special reason), reading the novels of Sábato and Fuentes, devouring Cortázar, Guimarães Rosa, García Márquez, translating all of Neruda. Here in the United States things are different. (3)

And yet, Monegal concluded on a more positive note, thanks to the appearance of a plethora of excellent translations of important works by major writers, the situation was changing, and for the better. Also important to the increasingly positive reception of Latin American literature in the United States were "the success of the new Latin American novel in Europe, the triumph of Borges," the "successful public appearances of Neruda, Paz and

Nicanor Parra," and increased coverage in such organs of scholarly and public opinion as *Time, Newsweek*, the *New York Review of Books*, and the *New Yorker*. As a culture, the United States was slowly beginning to give Latin American literature its due, to admit that it did in fact possess something more than mere "anthropological value," as Trilling, comfortably wrapped in the solitude of his ignorance, had so snidely declared.

Neruda and the Nobel Prize for Literature: Ending the Long Silence

Appearing in 1967 (one year after the Jonathan Cape edition), Tarn's sensitive rewriting of Neruda's Spanish original was instrumental in gaining Neruda the kind of recognition in the English-speaking world that would, in 1971, contribute to his being awarded the Nobel Prize for literature. Published in a bilingual edition and featuring a very helpful thirteen-page preface by Robert Pring-Mill, *The Heights of Macchu Picchu* uses the solitude caused by the rupture of twentieth-century America and its ancestral Native American past (in ways that, for many American readers, recall Hart Crane's *The Bridge*) to argue, in the poem's dramatic conclusion, for a new and revitalized sense of Pan-American identity, one that connects our past, present, and future in an unbroken continuum of human solidarity.[3]

In addition to the generally high quality of the translation itself, which was enhanced by Neruda's generous assistance with the proper interpretation of the original's many semantic ambiguities and complex structures of allusion and metaphor, the book benefits greatly from the kind of critical introduction that illuminates not only the Spanish text but the process by which it was translated. By shedding light on both the translation problems that had to be confronted and the rationale behind their resolutions, Pring-Mill's introduction makes a major contribution to our ability to understand and appreciate not only the original but its English version as well. In this sense, it, like Rabassa's introduction to Clarice Lispector's *The Apple in the Dark*, may fairly be regarded as a model for the kind of critical introduction we need more of for works in translation. Noting, for example, how Neruda's penchant for developing his poem through "a web of two-way syntax that creates conflicting patterns of associations around the imagery" (xii) represents a formidable problem for the translator, Pring-Mill introduces us not merely to one of Neruda's most characteristic poetic devices, an entangling and richly fecund line structure, but how he makes it produce the various effects he desires. Sensitive not only to the special importance of syntax in our interpretation of a line of Neruda's poetry in its original Spanish but to its critical importance to the translator, whose burden it is to try to reproduce it, semantically if not phonetically, in another language system, Pring-Mill's commentary brings us closer to both the original and the translation, which we can now see as both a re-creation of another text and a successful poem in its own right. In his view, rightly enough,

> Ambiguous syntax is one of the most fascinating aspects of Neruda's manner of proceeding in all his complex poems, yet it is a feature which is peculiarly tantalizing to translators. They can rarely hope to establish a corresponding ambiguity, and therefore have either to opt between layers of meaning, or else to give the grammatical sense of a single layer while trying to suggest the others by words which carry heightened and conflicting associations, as Tarn does. (xii)

Pointing out that sometimes "a word will have to be intensified because of a degree of abstraction which seems nebulous in English, requiring some kind of concrete rendering to achieve an equivalent impact," as in the cases of such "frequent terms" as *vacío*, *manantiales*, or *diseminado*, Pring-Mill argues that Neruda's vision, as expressed in his native Spanish, is "not necessarily imprecise because such terms seem vague" (xii). To the contrary, Neruda "has very often taken a fairly neutral word and loaded it with his own associations by using it in numerous previous contexts, whose cumulative effect has been to extend and clarify its field of meaning" (xii–xiii). The translator, Pring-Mill contends, must be alert to such tonal and semantic shifts, recognizing always that "such terms cannot always be translated . . . by a single intensified equivalent, since different shades of meaning have to be brought out in different contexts" (xiii). Finally, in a comment that both apprises us of another key aspect of Neruda's art and at the same time heightens our appreciation of Tarn's translation, Pring-Mill writes: "A further difficulty lies in the fact that Neruda's poetry has a natural setting whose grandeur obliges a translator to work close to the brink of what might seem hyperbole—a danger Tarn tries to avoid by using taut-phrased, sharp-edged images wherever possible" (xiii).

But poetry, characterized by George Steiner as "maximal speech" (233), the epitome of semantic concentration, covertness, and invention, is notorious for being the genre most resistant to translation. And so it is no surprise to learn that Tarn's efforts, laudable though they are in the main, have elicited some valid and perceptive criticisms, particularly from scholars fluent in Spanish and knowledgeable about Neruda's poetry and from other poets, writers skillful in exploiting the rich resources of mid-twentieth-century American English, the flexible and inventive voice in which much of the best of this criticism appears. The quality of this criticism, interestingly enough, had the effect of enhancing Neruda's reception by the American reading public. Citing the many interpretive difficulties posed by Neruda's richly polysemic, mythically charged work, M. L. Rosenthal, for example, believed that "Nathaniel Tarn's translation, conscientious and suggestive, misses some of the rhythmic and echoing cues and too often sacrifices a chance to evoke the sound and syntax of the original." At the same time, Rosenthal admitted, Tarn's re-creation of Neruda's lines does "catch the luxuriant ambiguity, the delicate exploration, and the power of many passages. Since the Spanish and English are given on facing pages, the reader may compete with the translator" (25). And in 1967 Dudley Fitts wrote in the *New York Times Book Review*:

> It is difficult to exaggerate the seriousness of the problems that must be faced by the translator of a complex, richly nuanced poem. Usually he must settle for approximations, even in passages of relative simplicity. In the work of Pablo Neruda, where language can be so dense, so ambiguous, and where, moreover, the poet's ecstatic élan is constantly setting up hurdles of rhythmic and syntactical dislocation and all sorts of crosscurrents of sound and metaphor, even approximation must fall short of the mark. (26)

But, like Rosenthal, Fitts finally came to judge Tarn's efforts in a positive light, as achieving the kind of overall fidelity to the sound and sense of the original that Steiner, in his seminal study *After Babel: Aspects of Language and Translation*, posited as the hallmark of the successful translation. "Mr. Tarn," declared Fitts, "is to be congratulated upon deciding to print the Spanish text opposite the English and to follow it, as nearly line for line as possible, in his version. No one knows better than he that the result is not Neruda's poem; but it is a poem, frequently an impressive one, in its own right," and the meticulous, culturally attuned reader will gain a true sense of the original (26). Tellingly, this is a conclusion also reached by James Wright, who, writing in *Poetry* in June 1968, noted: "The translation of Neruda into English is a problem which has engaged several poets. One of the most effective of these is Mr. H. R. Hayes, whose version of *Walking Around* remains, for me, one of the greatest poems in the modern American language. Mr. Clayton Eshleman has also done a Neruda notable for its daring and force. Now we have Mr. Nathaniel Tarn, the gifted English poet" (29). Focusing on Tarn's efforts, Wright concludes:

> He has tried to solve the most difficult poem by Neruda which involves not only the stylistic and imaginative brilliance of the great poet's lan-

guage but also his formal mastery of these elements which enables Neruda to illuminate for us some of the meanings of life. Although personally I would hem and haw over this and that detail of Mr. Tarn's translation, I have to confess that I think it is a beautiful poem in the English language, worthy of the noble and spacious poem which identifies Neruda as one of the precious few great masters of our time and of any time. (29–30)

In reading Tarn's version of *The Heights of Macchu Picchu*, then, the impression one gets is that he has re-created Neruda's marvelous original in such a way that one truly can gain at least a sense of the Spanish text's semantic and cultural complexity. If it is not perfect—the concept of perfection as it applies to translation is, of course, an illusion—it is a very faithful reproduction, one that afforded English-speaking readers in the late 1960s a reliable guide through the political, cultural, and aesthetic challenges of Neruda's daunting and controversial American vision.

Octavio Paz's Integrative Vision of the Americas and Implications for Translation

Another landmark Spanish American work, appearing a few years earlier in English translation, had actually set the stage for Neruda's panhemispheric sense of the American experience and for his unique sense of American solitude. In 1950 the influential journal *Cuadernos Americanos* had published a study by the Mexican poet and thinker Octavio Paz that was destined to become one of the decisive documents of inter-American study.[4] Revised and expanded in 1959 and reissued by the prestigious Fondo de Cultura Económica, Paz's groundbreaking book *El laberinto de la soledad* was finally translated, by Lysander Kemp, and published in 1961 by Grove Press under the title *The Labyrinth of Solitude*. In 1943 Paz had received a Guggenheim fellowship, which enabled him to travel and study in the United States, a sojourn that eventually led to the writing of *The Labyrinth of Solitude*.[5] An intellectual and a man of the world, Paz was later tapped to serve as Mexico's representative to UNESCO and as its ambassador to India (a post he resigned in protest of the violent methods employed by the Mexican government to quell student protests in Mexico City just before the 1968 Olympic Games). Coinciding with the Cuban Revolution, the discovery of Borges by the English-speaking world, the creation of *Odyssey Review* at Columbia University, and, perhaps most important of all, the emergence of Gregory Rabassa as a translator of Latin American literature and as an articulate, sophisticated advocate of it, the appearance of Paz's book was a landmark event. Ostensibly an examination of Mexican identity, *The Labyrinth of Solitude* made its case not by isolating Mexico but by arguing that the country had to be examined comparatively. In the process the book became one of our most revealing expressions of inter-American cultural relations. The often startling conclusions Paz reached had a profound impact not only in Mexico but in the United States as well. Except for academic specialists in Latin American literature and history, those Americans who chose to read Paz's astute critique of the two neighboring nations were startled to learn, for example, that Mexicans knew a great deal more about the United States than Americans did about Mexico. More than this, they were shocked by a writer from an "inferior" culture having the audacity to actually criticize some of the most salient features of American life, which Paz would compare, often quite incisively, with life in Mexico. Inherent, then, in Paz's exploration of Mexican identity was the role the United States played in it. Paz was thus pointing at a relationship that, in essence, typifies and justifies the entire inter-American enterprise.

Most surprising of all, however, was that while Mexico was clearly marked by a special kind of solitude, so too was the United States, a nation whose history, as Paz pointed out, gradually imposed upon it a kind of insularity at odds with the increasingly central role the United States was asked to play in world affairs. This revelation, almost totally overlooked at the time, would become more obvious to American writers, artists, and intellectuals who, as we have seen, began during the 1960s to question seriously the values driving their culture and to challenge the wisdom and morality of the new political and economic forces that had come to dominate it. As Paz suggested, the historical reasons for these two New World solitudes were quite different—seventeenth-century Puritan England versus fifteenth-century Catholic Spain, and the sociopolitical structures these situations imposed on their respective parts of the New World—though equally powerful and pervasive, and eventually they would have to be confronted, by both sides, if better hemispheric relations were to be achieved. Basking in the glow of its great victory over the forces of fascism in World War II and flushed with its newly won political and economic hegemony, the United States entered the decade of the 1960s optimistically, though sobered by the role it had to play in the Cold War, a conflict that, in the figure of Fidel Castro, would unexpectedly turn up only a few miles from its shores. But, as *The Labyrinth of Solitude* makes painfully clear, while the United States would be able to deal productively with its European allies, its relationship with Latin America would be much more problematic. Touching on issues of race, class, gender, and history as these apply, comparatively, to both the United States and Mexico, Paz argues early in his book that the modern Mexican suffers from both a feeling of solitude and a sense of inferiority, and that these have produced a latent violence that threatens, at any moment, to "break through his mask of impassivity." Extending this discussion to include the United States, Paz goes on to write:

> Man is alone everywhere. But the solitude of the Mexican, under the great stone night of the high plateau that is still inhabited by insatiable gods, is very different from that of the North American, who wanders in an abstract world of machines, fellow citizens and moral precepts.
> . . .
> Nothing could be further from this feeling than the solitude of the North American. In the United States man does not feel that he has been torn from the center of creation and suspended between hostile forces. He has built his own world and it is built in his own image: it is his mirror. But now he cannot recognize himself in his inhuman objects, nor in his fellows. His creations, like those of an inept sorcerer, no longer obey him. (19–21)

Going beyond the obvious economic differences between Mexico and the United States, Paz believes that while America's heritage is democracy, capitalism, and the industrial revolution, Mexico's is the Counter-Reformation, monopoly, and feudalism. From this, he argues that while the "self-assurance and confidence" of the American people permit them to offer criticism of their form of government and social organization that is "valuable and forthright" and "reformist" rather than revolutionary, things are different in Latin America, "where long periods of dictatorship" have made it an often lethal mistake for people to criticize their officials.

Contrasting what he sees as the basic optimism of Americans—an outlook that, if not tempered by an honest consideration of the facts, he believes often leads Americans into an "ingenuousness" that may include "dissimulation and even hypocrisy"—with the Mexican's "fondness for self-destruction," his "masochistic tendencies," and his "nihilism," Paz then catalogues a long list of differences between Mexico and the United States. Americans, for example, like fairy tales and detective stories and seek to understand reality, while Mexicans love myths and legends and prefer to contemplate reality (21–25).

When he wonders about the possible origins of such contradictory attitudes in two New World nations existing in such close proximity to each other, Paz, reaching back to North America's Puritan past, speculates that this engendered a belief that the world can be perfected, while in Mexico the world is something that, at best, can be redeemed. Further, in a comment that does much to explain American insularity and narcissism (and thus expose the problem of cultural arrogance that lies, still unresolved, at the heart of all inter-American study), Paz argues that the Puritan heritage "identifies purity with health" and endorses the "purifying effects of asceticism," which all but requires a careful segregation from the rest of the impure world and a disavowal of its beliefs. For the Puritans, Paz declares, every contact with the outside world constitutes a contamination. "Foreign races, ideas, customs, and bodies carry within themselves the germs of perdition and impurity." For Mexicans, and for Latin Americans generally, "there is no health without contact. Tlazolteotl, the Aztec goddess of filth and fecundity, of earthly and human moods, was also the goddess of steam baths, sexual love and confession" (24). From this radically different historical perspective, Paz concludes: "If the solitude of the Mexican is like a stagnant pool, that of the North American is like a mirror" (27).

The mention of the Aztec deity is significant because it underscores the final fundamental difference between Mexico and the United States that Paz discusses, the role played by indigenous culture in these modern states. Suggesting, though not actually carrying out, a comparison of early-seventeenth-century England with late-fifteenth-century Spain, a newly formed nation-state that, born of centuries of violence and authoritarianism, would renounce the future and close itself off from the West at the beginning of the Counter-Reformation, Paz argues that Mexico was born "of a double violence, . . . that of the Aztecs and that of the Spaniards" (100), unlike the United States, whose birth also required the destruction of native peoples, but not on the scale of the epic struggle between the Spaniards and the Aztec empire. Here Paz emphasizes the very different nature of indigenous culture as it has evolved in Mexico and the United States. Comparing the fate of the two countries' Native Americans in the light of the social, political, and religious ideologies brought to the New World by the Spanish Catholic Church after 1492 and the English Puritans in 1620, Paz contends that the Spaniards refrained from exterminating the Indians because their labor was needed on the haciendas and in the mines. The Indians, in short, were a valuable commodity that was not to be wasted (101–2).

Then, musing on the role religion played in the conquest and exploitation of the Native Americans, Paz argues that the ritual of baptism offered them a recognized, legally sanctioned place in Spanish colonial society (one that also afforded them some meager level of protection against abuse), but that a like opportunity to gain a new social and religious identity was not offered in the North American Puritan experience: "This possibility of belonging to a living order, even if it was at the bottom of the social pyramid, was cruelly denied to the Indians by the Protestants of New England. It is often forgotten that to belong to the Catholic faith meant that one found a place in the cosmos" (102). In both the United States and Latin America, the systematic destruction of the ancient gods and cultures left the Native Americans isolated, fragmented, and enervated.

Although the history of the Native American people remains one of inter-American literature's most important, if neglected, dimensions, there can be no doubt that the solitude Paz speaks of here, the one deriving from the near total destruction of the entire Aztec world, has endured through the ages to become a major shaping force in all aspects of Mexican art, politics, and culture.[6]

Carlos Fuentes and the Duality of the Inter-American Reality: Lessons for the Translator

Another very influential modern Mexican author, Carlos Fuentes, has also cultivated his culture's rich indigenous past while at the same time developing a distinctly inter-American perspective in his work. In his first novel, *La región más transparente* (1958; tr. Sam Hileman, *Where the Air Is Clear*, 1960), Fuentes spun a narrative web around Mexico City in ways that recall what Dos Passos did for New York City in *Manhattan Transfer* (1925), a novel Fuentes knew well and admired for its experimental techniques, its social consciousness, and its critical tone. The primary center of consciousness of *Where the Air Is Clear*, the revealingly named character Ixca Cienfuegos, represents the two halves of Mexican reality: its ancient Aztec past and its modern urbanity, a large part of which involves cultural and economic influences emanating from the United States. Indeed, it is no exaggeration to say that this basic conflict—between the bloody Spanish conquest and the indigenous heritage—underlies much of Fuentes's work, as it does that of Paz. A later work, *La cabeza de la Hidra* (1978; tr. Margaret Sayers Peden, *The Hydra Head*, 1978), was an international espionage novel dealing with Mexico's vast oil reserves and their manipulation by Arab and American interests. *El gringo viejo* (1985; tr. Margaret Sayers Peden, *The Old Gringo*, 1985) intensified and expanded the inter-American approach as it focused on the Mexican Revolution and its significance for the United States and, more centrally, the mysterious disappearance of Ambrose Bierce in 1913 in Mexico.[7] However, Fuentes's two most acclaimed novels, *La muerte de Artemio Cruz* (1962; tr. Sam Hileman, *The Death of Artemio Cruz*, 1964; tr. Alfred

Mac Adam, 1991) and *Cambio de piel* (1967; tr. Sam Hileman, *A Change of Skin*, 1968), are similar in that they both, in their different contexts, utilize solitude as a basic motif.

Still regarded by many scholars as Fuentes's best novel, *The Death of Artemio Cruz* was a major force in the middle years of the Spanish American Boom and one of its most influential texts. Ranking among Fuentes's most brilliant technical efforts, the story of Artemio Cruz, a peon who survives the Mexican Revolution and its aftermath to become a wealthy and powerful businessman, weaves together a conflicted past, a confused present, and an uncertain future in a rich tapestry of first-, second-, and third-person voices.[8] Although superficially a story of success, *The Death of Artemio Cruz* really amounts to a scathing critique of the Revolution and the betrayal of its noblest principles, and of the corrupting and alienating effects of an unremediated pursuit of personal ambition (a point not lacking in significance for American readers concerned about their own culture). Disgusted by his physical and moral degeneration, Artemio Cruz, symbolizing modern Mexico, is locked in a solitude that stems from his having pawned the progressive and democratic principles of the Mexican Revolution for the trappings of wealth and power, much of which comes from the United States. We learn, for example, of Cruz's traitorous past and how he accumulated his vast fortune through the exploitation of his own people and the servile facilitating of foreign investment, an activity that produces in him a feeling of both pleasure and shame:

> Yes: you will light a cigarette, in spite of the warnings you have had from your doctor, and to Padilla will relate again the steps by which you gained your wealth: loans at short terms and high interest to peasants in Puebla, just after the Revolution; the acquisition of land around the city of Puebla, whose growth you foresaw; acres for subdivision in Mexico City, thanks to the friendly intervention of each succeeding president; the daily newspaper; the purchase of mining stock; the formation of Mexican-U.S. enterprises in which you participated as front-man so that the law would be complied with; trusted friend of North American investors, intermediary between New York and Chicago and the government of Mexico; the manipulation of stock prices to move them to your advantage, buying and selling, always at a profit. (Hileman tr., 11)

Evolving, finally, into a kind of signature theme for Fuentes, this same concern for relations between Mexico and the United States, couched always in the larger context of Mexico's still vibrant native heritage, also appears in *A Change of Skin*, a very demanding novel that, with parts of it reminding readers of William Burroughs, appeared in the United States during the closing years of the Boom, to guarded acclaim. Part of the problem had to do with the extraordinary complexity of the novel, with its scope, its interlocking structures, its characterizations, and its shifting levels of perspective, diction, register, and tone. Showing his profound cosmopolitanism and erudition, Fuentes steeps himself, with this narrative, in Mexican history (including its bloody pre-Columbian past), European culture and history (particularly the Nazi experience), and American pop culture, which both fascinates and repels him. Indeed, while much of the novel consists of an all-out assault on the pernicious effects of fascism and violence in all their various forms and guises, another significant portion of *A Change of Skin* is devoted, as William Kennedy pointed out in a 1968 review, to excoriating the rapacious economic and cultural presence of the United States in modern Mexico, even though Fuentes is clearly "enthralled by American images and idols," especially our movies and our actors (71–72). But another sticking point, and one particularly germane to the book's reception in the United States of the late 1960s, was its translation, which, though generally solid and reliable, does at times tend to stray from the feel of the original. The question of style, always the most difficult aspect of the translator's art and the one that most resists being "brought over" adequately, comes into play here. In Sam Hileman's translation, a disparity sometimes arises between the novel's very serious thematic intentions and the linguistic vehicle that seeks to convey these. To be fair, one should note that the same tension between the novel's content and its language exists in the original, though it is also true that Mr. Hileman's heroic attempts to resolve this perhaps irresolvable dilemma may raise more hackles than it soothes, and that, in essence, is the nature of the translation problem here. Although it is not known how closely Kennedy compared the translation to the original, he generously concludes his review by writing, "In English the book owes a great debt to its translator, Sam Hileman. It reads as if Mr. Fuentes had written in English instead of Spanish. And given all its Pop-art language, its slang and handsome rhetoric, this is no ordinary feat" (73).

Anthony West, however, writing in the *New Yorker*, does perform a close comparative reading of the translation and the original, and comes to a very different conclusion. *A Change of Skin*, he feels, "is something quite different from 'Cambio de piel,' . . . the fascinating novel by Carlos Fuentes that was published in Mexico last year. It is not only that the book has lost its curiously haunting illustrations—they were, with one exception, bleached stills from movies of the thirties. Something else has gone, too" (73). Outlining the original's very complicated plot and structure, its shifting verb tenses, chronological linkages, and levels of tone, and the nature and function of its mysterious (and possibly Aztec) narrative voice,[9] and citing concrete examples of what he sees as mistranslations (the Spanish word *floreadas*, he notes, is rendered by Hileman as "rosy" rather than "flowered"), West is sharp in his criticism of the English rendition of this novel: "the reader who wants to find out what Carlos Fuentes does with his elaborately crafted structure and with his sinister theme is not going to get much help from the American version of the book" (75).[10] But, as West notes, the translation question is complicated by several additional factors, including the process by which the final version was agreed upon. "The translation," West contends, was "approved by Fuentes, who was frequently consulted in the course of its preparation, and who speaks excellent English." Regardless, he notes, "almost from the beginning it is clear that something is badly wrong," and, as the conclusion of his review makes clear, West, again citing specific textual examples, worries that the putatively Carlos Fuentes novel known as *A Change of Skin* is actually going to hamper the development of better literary and cultural relations between North and South America: "throughout the book one finds passages that are only to be described as improvisations in the approximate neighborhood of the Fuentes text. At one typical point, Fuentes's '*Y a ganarnos la vida que de repente es el único recuerdo que nos queda de nuestra muerte original*' becomes 'Middle age is not bitching. It's merely a bitch.'" West's concluding comments speak forcefully, then, not merely to the manifold problems, both linguistic and cultural, faced by the translator, but to the larger question of translation's crucial role in the development of inter-American literature as a field:

> It is more than unfortunate that this very distinguished Mexican writer's work should be presented to the American public in such a fashion, and this remarkable translation is symbolic of the tragedy of incomprehension and misunderstanding which constitutes the history of the relationship between the Gothic North and the Latin South on this continent. Even when we listen to what our neighbors say, we do not bother to make sure that we understand the words they use. (75)

Latin American Writers Reading and Rewriting Each Other

The theme of solitude is expanded, in Euclides da Cunha's *Os sertões* (1902; tr. Samuel Putnam, *Rebellion in the Backlands*, 1944) and in Mario Vargas Llosa's *La guerra del fin del mundo* (1981; tr. Helen R. Lane, *The War of the*

End of the World, 1984), two books that share a special relationship, the latter having been directly and extensively influenced by the former. The influence is so strong, in fact, that one could argue that the Vargas Llosa novel is actually, more than anything else, a strategic rewriting of the da Cunha narrative, a reworking of what the Peruvian novelist regards as the Brazilian text's most salient features. Strictly speaking, *Rebellion in the Backlands* is nonfiction, though in its gripping second half da Cunha clearly avails himself of the techniques of fiction in order to impart to his reader the true significance of the terrible events he narrates.

The story of a short though shockingly violent uprising that took place in the harsh and arid backlands of northeastern Brazil, the *sertão*, between December 1896 and October 1897, *Rebellion in the Backlands* focuses our attention not only on the solitude of Brazil as it seeks to take its place in a world that largely ignores it but the solitude imposed on people the world over by ignorance, poverty, and fanaticism. In many ways, this classic of modern Brazilian literature will recall, for American readers, James Agee and Walker Evans's *Let Us Now Praise Famous Men* (1941; see Fitz, "Comparative Approach"), while for those knowledgeable in Spanish American letters it brings to mind both Domingo Faustino Sarmiento's *Facundo* (1845) and Heriberto Frías's *Tomóchic* (1899). Framing its story in a variety of contexts, *Rebellion in the Backlands* is a narrative rife with solitude, a point not lost, as we shall see, on the novelist Mario Vargas Llosa. In part 1, which is driven by a powerful sense of determinism, da Cunha describes how life in the *sertão* has long been a function of the climate and geography, of the region's essentially feudal sociopolitical history, and of the inexorable laws of biology, which—or so the author, a victim of the bad science of the time, had been taught—decreed that people of racially mixed backgrounds were inescapably inferior. The structuring of part 1, in fact, moves the reader, deterministically, from the most general to the most specific, from almost cosmic considerations of the land and climate to issues of biology, heredity, and "race," to considerations of the sociology, history, and culture of the backlands region and the people who subsist there, and, finally, to the formation of a single man, Antônio Conselheiro, the charismatic leader of the insurrection and the end result of the forces that produced him. The dominant images used by da Cunha are borrowed from geology, with the rebellion and its leader presented as deeply buried anticlines suddenly cast up to the light of day by a cataclysmic earthquake. Overall, the determinism generated by the text implies that the events that the book describes were inevitable, the product of forces that no one could foresee or control; powerless to alter or avert their fate, the *sertanejos* (backlanders) were mere pawns in the game, a condition that intensifies the reader's sense of their isolation. Struggling to explain the bloody tragedy that unfolded at Canudos—the headquarters of Conselheiro and site of the revolt's final battle, in which the insurgents were annihilated—da Cunha finds himself, laboring under the weight of his era's faulty scientific pronouncements on this key point, forced to insert "An Irritating Parenthesis" declaring that

> An intermingling of races highly diverse is, in the majority of cases, prejudicial. According to the conclusions of the evolutionist, even when the influence of a superior race has reacted upon the offspring, the latter shows vivid traces of the inferior one. Miscegenation carried to an extreme means retrogression. (84)

Attempting to explain why the mixed-race *sertanejos* lived and conducted themselves as they did, he then tells us that

> miscegenation, in addition to obliterating the pre-eminent qualities of the higher race, serves to stimulate the revival of the primitive attributes of the lower; so that the mestizo . . . is almost always an unbalanced type. (84–85)

Isolated by time and circumstance, outgunned and outmanned and seemingly doomed by the inexorable laws of nature itself, the mestizo backlanders fought back, however, inflicting a series of stunning defeats on the state and federal troops sent to put down the revolt. Gradually, as the narrative gains in momentum, drama, and intensity, the author himself grows to respect and admire the backlanders as indomitable "Titans," even as he begins to grasp the terrible irony of the greater conflict that lies behind the bloodletting—the effective abandonment of poor, rural northeastern Brazil by wealthy, urban, and progressive southern Brazil, and the barbarization of the latter by the struggle itself. Examining, as a scientist might, the underlying causes of the tragic clash of the two Brazils, the backlanders' and his own, da Cunha mordantly observes:

> we ourselves are but little in advance of our rude and backward fellow-countrymen. The latter, at least, were logical. Isolated in space and time, the jagunço,[11] being an ethnic anachronism, could do only what he did do—that is, combat, and combat in a terrible fashion, the nation which, after having cast him off for three centuries almost, suddenly sought to raise him to our own state of enlightenment at the point of the bayonet, revealing to him the brilliancy of our civilization in the blinding flash of cannons. (280)

The problem of the "two Brazils," one wealthy and progressive, the other rural and poverty-stricken, slowly emerges as one of *Rebellion in the Backlands*'s defining motifs. Having himself traveled into the backlands to cover the rebellion for his newspaper, and recognizing the confrontation of two societies "each one wholly alien to the other," da Cunha writes that here, standing on the edge of the mythic heart of Brazil, he sensed "an absolute and radical break between the coastal cities and the clay huts of the interior, one that so disturbed the rhythm of our evolutionary development and which was so deplorable a stumbling-block to national unity" (405). The soldiers of the recently formed Brazilian republic (1889) who were charged with quelling the rebellion were, for all intents and purposes, "in a strange country now, with other customs, other scenes, a different kind of people. Another language even, spoken with an original and picturesque drawl. They had, precisely, the feeling of going to war in another land. They felt that they were outside Brazil. . . . What they were being called upon to do now was what other troops had done—to stage an invasion of foreign territory" (405–6). Framing the issue in ways that, for Americans, recall the great conflict between North and South that led to our own Civil War (albeit in geographical reverse), da Cunha does not fail to indict progressive southern Brazil for its abandonment of regressive northern Brazil. Observing the capture of a nine-year-old boy, da Cunha reflects on what the winners of the war would have to learn from the whole dismal experience:

> It was plain that the Canudos Campaign must have a higher objective than the stupid and inglorious one of merely wiping out a backlands settlement. There was a more serious enemy to be combatted, in a warfare of a slower and more worthy kind. This entire campaign would be a crime, a futile and a barbarous one, if we were not to take advantage of the paths opened by the artillery, by following up our cannon with a constant, stubborn, and persistent campaign of education, with the object of drawing these rude and backward fellow-countrymen of ours into the current of our times and our own national life. (408)

Sadly, as da Cunha himself notes, fully cognizant of the prowar hysteria that had gripped the capital in the South and that was calling for the federal forces to not only crush the rebels but punish their entire region, "under the pressure of difficulties demanding an immediate and assured solution, there was no place for these distant visions of the future" (408).[12] The heroic resistance of the supposedly inferior *sertanejos*, fighting on in the face of hopeless odds and, in the end, dying to the last man and boy in "a dreadful form of suicide" (474),[13] finally leads da Cunha—who once described himself as having a diverse racial background[14]—to question what he had been taught about people of mixed-race heritage and how this related not only to issues of Brazilian identity but to the political and cultural viability of modern Brazil itself.

Like Rabassa's *One Hundred Years of Solitude*, Samuel Putnam's *Rebellion in the Backlands* is a masterpiece of translation. Yet it must be noted that it differs from the original in two significant respects: First, Putnam employs the ellipsis less than da Cunha, who was perhaps following the example of Machado de Assis, exploiting the punctuation device to increase the involvement of the reader in the process of imbuing the text with meaning. Second, Putnam constantly restructures the original, the effect of which is to alter, slightly, the reader's reception of the original's often ironic and not infrequently outraged tone. To be sure, Putnam's English version definitely retains most, if not all, of this tone, but the form of its delivery has changed, perhaps to conform to the then standard rules of English nonfiction composition. A striking example occurs in the "Nota Preliminar" (Preliminary Note), in which the author lays out how and why his book was written. Here da Cunha devotes a paragraph to summing up the problem of the entire northeastern region of Brazil—its isolation from the rest of the nation—and, less often noted, to touching on one of modern Brazil's other great problems, its tendency to live "parasitically on the brink of the Atlantic in accordance with those principles of civilization which have been elaborated in Europe," even when these are incompatible with Brazilian social, political, and economic realities. He ends this discussion by noting that the backlanders were also "separated" from the rest of Brazil "by a co-ordinate of history—time" (xxx).

At this point, da Cunha's text dramatically offers up not another paragraph but three separate though tightly interconnected lines, each one more powerful than the one before and each one standing alone, as if it were a full paragraph in and of itself, a statement pregnant not merely with meaning but with a clarion declaration of the author's true motivation in writing *Os sertões*:

> Aquela campanha lembra um refluxo para o passado.
> E foi, na significação integral da palavra, um crime.
> Denunciemo-lo.

Because each line is like a punch to the reader's solar plexus, the structuring of the three lines, each of which functions on its own, generates a tremendous sense of force and drama, the genesis of which is not merely the meaning expressed by the words but their positioning in their respective lines, their relationship to each other, and their overall appearance on the page. Da Cunha's structuring, in other words, expands and intensifies his statement of purpose.

Putnam's translation successfully captures the author's basic intention here, but it gives up quite a lot in terms of commitment and dramatic structuring, which, again, is one of the most defining characteristics of da Cunha's original. As Putnam renders it:

> The campaign in question marked a backward step, an ebb in the direction of the past. It was in the integral sense of the word a crime and, as such, to be denounced. (xxx)

Although it has its own balance and rhythm, Putnam's double-clause translation of da Cunha's first line blunts its power just a bit. This tendency to extenuate, and to join together semantic units standing alone in the original, continues in Putnam's rendition of da Cunha's second powerful line, a more literal translation of which might be "And it was, in the full sense of the word, a crime." But the worst damage occurs in the linking of da Cunha's final, stunning line about authorial commitment and intention to his second line. The result, in Putnam's solid, semantically accurate translation, is the near total loss of da Cunha's personal statement, his decision not only to describe and even criticize the war waged against the backlanders but to denounce it. And to do so in a way that, grammatically speaking, forces the reader to take a position on the matter as well. The English translation, while capturing, albeit rather passively, the idea that the crime of Canudos was "to be denounced," loses the crucial point, clear in the original and its use of the imperative, that da Cunha is actively denouncing the crime and, with his selection of the first-person plural, insisting that the reader do so as well. A more literal translation, thus, might be "Let us denounce it." While these divergences are by no means fatal, and while they do have their own rhythms and patterns in English, they are significantly different from the original, and one wonders why, since they could have been structured so as to hew closer to the personal drama and outraged conviction inherent in da Cunha's very striking original. Still and all, one must regard Samuel Putnam's *Rebellion in the Backlands* as a brilliant translation, one that readers can rely on to chart the original's ironic and sometimes caustic tone and to inform them about the author's attitudes and positions with regard to the tangled, confused events of the terrible conflagration at Canudos, a bloody, barren ground whose tragic story should resonate in the sociopolitical consciousness of every inter-Americanist.

One American novelist, Peru's Mario Vargas Llosa, did find in da Cunha's epic work the germ of a novel that would speak not only to the fatal solitude of the *sertanejos* at Canudos but to a fundamental problem of the Americas generally, the struggle of our American nations to find viable, authentic identities and to take their rightful places on the world stage. While some have been more successful than others in achieving this goal, the quest for it has been a common denominator of the New World experience from the beginning. Appearing in Spanish as *La guerra del fin del mundo* in 1981 and as *The War of the End of the World* in 1984, the novel enjoys a special relationship with the 1902 da Cunha text upon which it was based. We have here the kind of perfectly legitimate inter-American literary study that scholars tend to ignore or forget about, the kind that involves authors and texts from the Americas other than the United States. All too often we simply assume that inter-American literary scholarship must perforce involve the United States, but this is simply not so, as excellent comparative work involving Spanish America and Brazil, or Latin America (both Brazil and Spanish America) and Canada, has shown. Very often, of course, the United States is involved, but this should not be regarded as a sine qua non of the inter-American paradigm. Read from this vantage point, it is clear that while *The War of the End of the World* does center on the disaster at Canudos and its larger significance to late-nineteenth-century Brazil, it additionally makes clear why the basic conflicts that caused it to explode are also pertinent to Spanish America, the United States, and Europe, and to relations between them. In this sense, one can argue quite convincingly that Vargas Llosa's novel is, in many ways, the epitome of the inter-American perspective.

The various forms and degrees of solitude encountered in *The War of the End of the World* fall naturally into three categories: an attempt (yet again) to explain what really happened at Canudos and why; the relationship between language and reality; and, finally, the nature of human relationships and the role that desire plays in them. If the first category is essentially a function of history and its ability to reconstruct and examine the past, the second takes up the epistemological problem posed by Saussurean linguistics (which forms the theoretical basis of both structuralism and poststructuralism), while the third explores the idea that the philosophical problem of solipsism (the ultimate form of solitude) lies, tragically, at the heart of our human quest for love. It is a mark of the novel's power that *The War of the End of the World* does not segregate these issues but, to the contrary, integrates them into a narrative that melds all aspects of the human experience. The tonal shifts that, in the original Spanish, mark such an undertaking are brought across in most successful fashion by Helen Lane, whose English version allows readers of *The War of the End of the World* to be confident of getting a textual response that is close to the one readers of *La guerra del fin del mundo* would receive. As in the case of Putnam's *Rebellion in the Backlands*, Lane's *The War of the End of the World* offers the English-language reader an accurate sense of the original's abruptly changing tones, registers, ironies, and levels of discourse.

Like Euclides da Cunha—a real person whom Vargas Llosa fictionalizes in the tragicomic figure of an unnamed "nearsighted journalist"—Vargas Llosa zeros in on the ongoing question of what really happened at Canudos. To appreciate Vargas Llosa's achievement, it is important to remember that he writes his text as a novelist, one skilled in the techniques and resources of fiction, and not as the objective reporter that da Cunha was trying to be. The problem involved here is one that lies as well at the base of history as a discipline and of all historical inquiry, and da Cunha was clearly aware of it. After writing part 1 as objectively as he could, he elected to write part 2, the ebb and flow of the war itself, and its implications for the participants and for all of Brazilian society, as if it were a novel. Apparently realizing that the methods of historiography were inadequate to his goal—explaining not merely *what* happened, which would be difficult enough, but *why* things happened as they did—da Cunha unhesitatingly turned to the techniques of fiction to tell his story and make his point: that what happened at Canudos was madness and a crime and could not be allowed to ever happen again. With this authorial shift in tactics or approach, part 2, the more celebrated part, reads like fiction, and, though it is clear that Vargas Llosa knows part 1 and builds its determinism into his plot, it is this second part that most inspires him and leads him to expand upon the many issues it raises. For the reader who knows both texts, it is quite instructive to chart which thematic lines Vargas Llosa elects to develop and, just as telling, which ones he chooses to ignore. For comparatists, the relationship between Vargas Llosa's totally fictionalized *War of the End of the World* and da Cunha's hybridization of fiction and nonfiction offers an extraordinarily fertile example of inter-American influence and reception, one that entwines not only texts and issues of aesthetics and literary theory but entire cultures and conflicting social and political systems.

The second category of solitude explored by Vargas Llosa links the problem of history and our ability to know the past with the more basic question of language as a semiotic system, as a reliable way of knowing the truth. Concerns over the tenuous relationship between language and reality abound in *The War of the End of the World*, to the point that they must be considered its second front, its "other" great theme. While our ability (and desire) to know with certainty what transpired at Canudos, and what it really meant, functions as the historical context for the novel's plot, Vargas Llosa here expands the concern over language that Rodríguez Monegal once declared to be the most distinguishing feature of the "new" Latin American novel of the 1960s and emphasizes its fundamental connection to the most crucial aspect of poststructural thought, its interrogation of meaning, how we regard it, and how we respond to its allure. This is why the problem of "seeing," in all its manifold forms, recurs so frequently in *The War of the End of the World*, becoming, finally, the book's most basic motif. If "see" is tantamount to "understand," then we do not understand very much at all, Vargas Llosa suggests, even when we are trying as hard as we can and even when we are looking directly at the thing we wish so desperately to comprehend. Being an eyewitness to events does not, Vargas Llosa insists, permit us even to say for certain what happened, much less why. Our desire to know is thus continuously thwarted by our inability to do so, and the resulting sense of frustration with which we must live becomes one of our most human characteristics. Like Clarice Lispector, Vargas Llosa is less interested in the jargon-filled theoretical debates of issues germane to poststructuralism than with its human face, the implications that its defining principles have for the human condition, for how we deal with the realization that we are lost in a world full of signs we can neither grasp nor understand. The poignant sense of solitude that stems from this sobering realization about language and our inability to make it do what we want it to do has been a hallmark of the best of Latin American literature from the late nineteenth century to the present time, and it is no accident that two of twentieth-century Latin America's greatest writers have confronted it and tried to come to terms with it. It is from this unique sense of solitude, the kind imposed by the failure of language, that much of the intellectual power of modern Latin American literature flows.

An extension of this outlook, the third category of solitude developed by Vargas Llosa in *The War of the End of the World* is, with one glaring exception, also the least obvious. Hardly mentioned in the extensive commentary on this well-known novel, the relationship between the Baron of Canabrava, his wife, Estela, and her maidservant, Sebastiana, allows Vargas Llosa to plumb the depths of the conflict between love and solipsism, between our desire to love another human being and our essential isolation, the perhaps irremediable solitude of human existence (a theme that poignantly resounds in García Márquez's *One Hundred Years of Solitude*). But, as we shall see, Vargas Llosa's handling of this issue is hardly romantic or sentimental. In fact, he couches the entire question in the volatile contexts of power, gender, and sexual desire, a tactic that greatly complicates the naive reader's response at the same time that it enriches and renders more profound our consideration of what transpires between the three characters and what meaning we ascribe to it. Coming, as it does, late in the novel, well after the other, more obvious issues have been if not resolved then at least played out to their logical conclusions, the culminating scene involving the relationship between the baron, his wife, and her maid serves as a kind of coda to all that precedes it. The positioning of this scene, and the way all the other issues raised previously seem to coalesce naturally in it, make the reader wonder if Vargas Llosa's intent here is to show that all the preceding intellectual issues—the problem of knowing, the problem of language and its relationship to reality, the problem of meaning—are not superfluous to the human condition but, in fact, essential to it. Focusing on these three characters, whose development in preparation for this pivotal moment can be easily mapped in the earlier sections of the novel, Vargas Llosa seems to want to show us that these issues are not just idle intellectual chatter but visceral concerns built into the very essence of human relationships, human identity, and human existence. Even in a state of love, when we expect to connect most intimately with another person, we cannot escape the problems of interpretation and meaning; even in a state of love, or desirous of it, we are not immune to misunderstanding what is before us, what we see with our own eyes, what we experience with our own bodies. Not even in the most intense moments of sexual intercourse, when we seek, physically and emotionally, to break out of our solitude and connect with another human being, can we be sure that we understand what is taking place.

Covering some seven pages of the translation, this extraordinary scene involves not only the concept of love but the baron's rape of Sebastiana, an event witnessed by Estela but complicated, the text suggests, by what may or may not be her willing participation in it. A further complication is that Estela and Sebastiana may themselves be lovers of long standing, a line of interpretation that can also be traced back through the novel and its development of their characters and relationships. What is not in doubt is that the episode is written almost entirely from the baron's perspective, a tactic that leads the reader to interpret the entire scene as an exercise in power and exploitation—and as a meditation on the fatal kind of solitude that the actualization of these imposes on a person. Regardless of the motivations that the narrative says are driving the baron at this juncture, his actions clearly point to abusive behavior with respect to issues of power, gender, race, and class—in short, to his life as a rich and powerful landowner in the very conservative *sertão*. The baron is accustomed to "possessing" things, including people, and to using them as he sees fit.

Complicating this relatively simple and straightforward line of interpretation, however, is the possibility that, overcoming differences of class and race, the two women, Estela and Sebastiana, have already paired off, united, perhaps, by what they (and the reader) regard as their status as chattel in the very masculine world of the baron and their love for each other. In the culminating moment of this powerful and very complex scene, the baron, performing cunnilingus on a sobbing and distraught Sebastiana, is interrupted by Estela, who, the text informs us, "did not appear to be frightened, enraged," or "horrified," but rather "mildly intrigued." The baron, "still holding the servant's legs apart with his elbows," turns to his wife and declares:

> Estela, my love, my love. . . . I love you, more than anything else in the world. I am doing this because I have wanted to for a long time, and out of love for you. To be closer to you, my darling. (539)

As if it were an indisputable sign of the correctness of his interpretation, the baron then observes that Estela's "forehead was not furrowed by that single deep wrinkle that was an unmistakable sign that she was greatly annoyed, the sole manifestation of her real feelings that Estela had never succeeded in controlling." Augmenting the reader's confidence in the baron's interpretation of Estela's response to his treatment of Sebastiana, the narrative voice at this point declares that Estela "was not frowning; her lips, however, were slightly parted, emphasizing the interest, the curiosity, the calm surprise in her eyes." The text then implies that the solitude of Estela's existence is pierced by her reaction to what she is seeing: "But what was new, however minute a sign it might appear to be, was this turning outward, this interest in something outside herself, for since that night in Calumbi the baron had never seen any other expression in the baroness's eyes save indifference, withdrawal, a retreat of the spirit" (539).

The alert reader, however, understands that this does not quite mean what it might, since, in an earlier scene involving a dispute over whether Sebastiana should be dismissed, the baron, suffering the pangs of jealousy over seeing "the camaraderie, the inviolable intimacy that existed between the two women," had a terrible argument with his wife, "the most serious one," in fact, "of their entire married life." In his mind the baron still had vivid images "of the baroness, her cheeks on fire, defending her maidservant and repeating over and over that if Sebastiana left, she was leaving, too." This memory, the reader learns, as if in anticipation of the later scene, had long been, for the baron, "a spark setting his desire aflame" (309). As a result, perhaps, of this earlier suggestion of intimacy between the two women, and the challenge to his control that it implies, the baron, in the later and more developed scene, finally elects in his time of personal and political crisis to put to the test his interpretation of the ambiguous relationship between Estela and Sebastiana by assaulting the clearly unwilling maidservant.

> "I always wanted to share her with you, my darling," he stammered, his voice unsteady because of the contrary emotions he was experiencing: timidity, shame, devotion, and reborn desire. "But I never dared, because I feared I would offend you, wound your feelings. I was wrong, isn't that so? Isn't it true that you would not have been offended or wounded? That you would have accepted it, looked upon it with pleasure? Isn't it true that it would have been another way of showing you how much I love you, Estela?" (540)

The narrative voice then tells us that, carefully watching his wife's reaction to this declaration, the baron "saw her turn after a moment to look at Sebastiana, who was still curled up sobbing, and saw that gaze, which until that moment had been neutral, grow interested, gently complaisant" (540). As if offering a clue to the reader's role in the process of interpretation, the narrator next informs us: "Obeying this sign that he had received from the baroness," the baron "let go of her hand," at which point Estela sits down on the bed and "with great care and precaution" takes Sebastiana's face between her hands while the baron proceeds to rape her.

Then—in a reference that parallels the problem of another character, one Galileo Gall, a European anarchist who has come to the *sertão* to help foment at Canudos the revolution envisioned by his particular ideology—we are told that, with the baron's desire now returned "like a mad fury," he "did not want to see any more" (540). As he climaxes, his life seeming to "explode between his legs," he manages to see Estela "still holding Sebastiana's face between her two hands, gazing at her with pity and tenderness as she blew gently on her forehead to free a few little hairs stuck to her skin" (540).

In the concluding scene, the baron wakes up alone several hours later and, covering himself with a sheet (as if feeling Adam's shame at being here cast out of the edenic world of the two women), goes into the room of the baroness and finds Estela and Sebastiana in bed together, sleeping, but, it is pointed out in a perhaps strategically embedded phrase, "their bodies not touching" (541). The translation, at this critical juncture, hews faithfully to the original, both tonally and semantically, retaining its central uncertainty as to what has happened here: "Ella y Sebastián dormían, sin tocarse, en el amplio lecho, y el barón estuvo un momento observándolas con un sentimiento indefinable a través de la gasa transparente del mosquitero." (543)

[She and Sebastiana were sleeping, their bodies not touching, in the wide bed, and the baron stood there for a moment looking at them through the transparent mosquito netting, filled with an indefinable emotion (541)].

Artfully done, Vargas Llosa's narrative thus manages to suggest both that the two women have long had a lesbian relationship, in defiance of all the baron represents, and simultaneously that they may well not have had a sexual relationship at all, though it does seem likely that they have some sort of emotional bond that has allowed them to support and comfort each other and, in so doing, defy at least some of the baron's power and control. The reader is thus offered several different lines of interpretation, all plausible and all consistent with what went before in the novel. The result, from the author's perspective, is the creation in this climactic scene of precisely the kind of ambiguity that has percolated throughout as the novel's basic theme. Here, however, it appears in its most distilled, most troubling, and yet most human form. Vargas Llosa makes so much use of the verb "to see" because, for him, the essential problem that *The War of the End of the World* speaks to is that although we can *see* physiologically, we cannot *understand*, or at least we do so only imperfectly. Or we misinterpret the meaning not only of the events we witness, or "see," but of those in which we are ourselves intimately involved, as evidenced by the case of the baron, Estela, and Sebastiana. What we most desire will forever elude us. Not even in the most intense moments of our existences can we escape from the essential solitude and myopia that plague us.

More than this, Vargas Llosa is showing us that the same problem afflicts us all: the characters who, like Gall and the "nearsighted journalist" patterned on Euclides da Cunha, are trying to understand what was happening at Canudos; the baron trying to understand what is happening with his wife and her maidservant; and the reader trying to understand what is happening in any given text. Is Estela, the reader wonders, really interested in a ménage à trois with her husband and Sebastiana? Or, paralleling the cases of Gall and the nearsighted journalist and many others in the novel—all of whom are puzzling over the meaning of something, even something they themselves have witnessed or participated in—does the baron see only what he wants to see? Does the baron interpret what he believes (or wants to believe) is happening between Estela and Sebastiana through the (distorting?) lens of his desire, just as Gall's European revolutionary ideology leads him to see what he wants to see at Canudos, and just as a reader's ideology or theoretical perspective can lead to misinterpreting, misreading, or distorting a text? This commanding final scene of the novel, then, can be said to stand as a grand if disturbing metaphor for the entire problem of interpretation and our quest for meaning: in historical events, in human relationships, in the act of reading, and in language use generally, whether the goal is to try to explain what happened in the past, to explain what is happening in the here and now, or to establish a definitive meaning for a text. The problem of interpretation, Vargas Llosa tells us, is the problem of life itself, and we have no alternative but to deal with it while aware, painfully and with great frustration, of being trapped in the unique kind of solitude that comes from realizing that, as human beings, we are indeed condemned to what Fredric Jameson calls the "prison-house of language."

Two additional Rabassa translations of Vargas Llosa are worth mention in the context of the "prison house of language": *La casa verde* (1965; tr. Gregory Rabassa, *The Green House*, 1968) and *Conversación en La Catedral* (1969; tr. Gregory Rabassa, *Conversation in The Cathedral*, 1975). The settings of *The Green House* are a provincial city and the hostile yet seductive environment of the Peruvian jungle, one that the author has used in several of his novels. The jungle and the institution of prostitution are the metaphorical prisons in this work, which is based on Vargas Llosa's travels with a group of anthropologists into the jungle, where Indian girls were forced to serve as prostitutes after being abducted from the coast. *The Green House* is the story of a house of prostitution that is burned and then rebuilt; in a parallel story line, a young girl from a jungle mission becomes a prostitute in Piura. Rabassa comments how in this novel Vargas Llosa "became one of that group practicing what would be called, for better or for worse, magic realism" (*Treason*, 77). While there is "nothing otherworldly" in the novel, the characters "have the proportions of monsters" (77).

Conversation in The Cathedral takes place in a cheap bar, The Cathedral of the title, where two characters meet and spend the afternoon talking about their pasts. The "prison" of the characters is their dialogue, which wraps them in layers of memory, narrative, interior monologue, and the external events around them. Essentially a novel of power and politics in the Peru of the 1950s, the book poignantly illustrates the grip of military dictatorship on a country. Rabassa comments on the difficulty of translating the verbs in the novel to capture the nuances of the various Spanish past tense forms ("two, sometimes three past tenses, each with a definite temporal connotation") (*Treason*, 79). He notes that he is happy not to have translated *The War of the End of the World*, because he "cannot see how anyone can improve on the novelistic reportage of Euclides da Cunha in his *Os sertões* (*Rebellion in the Backlands*). Any comparison always brings to mind Cervantes and Avellaneda" (81).

Translating the Land

Octavio Paz said in *Corriente alterna* that Juan Rulfo is "the only Mexican novelist who has given us an image, instead of just a description, of our landscape." Rulfo's classic Mexican novel *Pedro Páramo* (1955; tr. Margaret Sayers Peden, 1994) is set in an isolated village of rural Mexico called Comala. It is an oneiric tale that relates the search of a man for his father, and the father's obsession with a woman, Susana San Juan. In this story, comprised of the "murmurs" of many citizens of Comala, the town itself is the main protagonist, and it is a city of the dead. Carmen Boullosa notes how the novel has an "astonishing acoustic quality; its dialogues and interior monologues feel improvised, as if the author let the characters speak on their own. . . . The text's popular expressions, colloquialisms, idioms, sayings and proverbs give it an authentic lightness, a regional flavor, a very Mexican and picaresque *salsita*" (2). She also notes that the novel is at once "rural and cosmopolitan" and that it is the consummate representation of Mexico, the land and the people (2). Margaret Sayers Peden's remarkable translation captures the poetic and mysterious qualities of Rulfo's prose, as well as the numerous intertextual references that mark his writing, which draws on its Mexican modernist and surrealist heritage as well as the European and American writers who influenced Rulfo.

The Brazilian *sertão* and the multiple forms of solitude it imposes on all whose lives it touches take center stage again in one of Latin American literature's greatest novels, João Guimarães Rosa's epic masterpiece *Grande sertão: veredas* (1956). Little known in the English-speaking world except among Brazilianists, and not helped by its serviceable but flawed translation, called *The Devil to Pay in the Backlands* (tr. James L. Taylor and Harriet de Onís, 1963), it richly deserves its fame as one of the greatest novels ever produced in the Americas. As Rodríguez Monegal and Colchie describe it:

> The tale, set chronologically in the early twentieth century but belonging to the era of romance, plays tantalizingly with the theme of homosexuality in a way that recalls some of Thomas Mann's masterly exercises. But Guimarães goes even further than the German master. At the very center of the novel he places an episode in which Riobaldo believes he has met the Devil himself. The primeval search for the father, diabolical temptation, frustrated eroticism—all these motifs are so intricately intertwined and inter-related as to make *Grande sertão: veredas* one of the most complex works of fiction ever produced in Latin America. (2:678)

A language novel in the tradition of *Finnegans Wake*, but with a more clearly defined story line, *The Devil to Pay in the Backlands* is an extraordinary achievement. An unbroken monologue of some 624 pages in the original Portuguese, and of a linguistic inventiveness that parallels Joyce's work, the novel is narrated by one Riobaldo, a now retired and respectable *jagunço*, or backlands gunman, who is pouring out his life's story to a greatly respected though unnamed listener, a "senhor"—perhaps Rosa himself, or the reader—who will perhaps impart coherence and meaning to this now vivid and fast-moving, now hypnotic and meandering discourse. The facts of Riobaldo's life are, like the *sertão* itself, less important than the meaning we take from the experience of living there. A land of both great violence and great beauty, where nothing is what it appears to be and where everything changes constantly, the *sertão* is an enchanting if dangerous enigma. Riobaldo's probing, self-conscious narrative ebbs and flows and surges like a great river, casting up a welter of radically different speech registers, neologisms, deformed words, ordinary words used in unusual ways, great swaths of poetic prose, and long, sinuous sentences deliberately left uncompleted. The mystery and mutability of language, in fact, can be said to gradually emerge as the novel's greatest theme, one encapsulated in one of the novel's key motifs: in the *sertão*, "*tudo é e não é*" [everything is and isn't].

With these sorts of language issues so integral to the novel's success in its original Portuguese, it is little wonder that readers who know *Grande sertão: veredas* in its strange yet compelling Portuguese find its English translation wanting. For some, the linguistic virtuosity and mystery of the original have been leached out of the translation, leaving an exciting but routine Western adventure story about a war between rival outlaw gangs (some of whom carry American Winchesters) with a surprise twist at the end.[15] As William L. Grossman wrote in a 1963 review for the *New York Times*,

> The translators deserve our sympathy. How can one translate a book in which the substance is closely wed to a unique style? Rosa sometimes employs onomatopoeia, alliteration, rhythm and even rhyme. He uses archaisms, regional expressions and terms of his own fabrication; in some passages even erudite Brazilians find him hard to understand. (27)

Grossman, an expert in Brazilian Portuguese and one of the first to re-create Machado de Assis in English, goes on to say of *The Devil to Pay in the Backlands* that the translators, James L. Taylor and Harriet de Onís, "might have tried to devise an English style with a flavor as close to that of Rosa's

Portuguese as possible. The product would probably have been either brilliant or disastrous. They chose, instead, to employ a conventional style, with the result that much of the color is drained from the book. For example, where Rosa writes of the 'foamy spit' on the surface of swollen, dirty rivers, the translators merely write 'spume'" (27), an accurate enough image, but one that pales next to Rosa's more elaborate original. This sort of problem, plus the deletion of whole passages, makes for an English version of this great American novel that will turn heads but not for the right reasons. The Guimarães Rosa who is received by an audience via *The Devil to Pay in the Backlands* will be that unfortunate author whose greatness is not made manifest by the translation. Yet it is also true that to know Rosa even by means of an imperfect translation is better than not to know him at all. Such is the magnitude of this egregiously underappreciated 1956 novel, a landmark text in the history of the novel form in the Americas and one crying out for a new translation.

Though little known outside the Luso-Brazilian ken, the novel has been hugely influential in Brazil and, increasingly, in Spanish America and the rest of the Americas, where, slowly but surely, the affinities between Rosa's deeply mythic treatment of the *sertão*, where the timeless struggle between Good and Evil gets played out with backlands *jagunços* ironically conjuring up images of medieval knights hijacking the Western genre, and the larger New World experience are being recognized and applauded.[16] Recalling both Melville's *Moby Dick* and Faulkner's *Absalom, Absalom!*, Rosa's novel has the same mix of gritty regionalism, the strange beauty of chaos and violence, metaphysical seductiveness, and the expiation of guilt. Written in the tradition of da Cunha's *Rebellion in the Backlands* and anticipating by almost fifteen years Vargas Llosa's *War of the End of the World* with its treatment of both the ontological and epistemological dimensions of language, Rosa's *The Devil to Pay in the Backlands* shows the human creature slowly and painfully coming to realize that living is a lonely, uncertain, and "very dangerous business" (another of the novel's motifs), a great "travessia," or journey, across the cruel and indecipherable but always beautiful universe that is the *grande sertão*.

The final author whose work we would like to discuss in the context of the unique forms of solitude that pepper the literature of the Americas is Darcy Ribeiro. Renowned in his native Brazil as an anthropologist, a fiction writer, and a sharp-minded and often controversial social critic, Ribeiro will be examined here with respect to two of his best-known and most influential works, the novel *Maíra* (1978; tr. E. H. Goodland and Thomas Colchie, 1984), and his book-length study of Brazilian culture and civilization, *O povo brasileiro* (1995; tr. Gregory Rabassa, *The Brazilian People: The Formation and Meaning of Brazil*, 2000).

Ribeiro's first novel, *Maíra* deals with a question that, though it is accorded disgracefully scant attention throughout the Americas, is of the utmost urgency: the plight of our remaining indigenous peoples. While the English version is generally accurate and reliable in such elusive matters as tone and context, it does tend toward the literal and away from the creative, so that the reader may, on occasion, encounter seemingly awkward and unnatural constructions. Then, too, this is the kind of important text that would have benefited greatly from a detailed and discerning critical introduction, one that explained for the imperfectly informed reader the significance of the many references to Mairún culture that enrich the text. Indeed, it might also have sought to develop the kind of integrated Pan-American perspective that would help a too often neglected nation like Brazil feature its indigenous tradition while at the same time actually facilitating the entire inter-American project as it applies to our native peoples, past, present, and future. In such an introduction the translators could also have pointed out the linguistic conundrums they faced and how they elected to solve them, a tactic that would allow the reader to better appreciate what they were up against and how, at least in some instances, a more mechanical approach was the better one. Still and all, one must credit the translators with successfully capturing the many tones that color this narrative. By turns ironic, angry, and resigned, *Maíra* tells a tale in which one culture's vision of progress becomes another's extermination, and for that reason alone we in the Americas, with our miserable historical record on this point, need to know Ribeiro's novel better and to think, seriously and without romanticized misconceptions, about the issues with which it challenges us.

Focusing on the intertwining lives of two main characters—Isaías/Avá, a young Indian man who is returning to his Mairún people after rejecting an opportunity to become a Catholic priest, and a young white woman, Alma, who rejects the role assigned her as a woman in modern society to seek a more satisfying personal identity—*Maíra* also deals, by extension, with the larger issue of the perhaps fatal clash between Native American culture and Western ideas about progress and development. The personal frustration, spiritual anguish, and isolation suffered by Isaías/Avá and Alma suggest that Ribeiro, an international authority on Native Americans, foresees destruction, not assimilation, as their ultimate fate, as it would seem to be for Native American culture generally. Exploited and corrupted by the forces of capitalism and increasingly marginalized by technological advances, Native Americans in the New World do not have a bright future. An additional theme of the novel, one that is again distinctly inter-American, is the religious clash between the native peoples of the Amazon basin (and the rest of the Americas) and an especially rigid and apocalyptic stripe of conservative American Christianity. This issue, a powerful and disturbing subtext of the novel, takes life through the creation of two characters, an American evangelical missionary and his linguist wife, who are assiduously translating the Bible into Mairún. The reader gradually realizes, however, that the translators are much less interested in the welfare of the Mairún as a people than in forcing literal translations of the Bible upon them. The imposition of a particular religious ideology, rather than any genuine concern for Mairún culture and civilization, is thus revealed to be the real purpose of this endeavor, which pulses just beneath the surface of the novel and ties together many of its other forces and tensions. And while the evangelicals would claim that they are improving the lot of the Mairún by replacing a false religious system with the one true faith, a more skeptical reader might well note that, for the Mairún obliged to undergo this conversion, the resulting sense of loss seems consistently to outweigh any alleged gain. The Mairún, like so many other American Indian cultural groups, are thus being forced, by the combined forces of religion, politics, and economic policy, into the kind of cultural solitude that borders more on oblivion than on salvation.

A second line of inter-American interest is opened when another of the characters, a Brazilian politician who knows nothing of the lands inhabited by the Mairún, concocts a scheme by which he will eventually be able to gain ownership of all their territory, strip away the forest, and turn the land into a vast cattle ranch, a development that recalls one of Theodore Roosevelt's lesser-known (by Americans, at least) visions of how Latin America might eventually be put to good use, which is to say, how it might be made profitable for U.S. corporations investing in the region. This kind of activity has, of course, been all too prevalent, with developers seeing the Amazonian forest as a resource to be exploited and paying little or no attention to the fact that the rain-forest soil consistently proves too fragile to sustain the depleting usage entailed in cattle ranching. Such unthinking and uncaring development has been the bane of the Amazon basin, as in similar places and cases the world over, and this too emerges as one of *Maíra*'s most significant themes.

A third inter-American concern might be identified in the novel's steady exposition of the conflict between the distinctive and attractive but vulnerable Mairún social structure and the encroaching frontier of a rabid Brazilian expansionism, one largely driven, Ribeiro makes clear, by international economic institutions that he believes have been given excessive control over Brazil's political and economic well-being. Long a critic of the policies of the Brazilian "economic miracle" of the 1960s and 1970s that was used by the dictatorship to justify its brutal practices, Ribeiro demonstrates here that the notion of the "frontier" is not limited to the expansion of the United States, although the applicability of this term to the social history of the two nations is widely recognized. In *Maíra* the problem is presented primarily in terms typically associated with structural anthropology. A relentless prodevelopment push is pitted against the ways of native culture (the novel's title, *Maíra*, is the Tupi word for the creator of the universe), and the outcome of this struggle is never in doubt. The imposition, again by an outside force bent on domination, of Christianity on Mairún religious beliefs is, as we have seen, another of the novel's key conflicts, and its resolution very effectively conveys what Ribeiro believes the fate of the Mairún people will be in the noneconomic sphere. In short, as this elegiac yet prophetic novel makes poignantly manifest, the destiny of the god Maíra, beset by forces beyond his control, will spell out the destiny not only of the Mairún and the other indigenous peoples of the New World but the destiny of the Americas generally.

Turning from fiction to nonfiction, in 1995 Ribeiro published *O povo brasileiro*, a work judged questionable by many yet recognized by everyone as his final statement on the issue that had long preoccupied him and overshadowed all his other work: the nature of Brazil and its people. Elegantly translated into English by Gregory Rabassa, *The Brazilian People* confronts what the author sees as the basic paradox of Brazil: that a place and a people so bountiful in natural resources and potential remain so hamstrung by a rigid system of class segregation, unequal income distribution, and racial prejudice, patterns that were established during Brazil's colonial experience and that subsequent generations have not been able to dislodge (318). Working in the tradition of such thinkers as Vianna Moog, Samuel Putnam, and Gilberto Freyre, Ribeiro also considers Brazil in comparison with the United States. "The question arising," he contends, "is how to understand why the North Americans, so poor and backward, praying in their wooden churches without any prominence in any area of cultural creativity, rose fully into industrial civilization while we sank into backwardness" (319–20). For Ribeiro, the answer to this question lies in the differing systems of sociopolitical organization. "The bad thing here," he says of Brazil, "the effective cause of the backwardness, is the way in which society is structured, organized against the interests of the population, who are always bled in order to serve designs that are alien and even opposed to their own" (320).

If one applies these criteria to the reigning social, political, and economic policies of the United States in the year 2007, it is certainly legitimate to wonder, as many are already suggesting, whether the old bugaboos of hypocrisy, provincialism, and xenophobia are not moving the United States backward at precisely the time nations like Brazil and Canada are moving forward, gaining strength as open, tolerant cultures and as progressive, forward-looking political entities. Implying the urgent need for precisely this sort of inter-American dialogue and comparison, Ribeiro then asks, who are the Brazilians? (320). He answers his own question with this ringing declaration of Brazilian identity and legitimacy: "We Brazilians . . . are a mixed-blood people in flesh and spirit, for miscegenation here was never a crime or a sin. We were made through it and we are still being made that way" (321). Brazilians, Ribeiro proudly contends, are "a people in the making," in search of their destiny even today, and because of this they are "open to the future" (321) in ways that epitomize the larger New World experience. Suggesting, finally, that the historical isolation of Brazil is best explained in terms of both external and internal pressures, the result of a caste system of social organization, Ribeiro, confident of his nation's future (and sounding, on balance, like a nineteenth-century American), contends that, in spite of its myriad problems, Brazil is "the new Rome," a "new civilization" that is built of "mixed blood" and is "proud of itself" for "being open to all races and all cultures" (322).

As we have seen, the theme of solitude permeates the literature of the New World (which, of course, was already an ancient world to the millions of people living here when the Europeans arrived). Though varying greatly in its expression and its sociopolitical contexts, the theme of solitude invariably serves as a reminder that, while the entire concept of America turned on the idea that life could be better than it was in the Old World, the ensuing realities too often ended up being something else, something inimical to the vision. Perhaps because it *was* a European invention, rather than a fact, the New World was prone to corruption and failure from the beginning. In large terms, one can see that two very different European social, political, and religious systems, Jesuit Catholicism and Puritan Protestantism, were implanted in the Americas and that these would produce civilizations that, as many Latin American writers including Paz and Ribeiro in particular have noted, stood in often stark contrast to each other. And rarely is this expression of solitude more acutely felt than in the Native American people whose traditions and cultures, in both North and South America, have been systematically destroyed or marginalized in the name of European religious and cultural superiority. The presence of Native American literature is essential to the entire inter-American project, for without it we do not see what we, the winners, have chosen, in our smugness and bigotry, to destroy or disparage. The Native American presence thus becomes a marker not only of our own morality but a reminder that life in the Americas is not what it should be, that violence, disdain, prejudice, and exploitation still characterize what we once believed would be the edenic experience, our crowning moment, our paradise. Seen from this perspective, the theme of solitude really speaks, in the more comprehensive, hemispheric sense of the term, to the perversion of the "American dream," a term that must be understood as something greater than proudly "possessing" a five-car garage and being pleased with greed, deceit, arrogance, sanctimoniousness, and aggression as defining characteristics of self and of nation. Charged, restively, by a gnawing sense of failure, a realization that we have not created the kinds of tolerant, justice-seeking, and humane societies that, given the high ideals that originally drove us here, we should have created, the theme of solitude truly binds the Americas together. In so doing, moreover, it justifies the inter-American approach as few other themes can, though it does so in ways that sharply define the tremendous differences that both unite and separate us. Whether we and future generations can overcome these differences and nurture the forces that unite us remains to be seen.

Urbanization and the Evolution of Contemporary Latin American Literature into a Hemispheric Context

Changing Patterns of Influence and Reception

The increasing urbanization of Latin America has been catalyst to the growth of a sophisticated literary community, created in large part through the translation and assimilation of key works. Writers in the United States and Europe began to focus their attention on their inter-American counterparts, initiating a period of intense intellectual dialogue flowing between continents in multiple directions. The rise of an urban persona in inter-American literature confronted cultural stereotypes and posed new challenges for the translator, particularly the task of acquiring and transmitting the new voices of the Americas in a changing world context. The similarities and differences between the Boom writers of Spanish America and the Brazilian writers of the same generation have had deep implications for the work of the translator.

The Latin American urban narrative since the 1960s has challenged stereotypes about Latin American literature and culture. A corpus of works has been published that unveils a metropolitan Southern Hemisphere strikingly similar to North America and Europe, but also marked by distinct differences. While the term *Boom* refers to the literature that emerged from Spanish-language Latin America in the 1960s, there are commonalities that link the Boom writers with their Brazilian counterparts. The themes of alienation, anonymity, human frailty, solitude, and imprisonment play out on the streets and avenues of Buenos Aires, Rio de Janeiro, São Paulo, Curitiba, Salvador, Bogotá, Panama City, and Havana. The writers of and since the 1960s display detachment and irony while wielding a mordant sense of humor to express the inexpressibility of emotion. The short story and song become vehicles of protest against dictatorship and repression. Domestic drama is an allegory for social dysfunction of a larger order. Women evolve into the subjects, not just the objects, of artistic and literary creation. A chorus of new voices and attitudes is projected into the hemisphere by the works in translation of the Spanish American Boom and its Brazilian counterpart that will have a transformative effect on society and culture. Through the medium of translation, the Latin American urban writers of the 1960s stride onto the world stage, shattering the "silence" of a self-proclaimed "exhausted culture" (Sontag, 182, 187–88). In the post-Boom, postmodern era, the themes of imprisonment and release are replaced by those of globalization and displacement.

This sophisticated city voice from Latin America surprised the North American ear. It was expected that the exotic and regional would continue to be the subject of letters from the South. *One Hundred Years of Solitude* was misread by many English-language readers for this reason. The dark and haunting vision of the new urban writers emerging from the capitals of Brazil, Colombia, Argentina, and Cuba presented new challenges to the reception of Latin American literature in the Northern Hemisphere.

Jorge Amado: Transition to a Postmodern Inter-American Urban Ethos

Among the Brazilian writers who have contributed most to the emergence of a postmodern inter-American urban ethos are Jorge Amado, Rubem Fonseca, Ignácio de Loyola Brandão, Lygia Fagundes Telles, and Caio Fernando Abreu, as well as a host of masters of the short story including Dalton Trevisan, Moacyr Scliar, Murilo Rubião, and Victor Giudice. Each of these important figures has made a unique contribution to the new inter-American narrative. Jorge Amado (1912–2001) is both a transitional and a controversial figure. He is the most widely translated Brazilian novelist—his works have appeared in thirty-three languages—and the first Brazilian to achieve commercial success in the United States. His 1958 best seller *Gabriela, cravo e canela* (tr. James L. Taylor and William L. Grossman, *Gabriela, Clove and Cinnamon*, 1962) was listed as one of the top twenty-five novels published in the United States in 1962 (Brower et al., 1). He is credited with opening the international market to the postdictatorship generation of Brazilian writers. Amado has the longest list of English-language translators, including Harriet de Onís, Helen Lane, Margaret Neves, Samuel Putnam, and Gregory Rabassa. Barbara Shelby is responsible for at least six works, including his famous novella *A morte e a morte de Quincas Berro D'Água* (1962; *The Two Deaths of Quincas Wateryell*, 1965) and his later novels *Tenda dos milagres* (1969; *Tent of Miracles*, 1971), *Tereza Batista, cansada de guerra* (1972; *Tereza Batista: Home from the Wars*, 1975), and *Tietá do Agreste* (1977; *Tietá, the Goat Girl*, 1979).

The commonplace of Amado criticism is that his work is divided into two phases. The early "Marxist" stage covers the novels classified as the "cacao cycle"—*O país do carnaval* (Carnival country, 1931), *Cacau* (Cacao, 1933), *Suor* (Sweat, 1934), and *Terras do sem fim* (1942; tr. Samuel Putnam, *The Violent Land*, 1945)—and the early urban novels of Salvador: *Jubiabá* (1935; tr. Margaret A. Neves, 1984), *Mar morto* (1936; tr. Gregory Rabassa, *Sea of Death*, 1984), and *Capitães da Areia* (1937; tr. Gregory Rabassa, *Captains of the Sands*, 1988). The second, lighter period, includes his later novels centering on the figures of heroic women, Gabriela, Dona Flor, Tereza Batista, and Tietá do Agreste. His work is considered transitional because of the way his writings usher in a modern urban narrative through time-honored techniques derived from the Brazilian oral tradition (see Lowe, "New"). As Brower, Fitz, and Martínez-Vidal observe,

> One's opinion of Amado's skill as a novelist, in fact, can change rather dramatically if one considers works like *Tent of Miracles*, *Home Is the Sailor* [*Os velhos marinheiros ou o capitão de longo curso*], or *A morte e a morte de Quincas Berro Dágua* [*The Two Deaths of Quincas Wateryell*] as not exemplifying the traditional realistic novel, but what we might think of as a new genre, the oral novel, or the oral tradition reconstituted in written novelistic form. Reading *Tent of Miracles*, for example, is very much akin to sitting in one's favorite bar listening to a master storyteller spin out a great, sprawling yarn, replete with fascinating characters, endless subplots, and a constant commentary on the story-telling process itself, including the role of the listener/reader in it." (2)

The controversy around Amado is sparked by what some believe is sexual and ethnic stereotyping in his post-1958 works and the reinforcement of "paternalistic racial views" (Brower et al., 2). His reception, then, is very mixed. For his English language readers, he is a fascinating source of exotic and titillating narratives about the vast, unknown country of Brazil (a misreading), and for Brazilians, he is either "a great ambassador of Brazilian culture and civilization around the world" or a faux populist who thinly disguises sexist and racist attitudes behind charming prose (2). In this, Amado is akin to Darcy Ribeiro, who has been accused of similar contradictions. Indeed, says Bobby Chamberlain, Amado's signature tropes of "comical overstatement . . . sarcasm, class humor, playful anecdotes, and ribaldry" (32) not only set him up for misreading but also set the greatest challenges for the translator. "The novelist's propensity to caricature and his neo-romantic identification with the Brazilian masses are cited as proof of his literary naïveté. But his desacralization of canonical discourses and the perspicacity of his social satire frequently escape detection" (36–37). Joanna Courteau takes this a step further to describe Amado's narrative process as an "engineering" of a new "national discourse in which tradition coexists with change, being displaced by it without violence" (48). How, then, is it possible to translate Amado's "utopian vision" or "*malandro* heaven" into the English language, which, according to Lawrence Venuti, tends to be represented by publishers, professors, and even translators as "the transparent vehicle of universal truth, thus encouraging a linguistic chauvinism, even a cultural nationalism" (*Scandals*, 92, quoted in White, 47)?

The difficulty in translating Amado with full justice lies both in language and in point of view. The duality and personalism of Brazilian life, which Amado celebrates in his narratives, are difficult if not impossible to translate cross-culturally. Amado presents the "third, synthetic position" identified by Roberto DaMatta, which is grounded in Brazilian institutions such as the *jeitinho* (getting around a rule or roadblock, usually through personal connections) and the Brazilian "'relational' or integrational ethic" (Chamberlain, 38). The English-language reader can only interpret this as naive or fanciful. For all the apparent simplicity of Amado's novels, he requires a sophisticated and culturally connected readership that can discern the ambiguity of his characters and plots. As Lowe points out, "This crosscultural paradox is artfully explicated in Catarina Edinger's essay 'Dona Flor in Two Cultures.' Edinger demonstrates how the 1982 American film *Kiss Me Goodbye* turns *Dona Flor* into a situation comedy for a homogeneous American 'mass' audience which completely misses the theme of choice and ambiguity that makes Dona Flor an interesting character" ("Character," 128). The theme of choice and ambiguity is central to Dona Flor and consistent with the expression of Brazilian cultural and national identity that marks Amado and his generation. While the moral universe of the United States is, from the perspective of our neighbors in the Southern Hemisphere, "polarized," in Brazil moral distinctions are not as clear. This subtlety is difficult to translate into the North American black-and-white ethical code.

If one compares Flor to her predecessor, Gabriela, and her successor, Tereza Batista, it is possible to note an evolution of the female character as a symbol for a country in transition as well as a gauge of Amado's attitudes toward the Brazilian "puzzle." Basic to Gabriela's character is the possession of freedom to pursue the enjoyment of the sensual life. Flor, in redefining her relationship with her two husbands, achieves personal satisfaction and economic and political autonomy. Tereza Batista, described by Ellen Douglass as the "warrior maiden" (84)—albeit betrayed in the end by the patriarchal agenda—does not experience the growth expected of a modern character. Tereza's story is told within the conventions of *cordel* (troubadour) poetry and a strong overlay of Amadian parody of his own novelistic techniques. As a character, she can be seen as a parody of her predecessors Flor and Gabriela, and her happy ending is accordingly less powerful and significant than theirs, yet it emphasizes the theme of survival. The fact that Amado would resort to parody in this last novel of the women's trilogy could be interpreted as a shift of authorial perspective on the Brazilian situation, a lightening or jading of viewpoint on the national dilemma. This shift is practically impossible to render in translation. Text translation alone of Amado is inadequate; for a complete rendering of his work, he must be placed in full context, which is the broad historical, social, and spiritual environment of twentieth-century Brazil in which he lived, a country then and still in transition.

Rubem Fonseca: High Art in Low Language

Rubem Fonseca, the controversial and heavily censored icon of Brazilian city writing of the 1960s, is an author whose themes and language resonate with readers in the postmodern city on any continent. His works have been translated into English, German, Czech, French, Spanish, and Italian. In 2003 he was awarded the prestigious Juan Rulfo Prize and the Luís de Camões Prize, the highest literary honor for literature in the Portuguese language. While Fonseca is best known for his short stories, recently his novels and screenplays have attracted serious attention. His work began to appear in English in the 1970s in literary magazines—*Fiction, Review, InterMuse*, the *Literary Review*—and his 1983 novel *High Art* was translated by Ellen Watson in 1986. The Watson translation was complimented as "accurate and efficient," but the U.S. edition did not have the success enjoyed by the translations in other languages. *High Art* is a literary detective story set in Brazil, with political and historical overtones involving the established Brazilian power elite and right-wing vigilantes. Using "found" material from the newspapers and TV, Fonseca sets out to create a complex tale illustrating the proverb "Set a thief to catch a thief." The main character and narrator is a criminal lawyer living and working in Rio de Janeiro, who is known by his nickname, Mandrake. He is a cynic with few moral scruples, highly promiscuous, and a complete failure as a detective. He consorts with prostitutes—Fonseca always pairs the detective with the whore in a poetic liaison of the law seeking the human touch of the forbidden—while chasing down false clues, threats, suspects, and memories. The mordant social criticism is often achieved by the down-at-the-heels detective or "class C" character looking as an outsider into the luxurious apartments of the wealthy. The view from the bottom up is a frequent motif in the Fonseca repertoire.

While in Brazil Fonseca was fast becoming a literary phenomenon, he was praised by Mario Vargas Llosa as a brilliant writer who creates literature out of "materials and techniques stolen from mass culture." Fonseca's parody of the detective novel transforms the medium into "high art" because of the skill and intentionality with which the tale is told. "Perhaps this is the 'high art' of the title," wrote Vargas Llosa, "telling a story as incredible and excessive as this one with the Machiavellian cunning necessary to make us believe it all and find it quite natural" ("Thugs").

Fonseca's 1985 novel *Bufo & Spallanzani* was published in English (tr. Clifford E. Landers, 1990) after becoming a sensation in Europe. Reviewing it in the *Washington Post*, Alan Ryan declared: "Readers of Cortázar and Cabrera Infante should like it. . . . Lovers of Umberto Eco and Julian Barnes should like it. For that matter, fans of Jim Thompson should like it, because Fonseca writes like an intellectualized Thompson, one who has gone to good schools but survives with his senses—and his sense of humor—intact."

Fonseca uses the city as a metaphor for the alienation, anonymity, incommunicability, and fragility of human life in modern times, and he manipulates the context so that we see the realities of the city through the lenses of his characters, who are often the weak, underprivileged, and abused in a society of extreme inequality in the distribution of wealth and power. There is a keen awareness of a society in transition in Fonseca and his contemporaries, resulting in shifts between sentimental nostalgia for what is lost and cynical detachment and surgical dissection of society's ills. Fonseca, perhaps more than his contemporaries, creates a postmodern syntax of the city through spatial symbols—the apartment, prison, street, office, luxury hotel. Fonseca tells his stories in "pictures," which is perhaps why he has slipped so effortlessly into the diction of film. He enlists his readers, and of course his translators, into the creative experience, encouraging an interactive relationship with the readers that forces them to fill in the blanks. But the urbane familiarity, almost intimacy, that Fonseca invites is deceptive. For as much as Fonseca sounds and feels like a postmodern big-city writer anywhere—New York, Berlin, Paris—there is still something ineffably Brazilian about his writing that must also be captured in translation. Fonseca makes frequent and sometimes playful use of the rich repertoire of Brazilian obscenities, which are hard to replicate in English. Accused of being a pornographer by the censors in the 1960s, he makes poetry out of explicit sexual scenes and language in a very Brazilian manner that reminds one of Amado's treatments of sexuality. These translation challenges are coupled with the use of film language and techniques in his narratives, which demand similar treatment in the target language. "The writer must be essentially a subversive," says the narrator in *Bufo & Spallanzani*. "Our language should be that of nonconformity, nonfalsity, nonoppression. We do not wish to bring order to chaos, as some theorists suppose. We always doubt everything, including logic. A writer must be a skeptic. He must be against morality and good habits. . . . Every highly intelligent means of expression is mendacious" (107).

A later Fonseca novel, *Vastas emoções e pensamentos imperfeitos* (1988; tr. Clifford E. Landers, *The Lost Manuscript*, 1997), illustrates the prominence of film as theme and metaphor in the Fonseca oeuvre. Throughout, the film is both the subject and the medium of discourse. A film noir is contained within the novel, which itself mixes a satire of contemporary Brazilian society and its love of the media with a scholarly dissertation on the making and language of film. The hero in this and other Fonseca novels is often engaged simultaneously in dodging threats against his life, discussing film and literature, and philosophizing on the complex relationship between love, art, and life. Here the protagonist says, "When I see a film, I think things like: why did the scriptwriter have the character say such and such? When I read a book I also think the same thing: why did the author write that? The guys are professional phrasemakers; they should know what they're doing. And I also pay a lot of attention to people talking on the street corner" (255). Fonseca pays great attention to wordsmithing and works closely with his translators.[1] Fluent in English and widely read in the great authors of the Western canon, Fonseca consciously styles himself after some of the masters of the American short story and detective novel such as Dashiell Hammett, Donald Barthelme, and Nathaniel West. Urbane and well traveled, Fonseca spent considerable time in New York and various European capitals as an executive with a Canadian utility company. After retirement, he gave himself fully to the writing life and has made frequent trips to the United States, Mexico, and Germany to receive prizes and participate in literary events. Berlin became a frequent destination as his works captured the attention of the German audience. The Fonseca translator is obliged to understand these influences and take them into consideration. Furthermore, historical and literary allusions abound in the Fonseca text, and these must be appropriately and accurately rendered. Fonseca has little patience for those who are not well read, and even his lowest-tier ("class C") characters are avid readers of high art.

A Mexican writer whose noir fiction has had considerable success in translation, and whose work can be handily compared to Fonseca's, is Paco Ignacio Taibo II. Political activist, professor of anthropology and history, journalist, and president of the International Association of Detective Fiction Writers, he has won numerous literary prizes including the Dashiell Hammett award for the best detective narrative in the Spanish language. A prolific practitioner of the detective genre, PIT II, as he likes to be called, has more than thirty books to his credit, the majority of them featuring Héctor Belascoarán Shayne, a gimpy, one-eyed private eye. In an interview with Ilan Stavans, the author singled out the books he likes best: *Algunas nubes* (1985; tr. William I. Neuman, *Some Clouds*, 1992), *Sombra de la sombra* (1986; tr. William I. Neuman, *Shadow of the Shadow*, 1993), and *Cuatro manos* (1990; tr. Laura C. Dail, *Four Hands*, 1994). He describes his peripatetic main character as "rootless, a refugee of the middle class, madly curious, stubborn, full of humorous feeling toward his fellow Mexicans, a bit melancholic. . . . Belascoarán Shayne has become what he is over 15 years of backwardness." Taibo attributes his popularity with Mexican writers to his "exoticism. . . . I suppose Mexican readers find in my novels a broken mirror, a proposition that invites them not to surrender to an immoral reality." As in Fonseca's fiction, the solitary detective lives on the margins of society, and lines are blurred between the law and the outlaw.

City Writers Confront the Military Dictatorship

Ignácio de Loyola Brandão, like Rubem Fonseca, was a widely publicized victim of Brazilian censorship. His 1975 novel *Zero*, first published in Italy for lack of a Brazilian house willing to risk association with the book, was confiscated by the police one month before the prohibition of Rubem Fonseca's short-story collection *Feliz Ano Novo* (Happy New Year, 1977).[2] *Zero* received the Fundação Cultural de Brasília award for best book of the year. The novel has been compared to Cortázar's *Libro de Manuel* (1973; tr. Gregory Rabassa, *A Manual for Manuel*, 1978) and is a patchwork of fiction and fantasy. Characterized on the title page as a "prehistoric romance," it is in fact set in a not-too-distant future, really the here and now of a Brazil become Megalopolis. The book is similar to Sérgio Sant'Anna's 1975 novel *Confissões de Ralfo* (Ralph's confessions) in its brash, apocalyptic appraisal of Brazil's uncertain path to the future. Some critics feel that, as a pair, these two novels are as seminal to new Brazilian literature as Mário de Andrade's *Macunaíma* (1928; tr. E. A. Goodland, 1984) and Oswald de Andrade's *Memórias sentimentais de João Miramar* (1923; tr. Ralph Niebuhr and Albert Bork, *Sentimental Memoirs of John Seaborne*) were for the modernist generation. *Zero* was translated by Ellen Watson in 1983 and reviewed enthusiastically, if briefly, in the U.S. press. E. L. Doctorow called it a "wild, surreal novel, vulgar, funny, self-conscious, painful. It is done in short takes, each with a headline; a kitchen sink kind of book, envisioning the hideous nature of life under a repressive regime of the 1960s." The *Library Journal* commented on the "exuberant exaggeration, unusual typographical layout and artful juxtaposition of seemingly unrelated information to build a sharp denunciation of dictatorship" (Babel).

The short story writers of the 1960s in Brazil, including Rubem Fonseca, opened a new era in Brazilian letters that was marked by the political moment and their reaction to it. They became masters of the metaphor and used dramas of the city and suburban life to frame political messages.[3] With the departure of the military dictatorship and the election of a civilian president in 1984, the way was opened for the arts to reenter Brazilian life and, by extension, for Brazil's artists to resume a place on the world stage. As early as 1979, the arts scene started to push its way back into the public eye after two decades of overt repression. Literary conferences mushroomed all over Brazil, and the Week of the Brazilian Writer in São Paulo in March 1979 was greeted by Brazilian intellectuals as the Nova Semana (New Week) alluding to the Semana de Arte Moderna (Week of Modern Art) of 1922. This was followed by the Week of the Brazilian Writer in Bogotá, Colombia, in November 1979. The short story medium was particularly suited to conveying political messages by its portable form and accessibility to newspapers, magazines, and journals. Similarly, for translators attempting to export this fiction, it was easier to place short stories in literary magazines than to introduce new writers to trade publishers. Indeed, only four of these masters have made it into book-length translations in the United States. For the most part, they have appeared in English translation in magazines and anthologies.

Brazilian Vampires as Emblems of the Dark Side of City Life

Dalton Trevisan, a native of Curitiba, Brazil, is as elusive a figure as his main character Nelsinho, the Vampire of Curitiba. Trevisan has published well over five hundred "microstories." His first collection of short stories, *Novelas nada exemplares* (Not at all exemplary stories, 1959), won national recognition in Brazil. *O vampiro de Curitiba* (1965; tr. Gregory Rabassa, *The Vampire of Curitiba, and Other Stories*, 1972), demonstrates the central concern of his work with the dark underside of daily life in modern Brazil, particularly under the pall of the dictatorship. Trevisan has been translated into English, Dutch, German, and Spanish, for the most part in anthologies of Latin American short fiction. According to Gregory Rabassa, Trevisan can be considered a forerunner of postmodernism. "He is what we think of as a minimalist, to borrow a term from musical composition. He writes short stories and has said that his ultimate aim is to reduce the story to its essential haiku. The wickedness of his themes is based on marital fights and squabbles, often leading to murder and mayhem. This genre of his—the microstory—is almost his alone, which makes him a master of it. The characters are inevitably João and Maria—everyman and everywoman. He finally unmasks the bourgeois image of the happy couple and thereby the sham of our accepted relationships" (Stavans, *Mirror*, 234). Trevisan first began publishing his stories in pamphlets that he distributed privately. They are styled after the medieval apologue or example, in which a the moral, or the lack of one, is stressed over plot. The microstories contain worlds within them, and portray the city as an infinite composite of tiny microcosms, each with its inner core of suffering. Trevisan's Curitiba is a city outside the parameters of space and time. It is a provincial capital frozen in the 1950s in the cyclical fantasies of the narrator. Urban space and its influence on his characters are particularly important in Trevisan's fiction. His dark view of the city contrasts markedly with the 1960s' optimistic technocrat vision of modern urban Brazil. Like Joyce, Trevisan "runs into himself" on every street corner. He conjures up his stories from the fragments of city life around him, as he told *Veja*: "Police bulletins, a sentence in the wind, a medicine bottle, a small ad, suicide notes, my ghost in the closet, visiting friends. What they don't tell me, I overhear from behind the door. I guess what I don't know, and with luck I discover what, sooner or later, I end up writing" (8).

Gregory Rabassa's renditions of Trevisan's microstories capture the atmosphere of insanity accepted as commonplace by the characters acting within them. In "Tres Tiros na Tarde" ("Three Shots in the Afternoon") the description of murder by spouse is as matter-of-fact as it is chilling:

Primeiro ela deitou uma droga no licor de ovo—a garganta em fogo, João correu para a cozinha e tomou bastante leite. Depois ela misturou soda cáustica na loção de cabelo, que lhe queimou as mãos. O vidro moído no caldo de feijão ranjia-lhe nos dentes—e rolava no chão do banheiro, as entranhas fervendo.

Na poltrona da sala, o copo de uísque na mão, lia em voz alta o programa dos cinemas.

—Que filme gostaria de ver, Maria?

Um dos guris brincando a seus pés no tapete.

—Para você querido. Voltou-se e recebeu os três tiros no rosto—o filhinho abraçou-se no pai.

First she put a drug in his egg brandy—his throat on fire, João ran to the kitchen and downed a lot of milk. Then she mixed caustic soda in with his hair tonic, which burned his hands. The ground glass in his bean soup was gritty on his teeth—and he rolled on the bathroom floor, his insides all aboil.

In the armchair in the living room, a glass of whiskey in his hand, he was reading aloud the list of movies being shown.

—What picture would you like to see, Maria? One of the kids was playing on the rug by his feet.

—This is for you, dear. He turned and caught the three shots in the face—the little boy embraced his father. (Stavans, *Mirror*, 232–35)

The appeal of this recluse writer to the international audience lies perhaps exactly in his mystery and the secrets he reveals of a country, time, and place beyond the reader's experience or imagining. The figure of the vampire is particularly unexpected from a Brazilian writer and links his work to folkloric traditions of Eastern Europe. The vampire seems to resonate deeply with his readers, and most of the criticism of his work has focused on this element. The essential difference between Dalton Trevisan's vampires and their European models is that his are very much at home in their urban environment and the monster lives within his characters, not as an outcast from society (Gordus). Trevisan's vampires, unlike the Transylvanian prototypes, feed off the city and owe their survival to it, yet they have a discernible link to vampiric tradition. The Trevisan vampire is a "representation of a fear returned, one based in a feudalist authoritarian past. It is Brazil's inability to exorcise its past and its marriage to a capitalist economic system that has created the unique horrific world described by Trevisan" (Gordus). Thus Trevisan offers both the exotic and the familiar, in addition to a compelling metaphoric reminder that danger lurks too close for comfort and can strike at any time.

The Jewish Experience Rendered in the Fantastic Mode

Moacyr Scliar is a medical doctor from Porto Alegre, the capital of Rio Grande do Sul in Brazil's urban south, who writes of the Brazilian urban and Jewish experience in the fantastic mode. He is the author of more than fifty novels, short stories, and essays, which have been translated into numerous languages. Active internationally, Scliar has spent time in residence at U.S. universities and attends literary and translation conferences. He is often quoted in the U.S. press on issues related to the Jewish cultural experience. *The Collected Stories of Moacyr Scliar* (1999) and *Max and the Cats* (2003) were translated by Eloah F. Giacomelli, and *The Centaur in the Garden* (1985) was translated by Margaret A. Neves with an introduction by Ilan Stavans. Scliar's work has been compared to the writings of Franz Kafka, Nikolai Gogol, Philip Roth, Mordecai Richler, and even John Updike. His universality comes from his innate skill as a fabulist, and as a witness to the Jewish experience in Brazil. In *The Centaur in the Garden*, named one of the "100 greatest works of Jewish literature" by the National Yiddish Book Center, Scliar chronicles the destiny of Guedali Tartakowsky, a Jewish centaur born into a family of Russian immigrants in Rio Grande do Sul. Tragedy mixes with comedy in this allegorical tale and once again interweaves the global history of the Jewish Diaspora, and the myth of the Wandering Jew, with the prosaic and often comical reality of day-to-day life in a midsize city in Brazil's remote south. Linking Jewish tradition and roots with the post–World War II Jewish experience, Scliar's work translates equally well in the Northern or Southern Hemisphere. His *Collected Stories* is comprised of six collections. *The Carnival of the Animals* contains stories written during the military dictatorship, political fables that confront the themes of oppression, persecution, cruelty, and the play between good and evil. One of the most important stories in *Carnival* is "A balada do falso Messias" ("The Ballad of the False Messiah"), which places a false Messiah among a group of Jewish immigrants in Rio Grande do Sul on their way to settle a tract of land that has been donated to them. Even though the Messiah, Shabtai Zvi, is heralded by a prophet, Natan de Gaza, and succeeds in overcoming the devil, Bandido Chico Diabo, as well as turning wine into water, he is discredited, and the Judaic community goes on to make its fortune in business and in contraband in Porto Alegre. The false god, Mammon, displaces the false Messiah, seducing the chosen people from the Promised Land. The prophet Natan becomes a mafia lord and Shabtai Zvi spends his days sadly in a bar, turning wine into water. Scliar's "Ballad" develops the theme of the existential wait, or postponement, in the sense that, for the Jews, redemption is always postponed in the wait for the Messiah. This has political overtones, as it refers to the two decades in which Brazil lost its cultural soul to the military dictatorship. English-language readers of all ages have enjoyed the breadth of knowledge displayed in Scliar's tales—history, medicine, psychology, anthropology, Hebrew scripture—and the wide diversity of genres he commands, including allegory, fantasy, and magical realism.

Fables of Babel

Murilo Rubião (1916–1991) was discovered late in his career and is now considered to have been one of Brazil's most innovative writers. He published
four books of short stories, widely spaced in time but all linked thematically
and artistically. He interpreted the city experience in the fantastic mode, re-
creating the myth of Babel as a parable of the modern condition. He wrote
in the "prophetic tense" about cities that are a continuous urban sprawl,
stripped of greenery. Each of his stories is preceded by a biblical epigraph,
which is immediately fulfilled. The apocalyptic event occurs in a present-
tense narrative, or in a thinly disguised future-as-present. The theme of the
infinite, rendered by repetitive and circular action, reduces the future to
an eternal present. By this manner of narration, prophetic time (the pre-
sentiment of the Apocalypse or the memory of the Fall) is marked by the
character's recognition of revealing action in the past through dialogue in
the present. Rubião populates his stories with mythical animals, such as his
rabbit, Teleco, and dragons. The dragons become corrupted and abandon
the city, much as Clarice Lispector's horses function in *A cidade sitiada*.
Rubião is said to have written the same story over and over again. He has
declared, "I work over language to exhaustion in a desperate search for clarity" (Lowe, *City*, 149), and claimed to have rewritten his story "O convidado"
(The guest) for twenty-six years before it was finally published. The theme
of infinite repetition in his work, as in the Sisyphean search for a woman in
the story "Epidólia," complements his obsession with perfection of language.
Perfection in women is ironically presented with the figure of the prosti-
tute-saint, an inversion common in city literature. In "A fila" (The line) the
prostitute Galimene, a fisherman's daughter, cares for the protagonist during
a long vigil in the city night. In "O ex-mágico" ("The Ex- Magician") the artist
figure is also a victim of consumer society. In this story, the magician (artist)
who was "thrown into the world without parents, an infancy or a childhood"
tires of his astonishing and sometimes disturbing skills as a magician. He
hears from a "sad man" that being a civil servant is to commit slow suicide.
For that reason he applies for a job in the state bureaucracy. Gradually he
begins to miss his old way of life, but it is too late. "I had to concede defeat. I
trusted too much in the ability to do magic and it had been annulled by the
bureaucracy" ("O pirotécnico Zacarias"; Zacharia the pyrotechnist).

In 1979 Thomas Colchie successfully translated *The Ex-Magician, and
Other Stories*, which in 2002 became the inspiration for a London show de-
scribed as a "dynamic, sensory extravaganza" (Dende). What appeals about
Rubião is his "weird" brand of magical realism and the fantastic, which is as

sensual as García Márquez's, as cerebral as the master Borges's, and as clinical as science fiction. He wields hyperrealistic techniques such as the use of prose simulating technical documents complete with footnotes, characters with masks, labyrinths in which his heroes lose themselves, and counterintuitive inversions, such as the guest received by multiple hosts. Images of the infinite abound—mirrors, parallel train tracks, cell bars, endless lines, buildings under continuous construction, and women who procreate endlessly.

Post-Kafka Allegories of Man as Object

One author who did not make it into a full-length translation in English but who appeared in numerous literary magazines in English, as well as in many European languages, was the brilliant and little-known Victor Giudice (1934–1997). He did not travel as much as his contemporaries, since he was afraid of flying, but he did visit Bogotá for a literary conference at the Universidad Javeriana in 1979, and he traveled to Europe to attend a season of opera toward the end of his life.[4] His third published story, "The File Cabinet," from the 1972 volume *Necrológio* (Obituary), became his signature work. Other publications include several volumes of short stories and two novels, *Bolero* (1985) and *O sétimo punhal* (The seventh dagger, 1995). In addition to his literary pursuits, he was a music critic for the Rio de Janeiro daily newspaper *Jornal do Brasil*. An avid reader and student of music, he grew up attending concerts and opera at the Municipal Theater of Rio de Janeiro. He read everything from forbidden erotic literature to comics to Rider Haggard, Conan Doyle, Poe, Sartre, Camões, Balzac, Sophocles, and Machado de Assis. His fascination with detective fiction led him to his particular brand of the fantastic. His complex and concise narratives and their piercing interpretation of the transcendental themes of love, time, and death associate him intimately with the metaphysical fantastic of such precursors as the Argentine Macedonio Fernández. Like Rubião, Giudice spun allegories of postmodern man in no-exit situations. He was especially resourceful in inverting "normal" relationships, such as life and death. Some of his stories branch into the fantastic-marvelous, such as his supersonic romance "Salvataurus" or his utopian tale "The Points of Harmonisópolis." His erudition and elegant style, his mastery of the murder mystery plot and his taste for the macabre align him with Edgar Allan Poe, Ellery Queen, Ursula Le Guin, and Agatha Christie. One of the most verbally inventive of the contemporary Brazilian city writers, he peopled his stories with unconscious grotesques. The atmosphere of eerie insanity summoned by his narratives is all the more compelling because the stories are constructed with the precision of a sonnet.[5] Giudice once stated that "fiction seems absurd because it is reality stripped of all its lies" (Lowe, preface to *Os banheiros*, 8).[6] He also said, "Fiction is almost the same as reality. It's a reality without false vision" (*Necrológio*, back cover).

Giudice presents special challenges for translation. His fragmented and ultraexperimental syntax, the extreme depersonalization of character, and the abrupt concision of his stories demand great focus and concentration of the translator. An example is his signature story, "O Arquivo" ("The File Cabinet"), which starts on the book jacket and continues into the front pages of the book. In this Kafkaesque tale the protagonist, João, who is diminished in every way including by lowercasing his name, gradually is metamorphosed into the file cabinet in the office where he is demoted year after year in recognition of the firm's "indebtedness" for his loyal service.

> joão afastou-se. O lábio murcho se estendeu. A pele enrijeceu, ficou lisa. A estatura regrediu. A cabeça se fundiu ao corpo. As formas desumanizaram-se, planas, compactas. Nos lados, havia duas arestas. Tornou-se cinzento.
> joão transformou-se num arquivo de metal. (*Necrológio*, 1–2)

> joão walked away. His wilted lips extended. His skin hardened, turned smooth. His stature diminished. His head fused to his body. His forms became dehumanized, plane, compact. His sides formed angles. He turned gray.
> João turned into a metal file cabinet. (tr. Lowe 84–86)

While some of his prose is stripped down to the barest essentials, Giudice can also be incredibly dense and elegant. Some of his protagonists are nineteenth-century-style intellectuals, connoisseurs of fine food and fine wines, antiques and lyric opera.[7] Coupled with this cosmopolitanism is the acute irony of the banal day-to-day. Behind the mask of the common man is the corrosive secret that transforms his characters into monsters. The logic of this apparently insane world is summed up by one of his lines in "The File Cabinet": "There is no madness without emotion."

Women in the City Write about Women

Beginning in the 1960s, a trio of talented and visionary Brazilian women writers were elevated to the world stage. Two of them, Clarice Lispector and Nélida Piñon, are discussed in other chapters of this book. The third, Lygia

Fagundes Telles, focuses on urban themes and how the urban environment shapes her characters.

Lygia Fagundes Telles has spent much of her life writing and living in São Paulo, where she has become a cultural icon. Like Nélida Piñon, she is a member of the elite Brazilian Academy of Letters. She has represented Brazil on official cultural delegations to Europe and has received numerous prizes for her work. Telles is the author of many books of short stories, novels, screenplays, and memoirs. Her signature work, the 1973 novel *As meninas*, was made into a 1995 film with the same title, and was translated into English in 1982 by Margaret Neves as *The Girl in the Photograph*. Neves also translated Telles's best-known volume of short stories, *Seminário dos Ratos* (1977; *Tigrela, and Other Stories*, 1986), and the novel *Ciranda de Pedra* (1955; *The Marble Dance*, 1986). The *Literary Review* published translations of her stories "Just a Saxophone" (1978) and "Before the Green Dance" (1995). Telles has been translated into Czech, French, German, Swedish, and Spanish as well.

Telles writes about the condition of women in Brazilian society, particularly in the city and state of São Paulo. The protagonists reflect on their role in the family and the extent of their possibilities in their social environment. According to Susana Rossberg, "it is an exercise of self-reflection and self-definition, of a will to change the status quo and to widen the opportunities for action." *As meninas* deals specifically with the political reality of the military dictatorship of 1964–1984 from the female perspective and the doomed attempts of three young women in a convent school to rise above their condition. The three protagonists come from different social backgrounds. Ana Clara carries the stigma of a working-class girl and struggles with drug addiction. Lia, a political activist, plots the revolution. The naive Lorena, from an old landowning family, is psychologically crippled by her bonds to a decadent bourgeoisie. Telles reveals these characters and their inner turmoil through a complex narrative technique blending dialogue and stream of consciousness, a method that dramatizes the characters' inability to communicate with each other and to discover what they might have in common. Long inner monologues serve as windows on the characters' psyches and their emotional paralysis. The story unfolds during a strike at the university, metaphoric of the girls' emotional limbo, and ends as anticlimactically as the strike.

The Brazilian critic Fábio Lucas has written, in his introduction to *Antes do baile verde*, of the role of myth and magic in Telles's fiction. The use of myth and storytelling, or fabulation, is a device that allows the characters to survive psychologically in an alien environment. According to Lucas, modern man must practice "the heroism of conscience" as a defense against his inability to change the rules of the game. Interior conflict is stimulated by the very absurdity of life. Lorena makes up a false history for herself, which includes the murder of one of her brothers by another as a reason for her father's insanity. She convinces herself that this version of her family history is indeed fact. She also retreats into sexual fantasies and talks about sex to herself and others, even to the nuns. She falls in love with a married, unattainable man with a Latin name, Marcus Nemesius, who becomes the object of her increasingly frequent obsessions. Ana Clara's lies are more deliberate, and their purpose is to divorce her from her ugly lower-class life. She even lies to her psychoanalyst.

> Mentia tudo. Bem feito. Boa noite que a gente fala a verdade. Fala nada. Histórias sujas de dentes podres não quero não quero.

> I lied all the time. So what. It's a night when hell freezes over when people tell the truth. People lie all the time. Stories of people with rotten teeth, I don't want anything to do with that, I really don't.[8]

Peggy Sharpe states that Lygia Fagundes Telles's works "have introduced us to a whole cast of female protagonists whose attempts at self-reflection are obstructed by the characters' incapacity to integrate the process of self-reflection with the external context of their lives" (80). Renata Wasserman considers Lorena, Lia, and Ana Clara to be paradigms of the rural aristocracy, the middle class, and the subproletariat. Telles's women of whatever class, Susana Rossberg concludes, perpetuate their own imprisonment by clinging to the social codes they know, and also by spinning an imaginary world in which they live and fade away. This social allegory is one that can resonate with women in all cultures, especially in times of turmoil.[9]

The collection of stories *Antes do baile verde* (Before the green dance, 1970) is Lygia Fagundes Telles's most important work. The stories were written between 1949 and 1969, and they illustrate most vividly the use of the mythical and fantastic in her work. Turbulent narratives, with carefully sculpted prose and open endings, these stories surprise, confuse, and horrify. They always invite readers to use their imagination and to navigate for themselves the continuous flux between reality and fantasy. When reality becomes too intense or disturbing, then fantasy takes over. The stories are mostly about misunderstandings and lost opportunities: couples in constant conflict, beatific hallucinations, death, and betrayal. In "Natal na barca" (Christmas on the skiff) a mother crosses a river with her son on her lap, and the reader does not know if the child is alive. In "Apenas um saxofone" (tr. Eloah F. Giacomelli, "Just a Saxophone") a woman asks her lover to kill himself to prove his love:

> Onde agora? Onde? Tenho uma casa de campo, tenho um diamante do tamanho de um ovo de pomba . . . Eu pintava os olhos diante do espelho, tinha um compromisso, vivia cheia de compromissos, ia a uma boate com um banqueiro. Enrodilando na cama, ele tocava em surdina. Meus olhos foram ficando cheios de lágrimas. Enxuguei-os na fralda do saxofone e fiquei olhando para minha boca que achei particularmente fina. Se você me ama mesmo, eu disse, se voce me ama mesmo então saia e se mate imediatamente.

> Where is he now? Where? I have a house in the country, I have a diamond the size of a pigeon's egg . . . I was doing my eyes at the mirror, I had a date, I always had plenty of dates, I was going to a nightclub with a banker. Curled up on the bed, he was playing softly. My eyes began to fill with tears. I dried them on the saxophone's diaper and stood staring at my lips, which seemed to me particularly thin. "If you really love me," I said, "if you really love me, then go out and kill yourself right away." (233)

Skillful use of dialogue and internal monologue is Telles's greatest strength: the narrative threads come and go, weaving in and out with ellipses and abrupt suspensions, achieving the quality of oral history. This perhaps is one of the biggest challenges to the translator of Fagundes Telles, to re-create the ambience of magic accented by a cruel reality and to render this ambience with the dexterity of narrative technique modeled by the author.

With the talented Brazilian trio of Lispector, Piñon, and Telles, the Argentine journalist and writer Luisa Valenzuela can productively be included. Self-exiled in 1979 to New York, where she still lives and teaches, Valenzuela now divides her time between New York, Buenos Aires, and Tepoztlán, Mexico, all scenes of her fiction. A very productive writer, she has published six novels, as well as short stories and novellas, and has received numerous honors. Her work can be understood well in relation to that of Clarice Lispector, as her novels center on the political violence and patriarchal mores of Argentine society and the interrelated themes of politics, language, and women. She demonstrates in her narratives how language can be used to oppress and manipulate, and can change reality. Her writing explores the social role of gender as well as factors that determine women's identity and sexuality. Myth and dreams are central metaphors of political and social reality in her work. Valenzuela has been an active campaigner against repression and censorship both in her writing and in international human rights organizations. Gregory Rabassa, who translated *Cola de lagartija* (1983; *The Lizard's Tail*, 1983), comments on Valenzuela's "intelligent knowledge of people and how they feel," and adds that this book, one of the few he translated directly from the manuscript, is on his "short list of 'difficult' works," not just for the translation but for the reading (*Treason*, 130).

Escape to the Movies: Film as the New Literary Diction

Shifts between inner and outer reality mark the work of Argentine writer Manuel Puig. Here the escape is into the world of film, whereas in Lygia Fagundes Telles's works the fantasy is in the characters' minds. "The mass media, print and video," according to Mario Vargas Llosa, "stole their best tricks from literature, and a few contemporary novelists are now returning the favor." He cites the example of Umberto Eco, whose *Name of the Rose*, "a hybrid medieval thriller, adventure novel and erudite entertainment," demonstrates that literary experimentation can be combined with the realia of tabloid violence and voyeurism. In Latin America, he writes, Manuel Puig incorporates the media into his work and both mimics and trumps them in his themes and narrative techniques. The cinema plays a large role in Puig's narratives: "his books—simultaneously visual and spoken—make rapid jumps to the past and the future. Their cinematic allusions constitute a utopian alternative, a fantasy world where people can escape the degradation of their lives" ("Thugs").

Suzanne Jill Levine has translated Manuel Puig and Guillermo Cabrera Infante, and has written about the process of translating in her 1991 book *The Subversive Scribe*. This well-known work is one of the best available on the dynamics of translating Latin American fiction, by a brilliant translator who got ahead of the wave of the early years of the Boom and who translated not only these two important authors but many others as well. As she has aptly said, "You often seek in the foreign what you are drawn to, perhaps unknowingly, in the familiar." "We translate to be translated" (*Scribe*, v).

A New Yorker by birth, she relates her sense of familiarity when first discovering Havana and Buenos Aires, and the recognition she felt in realizing that the "words and images of the American movies of the Thirties, Forties, and Fifties" (ix) were a shared background for approaching the narratives of these two authors. Levine is conscious of the experience of exile in one's own language, and in one's own culture. The affinity between translator and subject sometimes comes from that spark of recognition that the translator finds in her author, whether it is a personal chemistry, an existential bond, or the sheer joy of finding oneself through the language of the other.

> The translator's fate dramatizes that of the writer caught between the language of writing and the Real, or the elusive past, a "foreign country". . . . "My" language (in which I am also a visitor) can never fully express the Spanish original, but now I must make mine "home" again, express as fully as possible the other in whatever is my version of American English, for we all have our own private lexicon, even grammar. (2)

Levine was attracted to both Manuel Puig and Guillermo Cabrera Infante for what they did for and with language.

> *Tres tristes tigres* is perhaps the first work to turn "Cuban" into a literary language spiked with slang, wordplays, and dislocations, a Spanish enriched by a specific region but also by many cultural and literary references. . . . Puig's writings can be considered even more "pop," less "literary": Within the stylized, parodic structures of his novels such as *Betrayed by Rita Hayworth* and *The Kiss of the Spider Woman* he reproduces and analyzes popular culture and the spoken Argentine language. (8–9)

Manuel Puig (1932–1990), whose life story is carefully documented in Levine's book *Manuel Puig and the Spider Woman: His Life and Fictions* (2000), apparently read a lot but "never talked about authors or books, and when a literary topic came up in conversation he would look bored and change the subject" (Vargas Llosa, "Saved"). He was especially well informed about films and had a detailed grasp of the history and mythology of film, as well as of the biographies of famous film producers and actresses. He came to writing after failing at a career in film. "He was a man of the movies, or perhaps of visual images and fantasy, who found himself shipwrecked in literature almost by default." He wrote autobiographical tales that came from his recollections of seeing movies in the small cinemas of his hometown in the Argentine pampa. With his two most famous books, *Betrayed by Rita Hayworth* (1968) and *Kiss of the Spider Woman* (1976), Puig attained international recognition. His universal appeal comes from his brilliant collage of Hollywood images superimposed over the drab lives of his protagonists. The popular culture is thoroughly Argentine—radio and television soap operas, the tango, the tabloid press, rancheras. Yet, as Vargas Llosa observes, "the innovation in Puig's work is that the artificial, caricatured version of life eliminates and replaces the other dimension and becomes the only truth. It is this that gives his novels their strange ambience; though Puig's vision is based on one of the most common human experiences—the flight from the real world to a dream world using all the forms of the imagination" ("Saved"). Puig's homosexuality contributed to his need to escape into the world of film, particularly in the *machista* environment of the pampa, where prejudice was expressed with brutality. Levine explains how *Betrayed by Rita Hayworth* and then *Kiss of the Spider Woman* are structured around the device of the main character re-creating a film "in ways that reveal or carry out his own fantasies" (*Scribe*, 32). In a Scheherazade-style narrative that extends during the entire novel, Molina, the gay window dresser in *Kiss of the Spider Woman*, relates for Valentin, a political prisoner, the story of a film he has seen. This draws them together and at the same time reveals the ugly reality of the political moment of the military dictatorship. This was the only way that Puig could approach the fact of the dictatorship, through metaphors of evasion. "Authority frightens me," he once said. "I hate it. I don't accept it, but at the same time I find great difficulty in rebelling against it, in facing it directly" (quoted in Levine, *Scribe*, 32). Molina says to Valentin: "The only thing I want is to keep my promise to you, and make you forget about anything that's ugly" (*Kiss*, 233).

Levine has written extensively in *The Subversive Scribe* about translation challenges, covering everything from titles to themes, cultural double entendres, and miscommunications. She speaks of the importance of the extent of the author's knowledge of the culture of the target language, English, and how this has influenced her work. Most interestingly, the book documents the exchanges between Levine and her authors, giving insights into the nature of the "tango" she dances with them. On the subject of translating tango lyrics, she explains the importance of the epigraphs at the head of every episode of Puig's *Boquitas pintadas* (1972; tr. Suzanne Jill Levine, *Heartbreak Tango*, 1973), posing the question "how to re-create in English the parodical effect that spoken Argentine has upon its intended reader? Let's examine the main impasse, which includes the translation of the title: how to reproduce in translation the 'flavor,' the function of the tango lyrics in the original version" (*Scribe*, 125). The different and in some cases opposing cultural perceptions of the tango within and outside Argentina become a major consideration in her choices. She concludes that the common ground for the North American reader, her audience, is not the tango but the mystique of Hollywood. Accepting this fact makes all the difference in how she treats Puig's texts.

Levine ascribes "revolutionary transcendence" to Puig's writing, according to Vargas Llosa, and he disagrees: "I believe it is more ingenious and brilliant than profound, more artificial than innovative, and too dependent on the fashions and myths of its time to ever achieve the permanence of great literary works like those of a Borges or a Faulkner" ("Saved"). Still, Levine's contributions to understanding Latin American literature go beyond introducing her authors. Edith Grossman, speaking of *The Subversive Scribe*, says: "What she has to say about the linguistic, personal, scholarly, and imaginative elements that the translator must bring to that process is an invaluable contribution to our understanding of translation in particular and creativity in general." Levine has brought to light certain commonalities of the inter-American experience through her translations and writing about her work. In discussing how transvestism and homosexuality link the three Latin American novellas in an anthology titled *Triple Cross*, she stresses how transvestism "unveils metaphorically a common Latin American experience shared by the three countries represented [in the volume], a search for cultural identity" (*Scribe*, 142). When addressing the question of whether the works of Cabrera Infante, Puig, and Severo Sarduy are worth translating, she states:

> English speakers today need to know the concerns expressed in other languages; North American readers need to hear the voices of that "other" America alienated from the United States by a torturous political history. But these readers also need to understand *how* Latin American writing is transmitted to them, and *how* differences and similarities between cultures and languages affect *what* is finally transmitted. Knowing the other and how we receive or hear the other is a fundamental step toward knowing ourselves. (xiv–xv)

An Expatriate Reinvents His Country

Álvaro Mutis is a Colombian writer who spent his early years in Brussels and has lived in Mexico since 1956, thus living as a Colombian expatriate for most of his life. However, he spent part of his childhood on a coffee and sugar plantation established by his grandmother, an experience that put an imprint on his literary imagination. He states: "All that I have written is destined to celebrate and perpetuate that corner of the *tierra caliente* [tropics] from which emanates the very substance of my dreams, my nostalgias, my terrors and my fortunes. There is not a single line of my work that is not connected, in a secret or explicit way, to the limitless world that for me is that corner of the regions of Tolima in Colombia" ("Himself"). The landscapes that his antihero, the seaman and adventurer Maqroll, travels are wild and varied, but the spirit of his work is rooted in urban angst and solitude. Like Rubem Fonseca, Mutis started his writing career late in life, after working first as Standard Oil's head of public relations in Colombia and then for twenty-three years in Mexico as sales manager for the television divisions of several Hollywood film companies. His was the well-known voice that did the voice-over in the Spanish-language version of the TV series *The Untouchables*. He started writing short stories and poems, and it was Carmen Balcells, the literary agent who has championed many of the important writers of the Boom, who decided for him that the three hundred pages he had sent her did indeed comprise a novel (F. Goldman, vii). He went on to complete seven "tales" collected as *Empresas y tribulaciones de Maqroll el Gaviero*, first published in 1993–1994 in Spain, and in 2002 he won the Neustadt Prize for Literature. The masterful English translation by the "tireless, versatile" Edith Grossman (Updike, 81), published in 2002, is titled *The Adventures and Misadventures of Maqroll*. In addition to the Grossman translations, there are translations of his prose works in French, Dutch, German, Italian, Portuguese, Danish, Swedish, Polish, Greek, and Turkish. Mutis has been described by Gerald Martin as belonging to the post-Boom, "a typically anticlimactic phenomenon of our current postmodern, poststructuralist, and, for some, posthistorical era of economic and cultural globalization and intellectual and ideological deconstruction ("Maqroll," 24). John Updike connects the dots: "Readers even slightly acquainted with Latin American modernism will hear echoes of Borges's cosmic portentousness, of Julio Cortázar's fragmenting ingenuities, of Machado de Assis's crisp pessimism, and of the something perversely hearty in Mutis's fellow-Colombian and good friend Gabriel García Márquez—a sense of genial amplitude, as when a ceremonious host sits us down to a lunch provisioned to stretch into evening" (Updike, 81).

Mutis's work is all about crossroads and destiny, and the worlds that Maqroll travels are everywhere and nowhere. The metaphorical journey is punctuated by episodes in the major seaports of the world, where the characters rest, revel, and brood, and where transitions in their lives take place. The sea is the conduit to these ports of passage. Rather than *soledad*, the great theme of his work is *desesperanza*, which in Martin's words is "untranslatable into English, neither 'desperation' nor 'despair' but a non-hoping, a never-hoping, something like a combination of the weak meanings of each" ("Maqroll," 26). Maqroll is, according to Martin,

> a character unique in Latin American narrative, . . . of indeterminate origin, nationality, age, and physiognomy. He is not evidently a Latin

American and does not—at first sight—represent anything particularly Latin American in character. Like postmodern fiction as a whole, he is thoroughly deterritorialized. Although he speaks in Spanish to satisfy the conventions of narrative, we do not normally know whether he is "really" doing so. Sometimes he travels in Latin America, sometimes not. The literary regions he journeys through, without ever staying for long, are not "telluric," fantastic, or magical. They are more reminiscent of the atmosphere of Graham Greene's novels, what some critics have called "Greeneland." (25)

John Updike's generous and detailed review of *The Adventures and Misadventures of Maqroll* in the *New Yorker* introduces Maqroll as a character who "presents himself as one of the bad guys, 'on the periphery of laws and codes,' and proposes that bad guys aren't so bad, as they smuggle and pimp and deal their way through the world" (84). This is the other side of the Janus mask of the good-guy heroes, the "Lone rangers, from Don Quixote to Sam Spade and James Bond" (84), or Rubem Fonseca's detective poets. Updike laments how sad it is that a bad-good guy "leaves the reader with no one much to cheer for, in adventures that aspire to the epic" (84). Martin, for his part, finds Updike's lament "profoundly satisfying" (27), and he further cheers the reader by offering his translation of Mutis's recipe for a "Maqroll":

Ingredientes:
   Un vaso de Carpano
   Tres pedazos de hielo
   Un vaso de Jack Daniels
   Media tajada de naranja
   Nota bene: "Hay que rezar el padre nuestro, porque la borrachera no la quita nadie."

Ingredients:
   One jigger of Carpano brand vermouth
   Three ice cubes
   One jigger of Jack Daniels brand whiskey
   One half orange slice
   Nota bene: "One should recite the Lord's Prayer [before imbibing], for drunkenness spares no one." (25)

Maqroll's hold on Álvaro Mutis is apparently legendary: Mutis informed William Siemens in a letter that "Maqroll had been demanding to be set free but that the author was afraid to let him go, because the adventures Maqroll wanted to get into just might result in his death this time" (Siemens, 31).

Indeed, Mutis tried to kill off Maqroll in several of his stories, but he kept resurrecting him. The importance of this relationship between author and character, and character and reader, in the postmodern novel is that the author has to make the character believable to the reader and likewise the reader has to identify with the character so that it is possible to enter into the state of suspension of disbelief required by the puzzling postmodern narrative. "Certainly," Siemens writes, "Maqroll is a stand-in for that part of us which, trapped in a postmodern world characterized by emptiness and meaninglessness, wishes to break free and find some *authenticity*, whatever the cost may be" (33). Maqroll, like many in our postmodern world, has to keep moving to prove to himself that he exists. Siemens suggests that Maqroll embodies the core theme of postmodernism, the quest for integrity and authenticity, and likens him to the character of Jason Bourne in *The Bourne Identity*, who must prove his integrity in the effort to recover his identity. Siemens closes by quoting García Márquez: "Maqroll somos todos"—we are all Maqroll (33).

Thus it is, as we center on the universalities of theme and character, that we come full circle to the role of translation of Boom and post-Boom Latin American urban literature. The translator is the agent who has recognized the familiar in the Other and who also has the passion and energy to make the foreign known to the reader. The modern translator has no need to escape a *patrón*, or boss. As equal partners in the "translation encounter," translator and author have bound us together as citizens of an inter-American world. As Ilan Stavans writes in *Prospero's Mirror*,

> There's little doubt that the region lives today in far less isolation, in far more dialogue, than, say, a century ago. Silence has been replaced by words, and words in one language have traveled to another. In that sense, Harriet de Onís and her successors are yet another crew of courageous explorers in the tradition of Sir Walter Raleigh and, why not, Álvaro Núñez Cabeza de Vaca: they reach out to the geography of the imagination; they penetrate latitudes forbidden to most people, they interpret, they make accessible the inaccessible—they help us be better by expanding our horizon. While the old saying *traduttore traditore* applies in that their effort entails a degree of treason (in order to make an imaginary reality available, they have to falsify, to personalize, to adapt its message to their own language and culture, and adaptation necessarily carries along a degree of distortion), in spite of that, their vision has been crucial to breach an abysmal gap: they reinvent, they enter an already furnished house and redecorate it, and their craft has

particular significance precisely because it applies to a region whose birth has been perceived as a colossal misunderstanding, a chaotic *mélange* of words, facts and acts. Ironically what was once lost in translation during the *conquista* of the Americas can now be reconquered by the exact same means. (xxiv)

Translation and the Ontologies of Cultural Identity and Aesthetic Integrity in Modern Brazilian and Spanish American Narrative

Some Key Texts

With the emergence of such pivotal writers as Jorge Luis Borges, Julio Cor-tázar, Severo Sarduy, Clarice Lispector, and Machado de Assis, the enthu-siastic reception of Latin American literature in the United States of the 1960s was largely effected by what American writers and critics like John Barth and John Updike were lauding as its intellectual sophistication, its startling cosmopolitanism, and its dazzling technical innovations. On the strength of translations by Gregory Rabassa, Suzanne Jill Levine, and Ronald Sousa, among others, Latin American writing was seen to possess a level of thematic complexity and a type of verbal brilliance that dramatically dem-onstrated how profoundly the writers of Brazil and Spanish America were attuned to—and, in the case of Cortázar and his groundbreaking novel *Ra-yuela* (1963; tr. Gregory Rabassa, *Hopscotch*, 1966), even in advance of—the literary implications of Saussurean linguistics and their impact on both structuralism and poststructuralism. A literary culture long thought to be inferior was suddenly projecting a level of seriousness and complexity that allowed it to alter permanently the old North and South lines of influence as these had come to define inter-American literary relations and, in so doing, begin to lay the groundwork for a radically new, more balanced, and strik-ingly comparative approach to the literatures of the Americas.

A Sophisticated New Literature Creates a "Boom"

One of the most remarkable aspects of the Boom literature of the 1960s was how worldly it was. The appearance of the artful and endlessly erudite Borges in English translation in the early 1960s was stunning to readers ac-customed to thinking of Latin America and its literature in the lowliest of terms.[1] So unprepared were most Americans for the autogenous brilliance of Borges that, at the time, a common way of praising him was to say that he wrote like a French intellectual, as if it were impossible for an Argentine, a mere Latin American, to write as he was doing. Roughly contemporaneous debuts in English translation of other Latin Americans like Neruda, Fuentes, Paz, and Cortázar elicited similar responses, both in the American academy and in the reading public. Even Juan Rulfo's deceptively simple tales of impoverished Mexican peasants or Asturias's deeply mythologized and poetically rendered Mayan Indians exhibited a technical polish and exuded a conceptual power that led the reader to feel a visceral connection between these hitherto forgotten or ignored beings and the rest of humanity. Whether in narrative, poetry, or drama, the experimental writing that was sweeping north out of Latin America during the Boom period was not merely novel, it was exceptional in its formal innovativeness, its intellectual capaciousness, and its richly cosmopolitan context. The case of Borges, however, is unusual in that his enthusiastic reception not only in the United States but in Canada as well—where people could have already been reading him in his French translations and discussing him in terms of what Gérard Genette and other prominent French critics were writing about him—can be regarded as one of the first major steps in the development of an inter-American perspective.[2]

In 1962, the year two seminal collections of Borges's short fictions appeared in English translation, the impact "was immediate and overwhelming. John Updike, John Barth, Anthony Burgess, and countless other writers and critics have eloquently and emphatically attested to the unsettling yet liberating effect that Jorge Luis Borges' work had on their vision of the way literature was thenceforth to be done," for the Argentine master was immediately recognized by readers around the world as "a disturbingly *other* writer" (Hurley, 81). Borges himself, later to become a professor of English and American literature at the University of Buenos Aires, was keenly interested in issues of translation and was throughout his life an active and skilled translator (see Kristal). During the 1930s, for example, he became a frequent contributor to Victoria Ocampo's very influential literary magazine *Sur*, rendering major works by such American poets as E. E. Cummings, Hart Crane, John Peale Bishop, Wallace Stevens, and Delmore Schwartz into Spanish. A culturally aware and aesthetically discerning reader of American prose writers like Hawthorne, Melville, Whitman, Poe, and Emerson, Borges also produced, in 1940, a Spanish translation of Faulkner's *The Wild Palms* that was judged by the prominent critic Emir Rodríguez Monegal to have captured the style and tone of the Faulkner text so thoroughly that it can be considered "as good as or even better than the original" (*Borges*, 373).[3] Even more important, Borges's sensitive and nuanced translation of Faulkner became one of the principal mechanisms by which his famous style would come to exert a liberating influence on the then youthful generation of writers who would later become the masters of the Boom. The Borges translation, maintains Rodríguez Monegal, "was not only faithful to the original but created in Spanish a writing style that was the equivalent of the original's English. For many young Latin American novelists who did not know enough English to read the dense original, Borges' tight version meant the discovery of a new kind of narrative writing. They had, in Borges, the best possible guide to Faulkner's dark and intense world" (373). At the same time, as Efraín Kristal has shown, Borges did choose to delete, in his re-creation of *The Wild Palms*, the abortion episode, an editorial tactic consistent with his approach to other texts that contained details he found "gory or distasteful" (185n73) or that he felt diminished the aesthetic "impact of another aspect of the literary work" (119). In more ways than one, then, translation played a decisive role in the development of the Boom in the Americas, just as it later would with the birth of inter-American literature as a discipline.

Beyond the human drama so vividly and passionately portrayed in his stories and novels, Faulkner was especially important to Borges because of his successful experiments with narrative time and structure and, above all, because of his passion for verbal exuberance, his belief in the reality of fiction as pure artifice—a topic that, as we shall now see, Borges was himself investigating at exactly the same time.[4] In a sense, Faulkner revealed to Borges both how potentially liberating this radically new approach to fiction writing could be and how it might be even further and more formally developed. The story of Borges's growth and development in English translation is an interesting one and suggests not only the originality and complexity of his "fictions" but the different ways he was received by his English-speaking audience, particularly in the United States (see Cohn, *Two Souths*), where, lecturing and teaching at various places across the country during the 1960s, he achieved cult status almost immediately.[5] Initially, some of his translations into English were stiff and awkward, at times actually obscuring the wry interplay of style and thought that characterized his very Argentine Spanish style. Frustrated by these translation infelicities, a young American, Norman Thomas di Giovanni, volunteered his services to Borges as a translator, editor, and general factotum. The result was a very fruitful collaboration that lasted several years and allowed a new Borges to (re)appear, one whose style in di Giovanni's translations (which, one assumes, were approved by Borges himself) was now more supple, closer to Borges's natural style in Spanish. And there was another, unexpected result. By entering into this collaboration on his English translations, Borges was also becoming a writer who worked in English, a role he had previously eschewed. "As a translator of his own texts," notes Rodríguez Monegal, "Borges seems old-fashioned, awkward. His Victorian, bookish handling of the English language does a disservice to the original's truly creative Spanish" (*Borges*, 460). While di Giovanni's native, mid-twentieth-century American English did much to mitigate the stiffness of Borges's slightly archaic and nonnative (though effectively fluent) English, the texts produced by the two of them seem sometimes a bit odd, at least for the student wishing to study them in comparison with other versions of the same texts.[6] Of their very productive collaboration—and underscoring the difference between the choices made by the translator and those made by the original writer—one can only agree with Rodríguez Monegal when he observes, "The result, from a literary point of view, is sometimes strange. If their translations cannot be objected to from the point of view of accuracy and scholarship (they are the best one can ask for), they are less than unique from a purely creative point of view" (461).

Fascinated by magic (understood in the anthropological sense, as an issue of epistemology) and given to the creation of labyrinthine plot structures and the mirroring play of interlocking yet offsetting structures, Borges is the quintessential verbal magus, the writer not of traditional *cuentos*, or short stories, a genre which for him still smacked of the realist tradition, but of "fictions," verbal structures that flaunted their artifice. A writer and intellectual enamored of such philosophers as Plato, Berkeley, and Schopenhauer, Borges understood that "in a fiction, 'reality' *is* purely mental and that it doesn't exist beyond the words used to create it" (Sturrock, xxiv). In the 1930s, then, at precisely the time he was reading, teaching, and translating Faulkner—and coming to understand the true nature of the similar revolution in prose fiction that the American had wrought in his own country—Borges would reject the, for him, now outmoded tenets of realism in favor of a new kind of narrative art, one that functioned as an elaborate intellectual game, as a closed and self-referential semiotic system, though one not lacking, for the knowledgeable reader, in sociopolitical significance.[7]

Appearing in the late 1930s, the first text produced by the new Borges, the writer now emancipated from the intellectual and artistic constraints of realism and committed to the creation of "fantastic" narrative (Rodríguez Monegal, *Borges*, 326), was "Pierre Menard, Author of the *Quixote*," a droll parable that itself deals with the most fundamental issues of writing, reading, meaning, and translation. So perspicacious is this famous *ficción*'s commentary on the process of translation that George Steiner lauds it in the most unalloyed of terms: "Arguably, 'Pierre Menard, Author of the *Quixote*'

(1939) is the most acute, most concentrated commentary anyone has offered on the business of translation. What studies of translation there are, including this book, could, in Borges's style, be termed a commentary on his commentary" (70). In an extraordinarily dense text, yet one leavened by a dry humor and a sly parodic wit, Borges allows the alert reader to key on two closely related, though thoroughly disguised, points: how the same words gain and lose meaning through time, and why the act of reading—not writing—is the most crucial factor in the game of literature. Of the first issue, Borges's narrator tells us (in James Irby's superb translation) something that surprises us because, at first glance, it seems both illogical and bizarre: that while "Cervantes's text and Menard's are verbally identical . . . the second is almost infinitely richer. (More ambiguous, his detractors will say, but ambiguity is richness.)" (42). Although this improbable utterance ends a paragraph and is not expanded on, its significance reappears—though again, in vintage Borgesian mode, very obliquely—in the text's final lines: "Menard (perhaps without wanting to) has enriched, by means of a new technique, the halting and rudimentary art of reading: this new technique is that of the deliberate anachronism and the erroneous attribution." On the chance that the reader has not yet caught on to the importance of the reader's role in the creation of a text and of its myriad meanings, the narrator offers one more clue, adding, again with reference to reading but still destabilizing reality with pure artifice:

> This technique, whose applications are infinite, prompts us to go through the *Odyssey* as if it were posterior to the *Aeneid* and the book *Le jardin du Centaure* of Madame Henri Bachelier as if it were by Madame Henri Bachelier. This technique fills the most placid works with adventure.

If the reader, tangled up perhaps in the deliberate mixing of real authors with false or fictional ones, has not caught the drift by this point it is too late, for Borges and his narrator effectively end the game by concluding the narrative with a still related but now much less obvious reference to the creativity inherent in the act of reading: "To attribute the *Imitatio Christi* to Louis Ferdinand Céline or to James Joyce, is this not a sufficient renovation of its tenuous spiritual indications?" (44). As Rodríguez Monegal notes, in "Pierre Menard, Author of the *Quixote*" we can discern the foundation of a radically new poetics for narrative, one based not on the author and the original writing of the text but on the reading of it (*Borges*, 330), on every reader's differing interpretation of it. It is thus no exaggeration to say that, in terms of the development of inter-American literature and literary studies, reader response theory begins in Argentina, with Jorge Luis Borges, in 1939.

Machado de Assis's Legacy of the Creative Reader

While Borges may have been the first New World writer to argue systematically in favor of the reader's role in the literary experience, he was not the first writer in the Americas to speak to this issue or to integrate the reader's active participation into his narratives. That honor goes to Brazil's Machado de Assis, who as early as 1880 with *Memórias póstumas de Brás Cubas* (tr. William L. Grossman, *Epitaph of a Small Winner*, 1952; tr. Gregory Rabassa, *The Posthumous Memoirs of Brás Cubas*, 1998) had definitively established the reader as a creative and dynamic force in the creation of a text's semantic possibilities. Going beyond the influence of Sterne and *Tristram Shandy*, a book he knew very well, Machado with his 1880 novel (or antinovel) undermined the realist tradition, which in Spanish America had produced an abundance of good but overly imitative novels, by creating his own brand of "fantastic" or "magical" narrative, one characterized not only by a new role for the reader but, presaging Borges by some sixty years, by the creation of a new reader-centered poetics as well. This is almost certainly Machado's greatest single contribution to narrative theory, and it shows that, had he worked in English or French or German, he would today be widely recognized as one of the Western tradition's greatest innovators. In terms of inter-American literary history, one can easily conclude that the first "new narrative" of the New World begins with the seriocomic tale told by the very dead but still very manipulative bourgeois Brás Cubas, Machado de Assis's self-conscious, egoistic, and ultimately unreliable narrator-protagonist. With Machado, then, the break with realism, and with the norms of realistic narrative, is dramatic, though it must be remembered that it fits into a larger pattern of national development that makes Brazilian literature unique in the New World and, perhaps, in the Western tradition generally.

Roberto González Echevarría, Enrique Pupo-Walker, and David Haberly write in *The Cambridge History of Latin American Literature*:

> Brazil's is the most independent, and perhaps most original, national literature in the New World. Whereas the United States' powerful literary tradition is, nevertheless, in some synchrony with that of England, its former metropolis, as is the case with the Spanish American literary tradition with regards to that of Spain, Portugal ceased long ago to be a significant presence in Brazil. This is ironic because, of all

the American nations, with the exception of Canada, Brazil is the one whose break from the mother country was the least painful and radical. Instead of becoming independent from the metropolitan government, the metropolitan government actually moved to Brazil. Brazil absorbed its origins, like some mythological figure who swallows its parents. (3:1)

A rich and heady brew made up of its European, indigenous, and African bloodlines, Brazilian literature begins, in a formal sense, with the arrival of Pedro Álvares Cabral's Portuguese fleet in the spring of 1500. From the beginning different from Spanish literature (and from the other European literatures and cultures of the time), and reflecting the very different outlooks of Spain and Portugal, Brazilian literature was, even at the moment of its historical foundation, more receptive to outside forces and influences.[8] Even the "Carta de achamento" (Letter of discovery) written by Cabral's very perceptive and able scribe, Pero Vaz de Caminha, differs dramatically from Columbus's inflated and rhetorical discovery document. And, in truth, Brazil's coherent and inventive narrative tradition stems directly from this candid and self-conscious foundational treatise. While Brazilian literature generally came into its own during the early 1800s, in the second half of the nineteenth century "Brazilian fiction was unequaled in the rest of Latin America in terms of production and quality" (González Echevarría, *Oxford*, 15), with a number of writers equaling or surpassing what their counterparts were doing in North America or Europe at the same time.

Out of this very fertile matrix emerged Machado de Assis, whom the comparative perspective now allows us to regard not only as "the best Latin American fiction writer of the [nineteenth] century" (González Echevarría, *Oxford*, 16) but as "one of the best of all time anywhere. . . . In the Americas he is certainly on the level of Melville, Hawthorne, and Poe. No one in Spanish comes close to his polish and originality" (González Echevarría, *Oxford*, 95). David Haberly likewise declares that "Joaquim Maria de Machado de Assis (1839–1908) is the greatest nineteenth-century novelist of Latin America and one of the most remarkable literary talents to appear in the Americas as a whole" (Introduction, *Quincas Borba*, xi). As a result of Machado and the rather unique narrative tradition out of which he arose, it is easier to understand why even today "The Brazilian novelistic tradition . . . rivals in richness that of all of Spanish America, as well as that in the United States" (González Echevarría et al., 3:1–2), a point that merits much consideration given the somewhat uneven reception of Brazilian literature, and especially Brazilian fiction, in the United States. Carrying this issue even further, and underscoring the validity of the entire inter-American project, González Echevarría avers that "Brazil's is, with that of the United States, the richest national literature in the New World" (*Oxford*, xii). What is clear with respect to our proper appreciation of Machado, an egregiously underappreciated master who is only now beginning to garner the international renown and respect he deserves, is that his technical sophistication and theoretical breadth, his interest in such destabilizing human motivations as sexuality (both male and female), egoism, jealousy, and altruism, and his grasp of the sham and hypocrisy of the social world put him more in tune with the luminaries of contemporary literature than with those of the nineteenth century. In fact, as González Echevarría contends, "not only does he usher in the twentieth century, . . . in many ways he anticipates and even exhausts it" (*Oxford*, 16).

A grand anachronism, then, a writer and theorist very much in advance of his place and time, Machado, like the Baudelaire of *Les fleurs du mal* (1857), introduces the malaise of modernity to our New World conscious-ness. Though not Latin America's first truly great writer—that honor goes to Mexico's Sor Juana Inés de la Cruz, the finest poet and the most daring intellect of all colonial America, North or South—Machado is nevertheless its second great writer (Borges would win the bronze medal) and the first to renovate, by means of radically new modes of creativity, New World nar-rative. Best known for his novels, and especially for the trilogy comprising *Memórias póstumas de Brás Cubas* (1880), *Quincas Borba* (1891; tr. Clo-tilde Wilson, *Philosopher or Dog?*, 1954; tr. Gregory Rabassa, *Quincas Borba*, 1999), and his masterpiece, *Dom Casmurro* (1899/1900;[9] tr. Helen Caldwell, 1953; tr. John Gledson, 1997), a work judged by Helen Caldwell to be "per-haps the finest of all American novels of either continent" (1), Machado was arguably even more revolutionary as a writer of the short story, a form in which he had few peers, then or now. Of his roughly two hundred stories, fewer than twenty are known to have been translated into English. Some of the most outstanding, such as "Midnight Mass," a story whose repressed female sexuality and perfectly poised ambiguity would have appealed deeply to Kate Chopin and Henry James, or "The Psychiatrist," lend themselves to comparative inter-American study. "The Psychiatrist," which dates from his pivotal 1881–1982 period, calls up comparisons with Twain's "The Man That Corrupted Hadleyburg" (1899), while also being linked, in a more interna-tional context, to Swift's *A Serious and Useful Scheme to Make an Hospital for Incurables*, to Pascal, and to Chekhov's "Ward Number Six" (1892).

Of his novels, however, it is *Quincas Borba* that most poignantly expresses Machado's deep skepticism about the infallibility of science (particularly as it degenerated into phrenology and social Darwinism, the latter philosophy being espoused by the madman whose name gives the book its title), progress, and the unrestrained free market system. The result, sharply felt in this historically underappreciated novel (or, again, antinovel), is a great disenchantment with the ideals of Western civilization as they were then being thrust upon nations and cultures not yet prepared to receive them, one of which was Brazil, a culture just beginning to suffer the social and political realities of "savage capitalism." As David Haberly points out in his excellent introduction to Gregory Rabassa's new translation of the novel, *Quincas Borba* lends itself to being read as an allegory not only of Pedro II, who ruled Brazil from 1831 to 1839,[10] but of the Empire itself, an ephemeral political construct that was made up of "misplaced ideas" regarding progressive, democratic societies (see Schwarz)[11] and that was, at bottom, "a fiction held together by its central character, Pedro II" (Haberly, xv).

This point illuminates not only Machado's ideas about how a new and basically antirealistic narrative might be written and what the reader's role might be in such a narrative—told, once again, by a glib narrator who proves to be utterly an unreliable guide—but how all of this antedates the similar though not identical contributions of Borges. For example, though it is clear that both Machado, with his breakthroughs in the 1880s and 1890s, and Borges in the 1930s understand that fiction is radically distinct from reality and must therefore be understood and evaluated on its own aesthetic terms as a self-referential system, Machado was more committed than his Argentine counterpart to building a discernable political dimension into his text.[12] This wedding of the purely fictive (the symbolic world created by the novel itself) with the political is, in truth, what facilitates and justifies our reading of *Quincas Borba* as a withering political allegory, though it is unquestionably the novel's sophistication and subtlety as fiction, as verbal artifice, that dominates and manipulates our response to it. As Haberly puts it, "After 1879, Machado stopped trying to be realistic in his plots and descriptions; he recognized that he was describing an apparent reality that was itself fundamentally fictional. . . . The singularity of *Quincas Borba* lies in its denial of the validity of the text as a version of reality" (Introduction, xvi, xxv). This was a concept that Machado had first tried out some ten years earlier with *The Posthumous Memoirs of Brás Cubas*, but it gets a fuller, more elaborate treatment here before finding its maximum expression in *Dom Casmurro*, a novel whose consumption by the reader is totally controlled by its own acutely self-conscious status as a text that is not only polysemic but ironically so.

Falling between these two novels, it is *Quincas Borba*, however, that captures the essence of the skepticism that so characterizes our modern age. In Machado's hands this radical skepticism, born of the painful gap that exists between a lofty, idealized language and the grim, dehumanizing reality lived out by people at the bottom of the socioeconomic ladder, portrays a deeply hypocritical society in which ideas (and ideals) are so twisted and perverted by ideologies and by an unquenchable thirst for power that they end up having little or no relation to the realities they purport to describe. The world Machado outlines in *Quincas Borba* is one that both Twain and Orwell would have understood well. And, rooted as it is in our inability—or perhaps our unwillingness—to separate fantasy from reality, it is one that goes to the heart of the entire New World experience, from 1492 to the present day. Keying on the reader's crucial role in this process, and on its connection to the modern condition, Haberly sums up:

> Through the narrator's betrayal, moreover, Machado betrays our expectations as readers and demands the unexpected of us. He presents us with the "tatters of reality" his narrator has stitched together into an ordered sequence, but the narrator's evident unreliability invalidates that order and forces us to create our own reality from those tatters. A unitary explanation of events, imposed by a narrator or an author, gives way to chaos—a potentially infinite number of possible readers and of possible readings. And, finally, each of those readings may fail to capture an ultimately unknowable reality, since our human vision of our own lives, of the lives of others, of the world in which we live, is vague, fragmentary, and formless. (Introduction, xxv–xxvi)

While Machado "retrieves from Cervantes the origins of the novel as illusion, play, ambiguity and adventure, where truth can result from folly and imagination can open a higher order of reason," and while he has created "superbly funny books" that dissect "the abnormalities of alienation, perversion, domination, cruelty and madness," he also deconstructs empire "with a thoroughness and an esthetic equilibrium that place him in a class by himself. . . . By using irony and parody to create emotional or intellectual suspense and comedy, Machado trumpets his modernity as a writer" (Jackson, "Madness," 15).

Transition to Modernity

The Brazilian modernist writers Mário de Andrade and Oswald de Andrade provide an interesting bridge between Machado de Assis and the writers of the 1950s. Mário de Andrade was one of the most important figures in Brazilian literature and culture of the twentieth century and was the architect of the Week of Modern Art in São Paulo in 1922, inaugurated with the performance of his collection of poems titled *Pauličéia desvairada* (tr. Jack E. Tomlins, *Hallucinated City*, 1969). The Week of Modern Art introduced the Brazilian modernist ethos, which emerged "at the intersection of theories of subjectivity, ethics, and aesthetics during the 1920s and 1930s" (Gabara, 33). Mário de Andrade maligned the bourgeoisie and was the armchair intellectual, while Oswald (no relation) was the man of action. Mário looked at Brazil's urbanization through the nostalgic lens of the Brazilian Indian legacy, using anthropophagic imagery to express the threat of the big city—"São Paulo, giant mouth of a thousand teeth" (*Pauličéia*, 33)—or to deride the "digestive intelligence" of the "good bourgeois" (Lowe, *City*, 95). Oswald sought a perspective on the new Brazil from his trips to Europe between 1912 and 1922. He then brought the modernist aesthetic back from Paris, where he had formed close relationships with a number of leading intellectuals and had been in the Continental vanguard (Lowe, *City*, 95).

Oswald's signature work, *Serafim ponte grande* (1929; tr. Kenneth D. [K. David] Jackson and Albert Bork, *Seraphim Grosse Pointe*, 1979), is a brilliant social satire as well as a wildly funny parody of traditional narrative arts. The central idea of Brazilian modernism was to claim Brazil's place in mainstream Western urban culture and to reinvent its people as the product of its natural and ethnic history as well as of European and North American influences. The big city, in the modernist novel, is cast as the "new backlands," a symbol of hope and despair, and the challenge to the artist formerly represented by the *sertão*. Modernists aspired to create a "literature for export." The antihero Seraphim is a kind of sex-crazed Don Quixote who travels to the capital cities of three continents to flout, with equally roguish characters, the established social norms of "home, family and mutuality" (Johnson, 25). The style prefigures the "gliglish" of Cortázar in the dizzy mix of puns, metaphor, popular speech, archaisms, poetry, paraphrase, testimony, nonsense, and "facetious dialogue." The task of translating *Seraphim* is not just specific to the work with its invented words and even phrases, which are "imitations rather than translations" (Johnson, 25). The task is also to decolonize the text, for if translation is perceived by some as a colonizing act—a very Brazilian modernist posture—then Jackson and Bork succeeded magnificently in accentuating the book's defiantly modernist anticolonialism. "In no way do they disfigure the Brazilian bohemian's character. They retain also the flavor and texture of the Portuguese version and perspicaciously incorporate a translation of Haroldo de Campos' enlightening analysis 'Seraphim, A Great Notebook,' which contributes to a better understanding of Andrade's objectives in writing his audacious, derisive, unconventional travel book" (Johnson, 25).

The city became symbolic of what modernists felt was a dispersion of national character, personified by Mário de Andrade's *Macunaíma* (1928; tr. E. A. Goodland, 1984). Like *Seraphim Grosse Pointe*, the translation challenge for *Macunaíma* is that the novel "ironically poses the problem of a Brazilian national character [in the context of] a geographic and linguistic amalgam, a composite of folkloric sources expressed in a collage like language nobody actually speaks" (Unruh, 126). The main theme of the book is New World man against the gods, which are metamorphosed from their Old World personifications into New World variations of the same hopes and fears. Described by Alexander Coleman as a "verbal rhapsody," the book at first did not gain wide acceptance principally because it was outside the experience or imagination of the audience. Coleman writes that the translation "brings the language across with descriptive passages of considerable eloquence" but feels Goodland has problems with register and dialect: "he cannot make Mário de Andrade's folk speak in English as they should. 'Fiddlesticks,' 'hell's bells,' 'gosh,' and 'high dudgeon' have no place in contemporary translation, and there are places where he lapses into the language of Sir Walter Scott, which has nothing at all to do with de Andrade's wild experimental work." A canonical text of modern Brazilian literature that should have wider readership in the Americas, *Macunaíma* is an example of a novel that would benefit from retranslation.

Julio Cortázar and the Liberation of the Spanish American Novel

While Machado precedes Borges by many decades and, moreover, represents a Brazilian narrative tradition that, in its historical development, differs significantly from its Spanish American cousin, another marvelously gifted Latin American writer, Julio Cortázar, is often considered part of Borges's literary legacy. As we have already seen, Cortázar's breakout novel *Rayuela*, or *Hopscotch*, liberated the Spanish American novel from its provincialism and stale rhetoric and from the overly imitative stance that had long impeded its formal development.[13] At the same time, it too called in a most unambiguous manner for a new kind of reader, one able to deal with the aleatoric structuring(s) of the narrative itself.[14] But beyond its formal inventiveness, *Hopscotch* was at bottom a very "cool" (in the argot of the time), very sophisticated, and very witty discussion of how the basic principles of French structuralism might relate to the organization and reading of a literary text, how these principles might inform the development of fictional characters, and how a reader might respond to them. An urbane and worldly character himself, Cortázar, who had resided in Paris since the early 1950s, was fluent not only in French (and English) but in the theoretical and artistic issues then being debated by the European intelligentsia. Given the eclectic nature of his literary interests, it is no surprise to find that *Hopscotch* is deeply informed by these concerns and discussions (which not a few American readers and critics of the time found boring) and that it seeks to bring to life, as literature, what had been, to that point, some very abstruse philosophical ideas, particularly about language, truth, and being.

Although it was largely missed at the time, it is clear in retrospect that the most compelling thematic feature of *Hopscotch* is its critique of structuralism and the problem of "the center," a concept that Jacques Derrida would not take up until 1966 with his well-known Johns Hopkins University lecture titled, in its English translation, "Structure, Sign, and Play in the Discourse of the Human Sciences." Since Cortázar's novel was first published, in Spanish, in 1963, we can see that it preceded Derrida's more famous challenge to structuralism by a full three years. Thus we are justified in concluding that what is now widely known as poststructuralism finds its first full expression in a dazzling Latin American novel of the early 1960s, Julio Cortázar's *Rayuela*.

How, exactly, do these two texts' basic arguments compare? Derrida, critiquing the "structurality of structure" and concerned with how, inescapably, the function of any structure's "center" is "not only to orient, balance, and organize the structure—one cannot in fact conceive of an unorganized structure—but above all to make sure that the organizing principle of the structure would limit what we might call the *freeplay* of the structure" (324), is engaging an issue that pulses, captiously, at the heart of *Hopscotch*. This interrogation of the "structurality of structure," as we shall see, is precisely the issue that *Hopscotch*, in its inimitably comic fashion, takes on, and with results that could lead to a reconsideration of Derrida's basic premise as it applies to literary creation. Somewhat later in his essay Derrida also says that "even today the notion of a structure lacking any center represents the unthinkable itself" (324–25). "Nevertheless," he continues, making a point that relates directly to Cortázar's experimentations in *Hopscotch*, "the center also closes off the freeplay it opens up and makes possible. *Qua* center, it is the point at which the substitution of contents, elements, or terms is no longer possible" (325).

In Cortázar's (anti)novel, one of the main characters, an educated middle-class Argentine named Horacio Oliveira who is living the expatriate life in Paris, is looking for something—a "center"—that he knows, or is coming to suspect, he can never attain. "Closing his eyes," the narrator, sounding like Derrida, tells us of Oliveira, "he managed to tell himself that if a simple ritual was able to excentrate him like this the better to show him a center, to excentrate him towards a center which was nonetheless inconceivable, perhaps everything was not lost. . . . He was not drunk enough to stop thinking consecutively" (*Hopscotch*, 49–50). Replete with its many references to Logos, even the text of *Hopscotch* leads the reader to consider the extent to which it is the play of language, and not some preexisting condition, some eternal, unchanging verity (Logos), that determines who and what we are. In Cortázar's long, talk-filled narrative, the "center" we humans so ardently seek in the hope that it will make sense of the "freeplay" of our existences by ordering or structuring—our logocentric urge—then turns out to be the eternally fluid, malleable, and creative force of language. Developing around two poles, Paris and Buenos Aires, and thus embodying the binary oppositions so dear to high structuralist thought (and so undermined by the poststructuralists), the novel nevertheless subjects these to a constant decoupling and rearrangement via the semantic anarchy of language, a facet of the text seen most vividly in its wildly imaginative dialogue, in the intellectual prestidigitation of its characters, and in its famously random structuring. As, indeed, the structural "deconstructivity" of *Hopscotch* continuously demonstrates, there is no stable, orienting center; the thing we humans (the "structuring animal") want is the very thing the text denies us. Worse, if there were some sort of "first principle" to organize the universe and thereby help us fend off the chaos and randomness of our lives—which, as the title suggests, is what *Hopscotch* is about—Oliveira comes to the conclusion that it would have to be desire, a force that, in its myriad forms, is always potentially decentering and destabilizing, capable of upsetting all our best laid plans, intentions, and relationships. More intimately related, perhaps, to selfishness and egoism than to altruism and human solidarity, the free play (or expression) of desire thus becomes one of the novel's most important secondary themes. Oliveira gradually comes to see himself as undertaking a necessarily inchoate quest to attain a "kibbutz of desire," a Nirvana-like state of being that he believes would allow him to experience life as he wishes it to be and not as it is or as, in his Western, logocentric (and, we come to suspect, phallogocentric) way, he and his reader have been taught to expect it to be.

Although the critical consensus regarding *Hopscotch* is that it is uneven, brilliant in some respects but less so in others, everyone agrees that its enduring claim to fame resides in the extraordinary creativity of its language, a feature that, as we have seen, Rodríguez Monegal identified early on as the crucial feature of the Spanish American "new novel," the one aspect of its technical sophistication that would gain for it an international status not previously accorded it. Given the difficulties produced by such drastic shifts of tone, timbre, and register, by the multiple, overlapping ironies, and by the many portmanteau words that populate the text, even a thorough reading of the novel in its original Spanish is a daunting task. All the more remarkable, then, is Gregory Rabassa's pitch-perfect (and prizewinning) translation, a rendition in mid-twentieth-century American English that, step for step, offers a virtuoso double of Cortázar's own verbal alchemy. There can be no doubt that the critical success of Cortázar and *Hopscotch* came about in large measure because—achieving that rarest of victories in translation work—Rabassa's version allowed the English-speaking reader to come away with a secure sense of the original's tone, its dazzling wordplay, its self-reflective semantic complexity, and its quicksilver tonal shifts.

At one point, for example, the characters Oliveira and La Maga (his mysterious, beguiling lover whose presence in the narrative is like a talisman) are talking to each other in "glíglico," an invented language of love. Rabassa, not missing a beat, adroitly translates this term as "Gliglish," a similarly invented term and one that captures perfectly the original's sly implications. Such tit-for-tat creativity, in the original Spanish and in the English translation, makes itself even more evident in this marvelous exchange:

> —¿Pero te retila la murta? No me vayas a mentir. ¿Te la retila de veras?
> —Muchísimo. Por todas partes, a veces demasiado. Es una sensación maravillosa.
> —¿Y te hace poner con los plíneos entre las argustas?
> —Sí, y después nos entreturnamos los porcios hasta que él dice basta basta, y yo tampoco puedo más, hay que apurarse, comprendés. Pero eso vos no lo podés comprender, siempre te quedás en la gunfia más chica.
> —Yo y cualquiera—rezongó Oliveira, enderezándose—. Che, este mate es una porquería, yo me voy un rato a la calle.
> —¿No querés que te siga contando de Ossip? —dijo la Maga—. En glíglico.
> —Me aburre mucho el glíglico. Además vos no tenés imaginación, siempre decís las mismas cosas. La gunfia, vaya novedad. Y no se dice "contando de." (*Rayuela*, 104–5)

> "But does he retilate your murt? Don't lie to me. Does he really retilate it?"

"A lot. Everywhere, sometimes too much. It's a wonderful feeling."

"And does he make you put your plinnies in between his argusts?"

"Yes, and then we trewst our porcies until he says he's had enough, and I can't take it any more either, and we have to hurry up, you understand. But you wouldn't understand that, you always stay in the smallest gumphy."

"Me or anybody else," Oliveira grumbled, getting up. "Christ, this *mate* is lousy. I'm going out for a while."

"Don't you want me to keep on talking to you of Ossip?" said La Maga. "In Gliglish."

"I'm getting sick of Gliglish. Besides, you haven't got any imagination, you always say the same things. Gumphy, that's some fine invention. And you don't say 'talking to you of.'" (*Hopscotch*, 85)

Rabassa himself says of this passage, "As can be seen, the best way to translate *glíglico* is to put it into Gliglish. In both cases the author's intent overcomes our lack of knowledge of the language and we know all we have to know concerning what's going on. This is a manufactured case of linguistic difference, but it does illustrate that sometimes language is unnecessary to convey meaning and mere utterance will do the job" ("Words," 85).

Clarice Lispector's Semiotics of Desire

Another Latin American novelist who humanized poststructuralist theory was Brazil's Clarice Lispector, a writer whose impact throughout the Americas, and the world, has grown with each passing year. To fully appreciate the importance of Lispector's groundbreaking work, it is instructive to compare her first novel, *Perto do coração selvagem* (1944; tr. Giovanni Pontiero, *Near to the Wild Heart*, 1990), to Borges's *Ficciones*, which were completed in the same year. Both offer up splendid examples of an innovative and engaging "new narrative," Borges in the form of "short fictions" and Lispector in the form of the novel. And both will change the ways narrative gets written in their respective traditions. Yet it is in the differences between them that we see more clearly the unique contributions of Lispector.[15] Merging her concerns over the ontological implications of language with her examinations of the social, psychological, sexual, and political status of women, Lispector created a new kind of writing for Brazilian literature, one that stressed the fluid, contradictory nature of human identity as an issue of semiotics and of desire, in all its forms. She is viewed in France "as an important contemporary philosopher dealing with the relationships between language and human (especially female) subjecthood" and a writer who, in her stories, novels, and *crônicas* (short, reflective, often very personal essays on a variety of topics), seeks constantly to probe the ambiguity of language and to make it "reveal what, in its structuring as a container, it seeks to hide" (Sousa, vii–viii). Lispector's highly idiosyncratic prose style, always immediately recognizable, presents unusual problems for her many translators. Speaking of his efforts to replicate one of her most important midcareer novels, *La paixão segundo G. H.* (1964; tr. *The Passion according to G. H.*, 1988), Ronald W. Sousa writes:

> I have subordinated the rendition of many of what would traditionally be called "literary devices" to delineation, first and foremost, of the intellectual positions set forth in the book, and only thereafter have I endeavored to reproduce such features as style variation and artful use—or violation—of language norms. In so doing, I have often made the translated text more conventional than the original, regularly had to paraphrase where no single term was readily available in English, and occasionally had recourse to philosophical terminology where the original uses more ambiguous, and therefore more powerful, formulations. The result is a text that has lost something of the ambiguity and idiosyncrasy that is part and parcel of the original from which it arises and has become more expository in tone than that original. I invite the reader to imagine a Portuguese text that transmits a much greater sense of potential language chaos than does the translation.
>
> The result may or may not be called "translation," but then that undecidability is only fitting in regard to a work that may or may not be called a "novel." (ix)

Epitomizing the poststructural problem of our human quest for the logocentric "center" that lies forever beyond our reach, Lispector's nameless narrator ponders, in this intensely poetic 1964 work, her elusive, ephemeral sense of being: "I don't know, I don't know. For the thing can never be really touched. The vital core is a finger pointing to it—and what is pointed to enlivens like a milligram of radium in the tranquil darkness. . . . For the dark is not lightable, the dark is a way of being: the dark is the dark's vital core, and something's vital core is never reached" (*Passion*, 131).[16] Again and again, G. H.'s divagations about human identity wind their way back to language:

> Reality is raw material, language the way I seek it—and how I don't find it. But it is from seeking and not finding that what I have not known is born, and I instantly recognize it. Language is my human endeavor.

I have fatefully to go seeking and fatefully I return with empty hands. But—I return with the unsayable. The unsayable can be given me only through the failure of my language. Only when the construct falters do I reach what it could not accomplish. (170)

Another of Lispector's major translators, Giovanni Pontiero, often called attention to the existential and comic features of Lispector's work. As a careful and sensitive reader of her texts, Pontiero also composed useful introductions and afterwords that are of considerable help to the reader, particularly with respect to Lispector's views on language, writing, and consciousness. Although the Pontiero translations have elicited criticism for their lack of accuracy and fidelity to the stylistic nuances of the original (see Braga-Pinto, 72–77), Pontiero must be credited with bringing Clarice Lispector, an internationally celebrated writer, to the attention of a greatly expanded new audience.

Lispector's most distilled narrative of this type, however, is undoubtedly her 1973 "fiction," *Água viva*, translated in 1989 by Elizabeth Lowe and Earl Fitz as *The Stream of Life*, the text that became the inspiration for Cixous' very influential theory of *l'écriture féminine*. Of *The Stream of Life*, in fact, Cixous maintains that while it is about many things—all of Lispector's most basic motifs figure into its composition: water, darkness, words, the body, immanence, the instant, being, identity—it is about two things in particular, female pleasure and writing. Reflecting on its connections to the philosophical systems of Heidegger, Lacan, and Derrida, Cixous believes that while "Pleasure is all *Água viva* is talking about," the problem being dealt with is that "to say and to have pleasure are not simultaneous. To say something always betrays something" (xi), and it is this unavoidable act of betrayal that serves as the catalyst for the text's unique tension, its dynamic interplay between orgasmic release and frustrated desire. "What is tragic," argues Cixous, touching on one of Lispector's most defining themes, "is that the word separates. There is a difference in language between the subject who has pleasure and the one who says it" (xi), and while Lispector's eponymous narrator desires to discover her essence, she wants to do so without possessing it in the traditional sense; paradoxically, she wants to "possess" beginning with herself but without the isolating and tyrannical (and masculine) conditions usually associated with this term.[17]

Rejecting essentialist positions about gender, Lispector nevertheless presents a fictional world in which her female characters develop as manifestations of a powerful and decentering "libidinal economy," one infused with the kind of bisexual energy and freedom that Cixous endorses in *The Newly*

Born Woman and that, in opposition to "the male economy of contention" (Braga-Pinto, 108), overflows conventional boundaries about what it means to *be,* as either a female, a male, or a pansexual being. Infused, then, with the élan vital of *jouissance* and on the verge of realizing her female *puissance,* Lispector's narrator cries out, in the startling assertion of self-liberation that opens her story:

> É com uma alegria tão profunda. É uma tal aleluia. Aleluia, grito eu, aleluia que se funde com o mais escuro uivo humano da dor de separação mas é grito de felicidade diabólica. Porque ninguém me prende mais . . . mas agora quero o plasma—quero me alimentar diretamente da placenta. (*Água viva,* 9)

> It's with such intense joy. It's such an hallelujah. "Hallelujah," I shout, an hallelujah that fuses the darkest human howl of the pain of separation but is a shout of diabolical happiness. Because nobody holds me back anymore. . . . but now I want plasma, I want to feed directly from the placenta. (*Stream,* 3)

Frustrated but desirous of becoming, of entering into some higher and more satisfying state of existence, the narrator continues, simultaneously involving both the former lover to whom she is writing and the reader:

> Eu te digo: estou tentando captar a quarta dimensão do instante-já que de tão fugido não é mais porque agora tornou-se um novo instante-já que também não é mais. Cada coisa tem um instante em que ela. (9)

> Let me tell you . . . I'm trying to capture the fourth dimension of the now-instant, which is so fleeting it no longer is because it has already become a new now-instant, which also is no longer. Each thing has an instant in which it is. (3)

The critical response to the English translation of *The Stream of Life* has been positive. César Braga-Pinto, for example, writes:

> *The Stream of Life* is certainly the translation which is most akin to Lispector's "thing," since it does not try to translate it into a "narrative". . . . It thus *echoes* the original work without having to *explain* its meaning. . . . Unlike other translations of Lispector's books, the translation of *The Stream of Life* is not the result of the translators' attempt to fit Lispector's text into a particular interpretation. It is, rather, a

re-creation of the author's original experience, its echoing and, at the same time, its celebration. (85)

Acutely aware of Lispector's signature style—it has long been said in Brazil that no one writes like Clarice—as well as of her philosophical and political concerns, the translators sought, in *The Stream of Life*, to hew close to her syntax and to replicate her unique sense of punctuation, giving the English version the same kind of unorthodox and unexpected couplings of words, phrases, and ideas. Prototypical of late-twentieth-century concerns with semiotics and textuality, poststructuralism, *écriture féminine*, and the nature of writing as ontological act, Lispector's work epitomizes a certain kind of theoretical thinking about language, meaning, and being. One can only agree with Cixous when, referring to *The Stream of Life* in particular, she writes, "If there is a subject of this text, or an object, it is on the question of writing. *Agua viva* is about writing, as a verbal activity. I write you. This is something active. The circulation of blood in this text, the vital theme of this text, is writing, all the questions of writing. Everything is organized around the mystery of writing. . . . All the questions of writing are right here" (xv–xvi).

The Post-Boom and the Parodic Narratives of Severo Sarduy

Bridging the gap between the boom and the McOndo generation are the writers referred to as the post-Boom, who include Sarduy, Antonio Skármeta, Ariel Dorfman, Luisa Valenzuela, Rosario Ferré, and Reinaldo Arenas. Donald Leslie Shaw has written about the writers who followed the Boom in the mid-1970s, and who have focused on the young working class with its pop culture and lifestyle unfettered by older bourgeois expectations. This group has been characterized as more optimistic and grounded in Latin American social reality, as opposed to the darker vision of the Boom (see Shaw, 1998). The dialogue about the post-Boom, in the context of postcolonial and postmodern writing, has involved a number of scholars, but with less consensus than the discussion of the Boom, which was seen as the rise to maturity of a literary culture (Williams, review, 75).

Severo Sarduy's *Cobra* (1972; tr. Suzanne Jill Levine, 1975) is an open, elusive, and self-consciously parodic narrative that "represents, in many ways, the culmination of the New Latin American Novel" (Levine, in *Cobra*, vii). Reveling in its semantic and morphological play, language in fact becomes the novel's protagonist, the most fundamental agent of change and transformation in human affairs. Though they develop them in very different ways, the parallels with Lispector and *The Stream of Life* are many and clear: both *Cobra* and *The Stream of Life* manifest a basic concern for the mutability of language and meaning, for writing, for comparisons between writing and painting, for eroticism and the body's role in it, for transformation, for the offsetting play of opposites, and for undermining the logocentric myths of semantic stability and the unified sign. The differences between them, however, are even more telling: *Cobra* is more chaotic with respect to structure and story, and is more deliberately self-conscious in terms of the transformative power of language; *Cobra* is also more overtly a demonstration of Barthesian semiotics and of the ideas associated with the journal *Tel Quel*, with which Sarduy, a Cuban residing in Paris, was closely associated; finally, *The Stream of Life*, by contrast, presents language more as an issue of a personal ontology than as literary theory. In *Cobra*, language per se emerges as the main character, while in *The Stream of Life* it presents itself as process and as the mechanism that engenders the psychosexual self-realization of an unnamed woman. But because this self-realization is also self-effacing (as is the very language that conveys it), her characterization is, as is nearly everything else in *Cobra*, developed as a constant process of change and transformation. "*Cobra*," as Michael Wood has written, "is not *about* language," it *is* language, and its events are unmistakably functions *of* language. The text of *Cobra* thus moves not from adventure to adventure, nor even from scene to scene, but from word to word and image to image as it chases the "paradise of words," as Barthes himself has described this narrative, that it posits as the true nature of reality (Barthes, quoted by Wood 28). American readers familiar with the main female character in Pynchon's *V.* may see commonalities with Sarduy's ever-mutating transvestite, Cobra, whose overriding desire is to transform her/his body and, through this, her/his identity as well. Transformation might, in fact, for a certain type of reader, be said to be the underlying "theme," because, as the text of *Cobra* tells us, albeit disdainfully,

> without a theme—*the Madam*: "Ah, because literature still needs themes . . ." I (who am in the audience): "Shut up or I'll take you out of the chapter"—this narrative cannot continue. (14)

Both Pynchon's heroine and Sarduy's transvestite function in their respective texts as verbal signs (more so in the case of Sarduy), floating, like unattached signifiers, through the various scenes of the novels, suggesting finally that their authors view human existence as eternal movement toward the ineffable (a point shared with Lispector) rather than as culmination or closure. Mixing a wildly baroque style (one that invites comparison with the techniques of the Québécois neobaroque novel of the 1960s; see La Bossière) with high camp, blending in heavy doses of early-1970s pop culture, and topping it all off with a heady eroticism, *Cobra* too involves the reader directly in the ideologies of twentieth-century literary theory and in the text's self-conscious presentation: "Soon we'll fall into Stajanovism!"—the Madam would protest. "We must correct the errors of natural binaryism"—she added, Benvenistian—"but *per piacere*, gentlemen, this is not like shooting fish in a barrel!"[18] (4n–5n). Sarduy's involvement of the reader intensifies later when he writes, in a way that, in a moment of ironic intertextuality, compares his work parodically with the canonical texts of the Spanish American Boom:

> Moronic reader: if even with these clues, thick as posts, you have not understood that we're dealing with a metamorphosis of the painter of the preceding chapter—if you haven't, look for yourself how he has retained the gestures of his profession—abandon this novel and devote yourself to screwing or to reading the novels of the Boom, which are much easier. (42)

As volatile and radically inventive as the original is, the exemplary English translation by Suzanne Jill Levine matches it to an extraordinary degree. According to the translator herself, *Cobra* could best be described in terms of *bricolage*, as

> a Frankensteinian tapestry, composed of many languages, of the "leftovers" of texts, from Góngora to the *Michelin Guide*, from Cuban slang to French poststructuralist jargon. His "characters" (not characters in the realist sense) undergo continuous metamorphoses, reflected in the verbal disfigurements and alterations that Sarduy perpetrates. *Cobra* and his fourth novel, *Maitreya*, both satirize quests, from West to East (or vice versa), in which the Orient functions as a projection of the West's own (mis)interpretation. (*Scribe*, 37)

Touching again on the issue of linguistic play that so permeates this novel and that so defines it, Levine then declares that translating *Cobra* "meant translating a 250-page pun," with the reader being required to "follow metonymic displacements from image to image, character to character, translating the text not into an explanation, a message, but into yet another fragmented, open-ended image of itself" (38, 39). Focusing, for example, on the "untranslatable" play between *opio* (opium) and *apio* (celery), Sarduy himself, in a letter of 18 April 1973 to the translator, writes:

The point here is to hide a serious misdemeanor or error ["falta"] under a slight one . . . in which both words are pronounced almost identi-
cally. That is, here [Eustachio] traffics in *opio* but pretends to traffic in
apio; only one letter changes the formula. Couldn't you find a solution
with the word *horse*, which I believe designates heroin in English, or
something with "snow." (40)

Fully cognizant that Sarduy sought always to walk the tightrope "between
trope and meaning, supplanting signifiers with 'floating' signifiers referring
us back to wordplay, privileging the graphic materiality of vocables, which at
the same time speak to us of language's continual slipping, both away from
and toward meaning" (40), Levine found a creative solution to the *apio*/*opio*
conundrum by substituting cocaine, a drug offering a cultural connection
with its "notorious role in recent North and South American relations" (41).
Since the American slang expression "coke" connoted both the drug and the
popular soft drink Coca-Cola—which, in its original recipe, actually contained cocaine, and which therefore possesses an element of transgression
itself—Levine "translated *traficante de apio* (celery smuggler) as 'bottling
coke without a license,' both expressions suggesting in different ways the
contradictory 'benign transgression'" so essential to the original and yet also
integrating into the English text "the invasive repercussions of North American commerce and popular culture" in the Latin American (and world)
sphere (42).[19]

Pointing out that in *Cobra* "the metamorphoses of the main character,"
a transvestite who eventually merges the cultural surfaces of the East with
those of the West in a kind of reverse Orientalism, "correspond . . . to the
metamorphoses of language," Rodríguez Monegal and Colchie remind us in
The Borzoi Anthology of Latin American Fiction that

language is finally the real, and only, protagonist of Sarduy's novels.
There is only language in his books; no significance is hidden behind
the surface of signifiers. Each signifier refers to another signifier, which
in turn refers to a third, and so on. An erotic writer who has redis-
covered (as Roland Barthes has pointed out) the pleasures of the text,
Sarduy is today not only the most experimental of all Latin American
writers but also the one who has completely erased the boundaries
between prose and poetry. His novels are constructed with the rigor
and the fantasy of poems. They are devoted not to the construction of
narrative . . . but to the "deconstruction" of language. (2:951)

A singular achievement, though one not likely to be ardently embraced by the casual reader, *Cobra* remains "a remarkable book, a nervous, flighty homage to the life of language" (Wood, 28) in all its lubricious human glory.

Before closing this chapter, mention must be made of four other works of a similar stripe: Osman Lins's *Avalovara* (1973; tr. Gregory Rabassa, 1979), Lins's *A rainha dos cárceres da Grécia* (1976, tr. Adria Frizzi, *The Queen of the Prisons of Greece*, 1995), Helena Parente Cunha's *Mulher no espelho* (1983; tr. Fred P. Ellison and Naomi Lindstrom, *Woman Between Mirrors*, 1989), and Nélida Piñon's *A república dos sonhos* (1984; tr. Helen Lane, *The Republic of Dreams*, 1989). All these books continue the concern with language, being, and identity that characterizes *Cobra* (and that has marked the best of Latin American narrative since the time of Machado de Assis and of Borges), and all are, again like *Cobra* and *The Stream of Life*, deeply erotic. What is different here—and it is a difference that signals a radically new development in the modern Latin American narrative—is that all concern themselves with female sexuality. To be sure, this topic had been broached by Clarice Lispector as early as 1944 with *Near to the Wild Heart*, in which the young protagonist Joana liberates herself sexually, psychologically, and politically from a repressive social structure. But these Brazilian novels put female sexuality squarely at center stage.

Brazil's Everyman and the Quest for Paradise

Osman Lins's *Avalovara* tells the tale of Abel, a Brazilian everyman whose quest for paradise (another one of New World literature's most basic themes) involves him, psychologically and sexually, with three very different and very powerful women: Roos, who is worldly, sophisticated, and remote and who is variously identified (again recalling *Hopscotch*) with certain cities; Cecília, whose carnally charged hermaphroditism holds a key to our understanding of the entire novel; and a mysterious female presence known to the reader only by means of her semiotic status, an ideogram whose powerful, life-altering eroticism transforms Abel and points the way not only to paradise but to a higher, more complete state of being. The apocalyptic end of the novel, in which male violence attempts to destroy love, actually survives this potential disaster to symbolize the apotheosis of union, sexually and spiritually. In final lines that merge his concern with (again recalling *Hopscotch*) our constant search for the center—expressed in the novel's open, interconnecting narrative structure—and the catalyst of female desire, Lins writes of the discovered lovers in prose that (in Rabassa's translation, we must remind ourselves) is equal parts poetry and philosophy:

> Olavo Hayano his black and white hair his large teeth and devoured gap on one side of his face turns the barrel toward us we see his gesture well and we don't know what it means, we know nothing beyond recognition and beatitude, the ancient figures redolent of flowers and old things kept in drawers their tight coiffures shirtfronts lace hats remain motionless and turned toward the Bearer, he opens the pernicious mouth and several dogs or abonaxis birds bark at once, our pacifying bird sings louder our embrace, a new lightning flash in the room and we hear irate full of irate teeth the barking of the dogs and we cross a border and we join the rug we are woven into the rug I and I banks of a clear murmuring river peopled with fish and voices we and the butterflies we and sunflowers we and the benevolent bird more and more distant barking of dogs a new and luminous silence comes peace comes and nothing touches us, nothing, we walk, happy, entwined, among the animals and plants of the Garden. (331–32)

As the lovers dissolve into the rug's edenic motif, they too are entering into a state of Nirvana, though here the quest for yet another "kibbutz of desire" comes to fruition, literally and figuratively. Although the reader understands that the novel's conclusion is not an end but merely another moving point on one of the spiral's moving lines, and that paradise, or Eden, or the Garden, could therefore all be either ahead of us or behind us, the final lines of *Avalovara* must be taken at the very least as a moment of unification and happiness, of solipsism finally overcome, on the road (or spiral) of life.

Although the novel's protagonist is, nominally at least, a male, its true theme can be said to be the liberating and life-giving power of female eros, in all its manifold forms and expressions. Alluding in its title to a great mythical bird—perhaps, as Rabassa suggests in "Osman Lins and *Avalovara*," the Great Speckled Bird, Avalokiteśvara—the novel employs the spiral, rather than the circle, as its basic structuring device, this in contrast to both García Márquez's *One Hundred Years of Solitude* and Julio Cortázar's *Hopscotch* (32) and to many other works worldwide. Built on the superimposition of a spiral on a perfect Latin palindrome developed by a slave in ancient Rome, *Avalovara* develops as both an allegory about the concept of the creator and the thing created (as in the universe) and about the artist and the work of art, this being as well the mechanism by which the text self-consciously comments on its own creation and on the reader's role in it. As Lins himself (or his narrative voice) outlines it for us early in the novel,

The idea of rigor and universe are present in the sentence that proved so costly to the Phrygian slave of Pompeii: "SATOR AREPO TENET OPERA ROTAS." "The farmer carefully maintains his plow in the furrows." Or, as it can also be understood: "The Plowman carefully sustains the world in its orbit." It is difficult to find a more precise and clear allegory of Creator and Creation. Here is the plowman, the field, the plow, and the furrows; here is the Creator, His will, space, and the things created. . . . Identical is the image of the writer, given over to the obligation of zealously provoking in the furrows of the lines the birth of a book. (53)

Noting the connection to the Buddhist concept of "continuation and multiple, even conjunctive form, which in the end really has no shape as such," Rabassa calls our attention to *Avalovara*'s peculiar shape and how its characters simply appear, as in life, out of nowhere on the spiral's "wider loops" before they "descend (or ascend, catabasis and anabasis here being one and the same) to the resolution, which is but a moving point on the continuing spin," with the spiral itself continuing on indefinitely, making the text seem infinite (32) and in ways not entirely alien to the more deracinated (but much less carnal) worlds of Borges or, to a lesser degree, Cortázar.

Assembled with a mathematical precision, and functioning, structurally speaking, as a palindrome does, *Avalovara* is a love story in the most complete sense of the term, one that involves a total melding of body, mind, and spirit. But for all its formal complexity, *Avalovara* also offers up a compelling story about the human quest for unity, for wholeness in the face of chaos, and for the creation of order out of disorder, and in this sense it can be taken as a kind of alternative to both *Hopscotch* and *Cobra*. Calling our attention once again to the aleatory nature of life, Lins's challenging, sensual narrative reminds us that "a novel is but a collection of words and devices until it is read," and that it is quite likely because of their literary forebears, Machado de Assis and Borges, that "the Latin American writers are the ones who have come closest to this essential understanding of the importance of collective creation in literature the same as in the other arts" (Rabassa, "Osman Lins and *Avalovara*," 35). Exemplifying the best of the novel form's most imaginative permutations at the end of the twentieth century, and offering its readers a unifying and holistic semiotics of being, *Avalovara* is a text that, in both Portuguese and English, richly rewards and delights its rapidly growing international audience.

The Queen of the Prisons of Greece is Lins's last finished novel and, according to the translator, Adria Frizzi, is a "departure from and continuation of his previous books" (150). Distinguished by structural and lexical innovations that continue the author's postmodernist poetics, it has a structure that Lins described as "almost the opposite of *Avalovara.*" The novel is written in the form of a journal, dated according to the days it was being written, and, said the author in an interview shortly before his death, is a work "strictly connected to everyday events. *Avalovara* pointed to the cosmic order. *The Queen*, without denying the preoccupation with the universe and eternity, is more attuned to the quotidian, the temporal, the ephemeral. A contrast and a continuity. Characteristic of my restlessness. For me, the act of writing is an act of discovery. Hence the necessity for an initial plan and a margin for the imponderable. Before I begin to write, it's as if the world were black. Through writing, I gradually unveil the paths I want to travel" (Van Steen). The underlying technique is that of pastiche, "present in *The Queen* in several forms, involving virtually every element of narrative, from genre and discourse to characterization, from literature (texts and authors) to literary theory, from theme to space and time and the issue of authorship itself" (Frizzi, 150). The main character, Bacira, is the personification of this technique, since she herself is made up from the elements of the book's twenty-seven other characters. Frizzi's critical acumen in her writings about Lins carries over into her translation, and she deftly renders the postmodern pastiche of this difficult and little known, but worthwhile, writer into a cosmopolitan contemporary English.

Feminist Fiction and the Afro-Brazilian Paradigm

Another Brazilian text to work the same ground is Helena Parente Cunha's powerful 1983 novel *Mulher no espelho*, beautifully translated into English by Fred P. Ellison and Naomi Lindstrom as *Woman Between Mirrors*. The story of an upper-middle-class woman who, as she enters midlife, finds herself more and more at odds, psychologically and sexually, with the conservative mores that have long governed her sense of self, *Woman Between Mirrors* uses Afro-Brazilian culture as the mechanism by which the unnamed female protagonist confronts the many unresolved conflicts that have rendered her an inauthentic and deeply unfulfilled human being. While the prejudices of race, class, and age all come into play, it is female sexuality that functions as the novel's prime mover. More specifically, it is the protagonist's discovery of her own aging but still sexually vital body that serves as the basis for all further discoveries of Self and of Other. When, in the novel's climactic moment, the woman gives herself an orgasm, she is also seen to be shucking off the years of repression and frustration that have plagued her and tormented her sense of identity and being:

> A warm feeling of freedom runs through my images. I touch my breasts, I touch my sex. Alive with desire. A lewd smile surprises my face in the mirror. . . . My hands, circling around my breasts, gently reach the erect tips, they've only known the fat sweaty hands of one man. . . . My hands run on down to my waist, to my buttocks, sink into my sex, ripe humid flesh cradled away from soarings and divings. Now, ready at last for the soarings and divings? Yes, it's really me. (81)

Poetic, carnal, and packing a political message about the damage wrought—on both men and women—by patriarchy and racism that is not lost on even the most casual of readers, *Woman Between Mirrors* embodies a great deal of late-twentieth-century literary theory, especially French feminist and Lacanian thought.[20] By inventing her own body, "a body not young" yet "ready to claim its birthright of pleasure" (81), the protagonist simultaneously invents herself, a woman no longer young but a woman now free to enjoy herself and to make her own way in the world.

The second plot conflict comes to a climax late in the novel, when the protagonist, who has used Afro-Brazilian culture as a vehicle for self-liberation and rebirth, finds herself obliged to decide whether that same culture, which has exerted such a positive and liberating force in her life, has now become merely another form of imprisonment. This conflict, which speaks to the larger ontological questions regarding the nature of freedom and identity in a pluralistic society, accounts for the peculiar tension and ambiguity that dominate the novel's final scene, when the reader must decide for herself what path the protagonist will take. Emphasizing once again, in quintessentially Brazilian fashion, the productive power of synthesis,[21] the narrator, reflecting on the many conflicts that have tormented her existence and her identity, sums up her situation: "My story is just about over. Everything I could have wanted to try, I tried. . . . My face in the mirror is her face. I'm her. She's me. We are one" (132). Invoking one final time the many images and motifs of Afro-Brazilian culture that have, to this point, provided the protagonist with a life-affirming vitality and sense of personal liberation, the novel's final paragraph suddenly puts these into play, suggesting to the reader that they are no longer the positive, nurturing signs they had been and that, though not forgotten, they too must be left behind as the protagonist moves on to new identities and modes of being:

Suddenly a lightning bolt streaks across the dark sky. The mirrors shatter into a thousand pieces. On the floor, shards of mirror wet with blood. Wet with rainwater. A flicker of fire shoots skyward. I see an entire face in a shard of glass. A single face. I can't identify the smell coming in on the wind. The face. Me. The gentle wind from out of the heavy storm. (132)[22]

Do the mirrors serve here (and elsewhere) as a symbol or image of the narrator's own splintered, conflicted psyche, with all its repressed conflicts and desires? The reader also wonders, does Xangô, an Afro-Brazilian deity symbolized in the lightning, here liberate the narrator in some ultimate sense—an interpretive line that would complete the quest for liberation that has characterized her development throughout the narrative—or does he finally reveal himself to be merely one more form of tyranny, of a continuing male control over the female "I" who narrates this story and other stories like it? From this perspective, the reader wonders whether the novel is a kind of self-induced psychotherapy, a writing-intensive version of Freud's "talking cure," or whether it should be taken as a demonstration of the narrator's determination to become truly free, to reject any form of dependency or possession by anyone or anything.[23] Though no less sweet for being, at this point in her life, the "ripe fruit" of the sacred mango tree, the narrator, like the reader, is faced with a future in which she will have to fight to maintain a sense of wholeness and integrity and humanity in a world bent on making us all conform to its rigid, fragmenting demands.

Nélida Piñon's Exploration of Nationhood as a Projection of the Feminine Psyche

Although it is not as obvious as it is in *Avalovara* and *Woman Between Mirrors*, female *jouissance* is also a transforming presence in Nélida Piñon's epic masterpiece *The Republic of Dreams*, where it is closely identified with Brazil's development as a nation and a people. Of Madruga, the family patriarch, and his sense of Brazil, Piñon writes: "On certain summer nights in Rio, Madruga dreamed of Africa, one of the burning-hot wombs of the country called Brazil" (49). This is appropriate, since Brazilian literature, like Canadian literature (see Irvine and Lewis, 326, 332–33), has long featured a place for women, as strong, assertive characters and as creative writers, in its literary development (see Payne and Fitz). *The Republic of Dreams*, moreover, resonates with a sharply inter-American dimension, one that invites a variety of comparisons with the United States. European settlers in both Brazil and the United States, for example, originally conceived the New World as an earthly paradise and as a utopia, with the two concepts figuring prominently in Piñon's great, sprawling family saga. Both nations, moreover, suffered a corruption of the dream (one early, the other late), both are made up largely of immigrants, both engaged in the destruction of native peoples and the subjugation of African peoples, and both experienced a westward expansion, one that, in each case, elicits a sense of the frontier as an especially decisive feature in the process of national formation. For an American reader of *The Republic of Dreams*, however, the experience is unsettling, a bit like looking into a mirror, and the sense of déjà vu is overwhelming. Yet, as Piñon makes clear, the differences are in some ways even more striking: the story of Brazil has always featured sexuality as a basic motif (though Piñon completes the traditional portrait by granting female sexuality its due), miscegenation as a fundamental element of its cultural identity, and a powerful and vital African presence, one that the author develops as the heart and soul of modern Brazil.

A most striking aspect of *The Republic of Dreams*, at least for the American reader, is that Brazil is constantly conflated with the larger, more metaphoric concept of "America." This vaguely defined geopolitical place is also, and much more importantly, a state of mind, corrupted by the cancer of slavery but, in the case of Piñon's Brazil (*her* "republic of dreams"), also conceived and erected upon the body of Africa and driven forward by an extraordinary fusion of sexuality and politics. We read, for example, in a scene not entirely compatible with accounts of the Puritan formation of America:

> Madruga did not even know that Brazil . . . was dripping genitals exhausted from fornicating. Collective orgasm thus constituting the single public act compatible with its precarious legal institution. . . . Till the day when this great fuck would become confused with the exercise of political power, and substitute once and for all parliamentary rule. (70)

From this potent matrix, female solidarity slowly emerges as the novel's secondary theme, and it comes to animate and alter our perception of everything else. Although the female sexual energy that permeates *The Republic of Dreams* is not limited by race, age, or class, or by conventional notions of propriety or orientation (the solidarity achieved by female homoeroticism represents another very powerful force in the novel), it is the body of the black African woman that carries the story along and that, for Piñon, eventually takes charge, metaphorically speaking, of the birth of the nation (549 et passim). The same motif, the black African woman birthing Brazil, appears earlier in the novel, but here in the context of a homoerotic bonding between Odete, the family's black housekeeper, and one of its female scions, Breta. Embracing the black woman, whose arms are thrown around her and whose head is resting on her belly, Breta experiences something of a racial, sexual, and political epiphany:

> There Africa was, resting firmly in the middle of my belly. The Africa that had borne us and cradled us and that we were ashamed of. . . . At that moment, it was all too much for me. I experienced toward Odete a feeling as powerful as the one that assailed me when the thought came to me that I had Brazil in my hands, my body, my own genitals. It seemed to me then, in those hours of emotion, that Brazil palpated me with exaggeratedly minute precision, not scrupling to penetrate even the intimate parts of my body, going up inside my vagina, where it turned round and round. (115–16)

But *The Republic of Dreams* also pulses with the sexual potency and pleasure of white, upper-class women as well (while, as we have seen, not failing to show close bonds of affection, respect, and support developing between black servant women and their female "masters"). The young woman Esperança struggles for psychosexual emancipation, determined "to overcome her condition as a woman" (601) in a society ruled by men and by male law. "Esperança . . . palpated her body, in her eagerness to make intense use of it" (601). Later, when she discovers her mother's secret diary, in which the older woman recorded her own quest for psychological, sexual, and political freedom—a freedom feared by patriarchal culture, whether in Puritan New England or in colonial Brazil—we read:

> Father threatens to punish me if I give myself over to the pleasures of love. He is my torturer. As my revenge, however, and in proof that I am mistress of my fate, at night, in the bedroom, I slide my fingers down to my sex and let myself go. I penetrate myself and hit the mark exactly. (601)

Reasoning that God must have given women "these intense genitals" for a purpose, Esperança declares that she "will no longer tolerate the absence of pleasure," that she will no longer feel "bashful or ashamed" of her body, and that henceforth she will no longer accept "an inferior and submissive reality" (602).

In the modern period, then, and especially since 1944 and Clarice Lispector's landmark novel *Perto do coração selvagem*, we can see that Brazilian women writers have consistently used their bodies as the original site of identity and becoming, with the act of masturbation—literally taking their bodies into their own hands—serving very frequently as the key motif, the definitive act of female self-empowerment. While the growth and development of women's writing has been an international phenomenon in the final decades of the twentieth century, in the Americas there is a particularly strong parallel between what was happening in Brazil during the repressive military dictatorship of the 1970s and in the same period in Canada, and most especially in Québec, where a feminist writing that was both politically charged and theoretically sophisticated was taking solid root. For scholars interested in new possibilities for inter-American scholarship, this is an area of tremendous potential. As in the case of translation studies, these two very distinctive New World cultures have taken the lead as well in the cultivation of women who write and in the nature of that work as it relates to the condition of women specifically and to their place in society as a whole. In this modern Canadian and Brazilian women's writing, the theme of sexuality looms strikingly large, its conceptualization providing a fascinating point of comparison between such writers as Clarice Lispector (often linked to Nicole Brossard), Hilda Hilst, Márcia Denser, Lya Luft, Helena Parente Cunha, Nélida Piñon, Marie-Claire Blais, Claire Martin, Louise Maheux-Forcier, Louky Bersianik, France Théoret (much of whose work has an openly and militantly inter-American bent to it), and Jovette Marchessault (whose texts reconnect us, by means of a revitalized sense of social responsibility, with our Amerindian heritage). With its emphasis on lesbian love, Denser's landmark collection of stories *Muito prazer: contos eróticos femininos* (1982) makes, along with Sylvia Molloy's *En breve cárcel* (1981; tr. Daniel Balderston, *Certificate of Absence*, 1989), for an interesting comparison with Brossard's *L'amèr; ou, le chapitre effrité* (1977; tr. Barbara Godard, *These Our Mothers: Or, The Disintegrating Chapter*, 1983). Like the two Latin American texts, *L'amèr* "reads as a positive lesbian utterance as well as an invitation to reflection, an intellectual yet poetic attempt to engage the reader in a series of contemporary reflections on women as mothers, daughters, and lovers of other women" (Gould, 221–22). Recalling once again Lispector, whose erotically fluid and probing narratives, as we have seen, provided Cixous with the prototype of *l'écriture féminine*, "*L'amèr* offers both a deconstructive and an affirmatively lesbian approach to writing in the feminine that has paved the way for Brossard's later theoretical fiction" (Gould, 222). While also underscoring "the specificity of women's relationships to language and to the process of writing" (222), an issue that characterizes much modern Brazilian and Spanish American women's writing as well, the leading practitioners of Québécois feminism have understood how a "decolonization paradigm" could, by identifying with Third World liberation movements in such places as Algeria, Chile, Vietnam, Argentina, and Brazil, create "an international frame of reference for women's political analyses" (210), one ripe with inter-American potential and one profoundly involved with both the art and the political importance of translation. Writers throughout Mexico, Central and South America, like those in Québec, are linking an awareness of "women's oppression under patriarchy with the struggles of developing countries subjected to the dominance of foreign capital" and pointing to "the connection between feminism and Third World resistance to Western imperialism" (210).

In the 1960s and 1970s, the best of the new writing that was emanating from Canada and from Latin America was revolutionary not merely in form but in content as well. The entire concept of what it meant to be "American," to be a part of the New World experience but not lost within it, was once again in play.[24] Though originating in nationalistic trends and issues, in what the Québécois writer Jacques Godbout termed the *texte national* (a term that might well apply to the Latin American literature of the same period), Canadian and Latin American literature during this extraordinarily fecund period stood out because it was profoundly philosophical and worldly, deeply informed by the intellectual, artistic, and political issues of the time. It was, to invoke Godbout's term once again, both nationalistic and international at the same time, able to demonstrate vividly and compellingly that the long-ignored cultures of Canada and Latin America were, in truth, much more cosmopolitan and sophisticated than readers in the United States were expecting.[25] Although Canadian literature did not catch on in quite the same way that Spanish American literature did, it could have and it should have. In fact, the Quiet Revolution produced some astonishing texts, from Leonard Cohen's *Beautiful Losers* (1966) to Gérard Bessette's somewhat Borgesian (in the use of labyrinths) *L'Incubation* and Marie-Claire Blais's *A Season in the Life of Emmanuel*, both appearing in 1965—truly a banner year for *la littérature québécoise*, which was busy distinguishing itself, on political and linguistic grounds, from the old appellation of French Canadian literature.[26] The explosion of inventive and sophisticated literature pouring out of Francophone Canada during the 1960s was accompanied by a "veritable flood of translations" into English (Shek, 136), many of which were of the highest quality, thus providing American readers with a reliable window into a neighboring literature and culture about which they knew very little. That Canadian literature did not have a more enthusiastic reception in the United States of this period remains one of inter-American literature's most complicated and perplexing questions. As in the case of Brazil and Spanish America, the problem facing Canadian literature in the 1960s was not the quality of the writing being produced and exported but the low esteem in which (another victim of cultural stereotyping) it was held in the United States, a culture still locked in the solitude of its insularity and hubris. In spite of this, however, the seeds of inter-Americanism had been sown, and with Canadian and Latin American writers now reading and reacting to each other, the traditional lines of literary and cultural influence were rapidly changing. The foundation of a new discipline had been laid.

Translating the Voices of a Globalized Latin American Literature

The McOndo Revolution and the Crack Generation

New Latin American literature is being produced by globally connected "third-culture kids" of the digital age who are equally at home in Los Angeles and Mexico City.[1] Two movements give shape and purpose to this literature: the McOndo Revolution and the Crack Generation. Both seek to push their way out from under the shadow of García Márquez and his magical depiction of Latin American life. These writers, headed by Alberto Fuguet and Jorge Volpi, project Latin America as a borderless society, invaded by McDonald's, condos, and strip malls and accessible by cell phone. The task of the translator is to find a voice for this new Latin American narrative that intelligently reflects its mix of pop vocabulary, exacting hyperrealism, and classical intensity.

The young voices from the inter-American world are producing a new "sound" that is familiar and also distinctly different from that of their precursors. These new writers, third-culture kids who have lived and traveled across the hemisphere and around the world, carry iPods and go to Starbucks and live in an altered reality that has vestige characteristics of Latin American magical reality but has more in common with Miami or New York. When Alberto Fuguet baptizes this space "McOndo," he is playing not only on the obvious Macondo and McDonald's but on "condo," "onda," and Macintosh. These new realists, led by Chile's Fuguet and Mexico's Jorge Volpi, have abandoned "magical" realism for a personal virtual-realism that is apolitical and unapologetically "universal." Indeed, many of their stories take place in the United States or Europe. Fuguet says that he "never related to the canon" of García Márquez, Vargas Llosa, and Cortázar. In an article in *Foreign Policy*, Fuguet writes about the "Magical Neoliberalism" of his precursors, and to the *New York Times* he refers to them in the language of the Information Age: "I'm a really big fan of Márquez, but what I really hate is the software he created that other people use. They turn it into more of an aesthetic instead of an ideology. Anybody who begins to copy *One Hundred Years* turns it into kitsch" (LaPorte).

Fuguet was raised in southern California and moved to Chile when he was eleven. He spent a brief time at the Iowa Writers Workshop, where he was told that his work was not "Latin American enough" (LaPorte). His 1991 novel *Mala onda* (tr. Kristina Cordero, *Bad Vibes*, 1997), which has a character who does not recognize "the guy in the beret" on a Che Guevara T-shirt, turned Fuguet into a celebrity among Latin American youth. When it was first published in Chile, it sold 35,000 copies and triggered a secondary sales boost for the previously censored book *The Catcher in the Rye*. The main character is an Americanized seventeen-year-old boy named Matias, who is part of a clique of upper-class Santiago youth and who is the personification of alienated adolescence. He reads *Rolling Stone* and J. D. Salinger. *Bad Vibes* has been described as "a visceral, energetic read that shatters preconceptions and destroys stereotypes" (Spillman).

The 1996 anthology *McOndo*, coedited by Fuguet and presenting fiction by young Latin American writers, had as its objective the displacement of magical realism. The McDonald's and the condos that have invaded the hemisphere have made it more like Miami than the legendary Macondo where grandmothers levitate and butterflies have surreal qualities. Thomas Colchie has said that Fuguet and his followers "have a sort of darker vision that's more urban and has a lot more sense of humor. It's different from the facile magic realism, where on every other page you have an amorous iguana or a flying dictator. A lot of younger Latin American writers coming up from an overly intellectual tradition say: 'Enough of that stuff. Let's have some fun'" (LaPorte).

Fuguet has also demonstrated his mastery of the contemporary short story, a narrative form that has enjoyed tremendous popularity in Latin America during the late twentieth and early twenty-first centuries. In *Cortos* (2004; tr. Ezra E. Fitz, *Shorts*, 2005) he offers a collection of spare, sometimes very poignant tales that, recalling both Manuel Puig (because of his use of popular culture from the United States) and Borges (because the pieces that make up the collection are formally quite innovative), show us the lives of disconnected young people from Chile's upper classes. Though thoroughly hip to such international phenomena as American music and movies as well as the American sitcom and the Zeitgeist that goes with it, these privileged but disaffected kids are, as the thematically interconnecting stories make clear, grappling with the cultural, political, and psychological implications of being adrift. They are a uniquely inter-American "lost generation."

With *Shorts*, Fuguet also demonstrates his skill at merging a wry, laconic style with a presentation of young characters struggling to find themselves in a now deeply Americanized cultural milieu that, disturbingly, has internationalized them without first having allowed them to be nationalized. Indeed, *Shorts* represents, in its original Spanish, something of a stylistic tour de force, and on this key point the author has once again been well served by his English-language translator, who has been able to faithfully reproduce the many tonal shifts that animate the tales in *Shorts*. Just as "Fuguet's Spanish is clipped, exact, unpretentious, capable of assimilating a pop vocabulary without making it sound jarring, allowing it to mesh with passages of formal classic beauty," notes writer and critic Alberto Manguel, so too "Ezra E. Fitz has produced a translation of miraculous clarity, intelligence and immense readability. Thanks to him, none of the difficulty of rendering Fuguet's style into English remains evident."

Ezra E. Fitz has followed his father Earl's footsteps into the world of inter-American literature. About the same age as Fuguet, Ezra Fitz has been able to capture Fuguet's irreverence and trendy globalism to perfect pitch. His translation of Fuguet's 2002 novel *Las películas de mi vida* was published by HarperCollins in 2003 as *The Movies of My Life*. Fuguet can be linked with Manuel Puig, Rubem Fonseca and Walker Percy in his use of film as metaphor and device in his fiction. In this novel Beltrán, a Chilean seismologist, evokes his expatriate childhood through a rerun of fifty favorite films, all of which resonate with both U.S. and Latin American culture. His mother's affair with a married man is coupled with *An Unmarried Woman*, and the missing people in Pinochet's Chile are compared to the disappearances in *Soylent Green*. The theme of family dysfunction and dissolution is supported by the film references, but what is most important is how the characters react to the films. In this regard the film metaphor is less central to Fuguet's novel than, say, to Puig's *Betrayed by Rita Hayworth*, where the movies are a vital part of the plot. Beltrán, however, compares Chile and the United States in cinematic terms: "Life in California was so uneventful that we turned to the movies to give us everything we couldn't find in the neighborhood; in Chile, however, everything was so intense—so completely strange and inexplicable—that people went to the movies only when they wanted to kick back and relax" (Fuguet, *Movies*, 183). With these acute cultural observations the novel offers fascinating glimpses into the expatriate life and the psychology of the third-culture kid. Beltrán reflects:

> I was cursed with knowing two languages and feeling, secretly, that I wasn't completely at home in either. Now I could look at things comparatively, and suddenly, everything was multiplied by two. In every

case, I ended up choosing a remote point of view. Now, wherever I may be, I always see things as if I'm a foreigner. (165)

The family is itself an emblem of globalism, with the Jewish grandfather, the aunt who marries Yul Brynner, and the parents who go to concerts of Claudio Arrau at the Hollywood Bowl.

So there they were, in California, under the palms and the sun, fresh off the plane, smiling for the camera, living on the wild side, drunk and addicted to the American dream. They worked odd jobs and lived four to a room in a house on Los Feliz, enjoying the easy money, cars and women who gave themselves to them; life was good, it was better to wash malt glasses at Ben Frank's Drive-In on Sunset (once it was Natalie Wood; another time it was Ricardo Montalban who spoke to them in Spanish and left a five-dollar tip) than to drink pisco and Cokes at Charles' Drive-In on Las Condes, Santiago's ritzy neighborhood. (75)

While they adapt readily to life in the States, Chile remains "a wound, a myth, an anxiousness, a weight; it was too many things for all its people unable to process so many conflicting emotions." The Soler family finally returns to Santiago after Allende's government falls and is then persuaded to stay in Chile by the mother's extended family. There "nothing turns out as planned," and the family finally falls apart. As his parents spin off into unrepentant adultery, Beltran feels displaced and homesick for the United States. He has become the eternal expatriate, afflicted with the unquenchable need to return, and finding that home is no place and every place. Michael Dirda in his review of *The Movies of My Life* in the *Washington Post* highlighted the "double-whammy of the novel's final pages," and identified Fuguet's "greatest strength" as "evoking the joys, traumas, fears and hopes of childhood and adolescence . . . transcend[ing] any nationality."

Edmundo Paz Soldán, a Bolivian professor at Cornell University and a contributor to the anthology, has said of *McOndo*, "I think we made a strong connection with readers, but the critics, especially the old guard, said that we sold out and that we were a Latin American version of Generation X. They said we used too many references to American pop culture and that we were too obsessed with the depiction of urban reality. . . . You can call us alienated kids who are sold out on American pop culture, but it's the truth of our times. We grew up watching *The Simpsons* and *The X-Files*, and this comes out in our writing" (LaPorte).

Edmundo Paz Soldán, born in Cochabamba, Bolivia, in 1967, was awarded the Bolivian National Book Award for *Turing's Delirium* in 2002, the prestigious Juan Rulfo Award, and a 2006 Guggenheim Fellowship, and was a finalist for the Rómulo Gallegos Award. He has spoken about the McOndo movement to the American media and at academic conferences.

Paz Soldán's second novel to be translated into English, *El delirio de Turing* (2003; tr. Lisa Carter, *Turing's Delirium*, 2006), is set in his fictional hometown of Río Fugitivo in Bolivia. The book opens with a meeting of a group of cryptanalysts called the Black Chamber, who have as their mission to protect the dictatorship from the "cyberhactivists" of the Resistance, and who want to deal a blow to globalism and "the System." The characters meet in a fictional online environment called the Playground. As in other McOndo writings, critical events take place online or in Internet cafes. In a previous Paz Soldán novel, *The Matter of Desire*, the protagonist frequents a Bolivian coffeehouse called Berkeley to meet with a local band called Berkeley about his late father's code novel titled *Berkeley*. *Turing's Delirium* introduces a drug-addicted prostitute, who sometimes dresses up as a cheerleader, at a McDonald's. Lisa Carter's translation was reviewed as "supple and not without potential" (Iyer), and the book itself has been greeted with surprise by reviewers who still expect the exotic from Latin American letters.

Crack Follows the Boom

In spite of their perception of rejection by the literary patriarchs, the new generation have a big supporter in Carlos Fuentes. In a 2003 interview Fuentes said, "I really support what they're doing, which is eschewing nationalistic themes and writing openly about what interests them in the world" (LaPorte). He is a special advocate of the Crack group, McOndo's Mexican brother, with its distinct aesthetic that identifies with European literary and intellectual traditions. The "Manifesto Crack"—with Crack meant as a riposte to Boom—declaims against "the early 1990s vogue for literary entertainment known in Mexico as *literatura light*" and lays claim to the intellectual legacy of the Spanish American vanguard of the 1920s (Anderson, 10, 1, 16–17). Leaders of this group are Jorge Volpi, Ignacio Padilla, Eloy Urroz, Enrique Serna, Cristina Rivera Garza, and Xavier Velasco.

Born in Mexico City in 1968, Volpi has a law degree from the Universidad Nacional Autónoma de Mexico. He was an observer of the turbulent years of Carlos Salinas de Gortari's presidency (1988–1994) and then the Zedillo administration when Salinas and his family were implicated in murders, drug trafficking, and money laundering. Many in Mexico began to speak of the "crack" that broke dreams of prosperity (Anderson, 16n6). Volpi moved to Spain in 1996 and now lives in Paris. He is the author of the prizewinning novel *En busca de Klingsor* (1999; tr. Kristina Cordero, *In Search of Klingsor*, 2002), a historical spy novel set in postwar Germany. His work has been categorized as "postmodern detective metafiction" (Vinarov). Written in high-culture, pseudoscientific diction laden with historical and technical data, the book echoes the complex and highly intellectualized narratives of Jorge Luis Borges. Volpi "has adopted Borges's definition of his Argentinean identity as a cosmopolitan curiosity about the world, rather than as a patriotic duty to prove his roots" (Wilson). *Klingsor* is the story of a military intelligence operation based on the real-life Alsos mission, which had as its purpose to round up the scientists who worked for Hitler on the atom bomb. During the period of the Nuremberg trials, a young American physicist with the ironically intended name Francis Bacon loses his post at the Institute for Advanced Study at Princeton, where he has worked under Albert Einstein. After a scandalous affair with a black woman and a broken engagement, Bacon is rescued by his mentor, who seems to understand his "carácter . . . *demasiado* inquieto," his *too* anxious character. The mentor gets him a military commission, and Bacon is sent to Germany to participate in the Alsos mission. Bacon's assignment is to learn the identity of Hitler's chief science advisor, the man with the code name Klingsor, who controlled the Nazi science agenda, including experimentation on human subjects and development of the atom bomb. Bacon defines himself as "un detective encargado de perseguir hombres en lugar de ser un físico que persigue abstracciones" [a detective in charge of following men instead of being a physicist who follows abstractions]. The plot becomes complex when Bacon is paired with Gustav Links, a German mathematician in custody of the Allied forces, who has talked about the existence of Klingsor to his captors. As part of their investigations, Bacon and Links make appointments with the Nobel Prize winners of the day: Max Planck, Max von Laue, Werner Heisenberg, Erwin Schrödinger, and Niels Bohr. To his downfall, Bacon falls in love with Irene, a neighbor who is actually a Russian spy. She inserts herself into the team, and eventually Bacon must choose between Irene and Links after he discovers her connection to Russian intelligence. At Irene's instigation, Bacon hands Links over to the Russians, claiming he is Klingsor. Links is put away in a Russian asylum, and it is he who narrates the novel in November 1989 during the fall of the Berlin Wall (Anderson, 11).

Volpi's novels are about the search for identity, knowledge, and the multiple possibilities suggested by scientific theory.[2] Each novel is written in the discursive style of the genre of knowledge it is exploring, such as quantum mechanics or game theory, as in *In Search of Klingsor* (Anderson, 1). Most of the novels employ the conventions of the thriller. Volpi's fundamental interest lies in his characters and their actions; he speculates on the choices characters make and the natural consequences of those choices. As Danny Anderson writes,

> Volpi's novels do not represent knowledge attained. Rather, they portray a search: knowledge is a possibility, a journey never completed. Moreover, the paths on such a journey cross a common terrain: the enigmas of identity and human behavior. Volpi's novels, with their focus on the poetry of actions, explore what was once called "human nature". . . . Volpi usually writes about identity in terms of *carácter,* *temperamento,* and *voluntad* (character, temperament, and will). Although his novels point toward a philosophy of uncertainty, they nevertheless enact a search for an underlying arithmetic of identity and behavior. This arithmetic of character develops from a simple relationship between subject and object into a complex view of situated actors in a social field of interacting forces. (2)

Ultimately *Klingsor* offers a perspective on a period in world history in which scientists were learning about the ethics of research and how human emotions such as vanity, pride, and competition corrupt the scientific endeavor. Unlike many novels of the Boom period that are constructed around descriptive narrative, Volpi's novel is almost entirely built on dialogue, in the case of *Klingsor* a long Faustian reflection on good and evil and the total unpredictability of human behavior.

The Antimagical Realists

Colombia's new urban writers align with the Crack and McOndo writers in their emphasis on the harsh reality of the postmodern Colombian city. Led by Mario Mendoza, who is in the anthology *McOndo,* and Jorge Franco, the group includes Ricardo Silva, Enrique Serrano, and Efraím Medina. They have been awarded prestigious literary prizes and honored at international writers' conferences. Franco's *Rosario Tijeras* (1999; tr. Gregory Rabassa, 2004), set in Medellín after the capture of Pablo Escobar, was recognized with the 2000 Premio de Novela Dashiell Hammett in Gijón, Spain.

Jorge Franco recounts that this new generation of Colombian writers had to struggle to work their way out of García Márquez's grip on a reading public that expected more of the same magical depiction of Colombian reality and was not interested in the existentialist musings of the younger writers. Jorge Franco is credited with reversing the trend and changing the focus of new writing to a recognizable Colombian reality. The remarkable story of how he got the book published—through sheer tenacity by giving a copy of his manuscript to the wife of the editor of *El Tiempo*—is recounted by Silvana Paternostro in an article in *Críticas*. He wanted to write about the place he grew up in, which was Medellín in the 1980s during the height of the drug cartel's control of the city. Franco's novel *Rosario Tijeras* is about the culture of drugs and violence. Its heroine is a female "hitman" whose nom de guerre comes from her use of scissors to castrate a man who raped her. In a narrative that evokes Carlos Fuentes's novel *La muerte de Artemio Cruz* and Faulkner's *As I Lay Dying*, one of her upper-class lovers narrates her difficult life in a series of memories that reveal both his empathy for her "anguished solitude in this world" and his obsessive love for her. Full of melodrama like Puig's novels, *Rosario Tijeras* is the story of a city held hostage by drug lords, told through the icon of the female superhero who personifies Colombia with her intimate knowledge of death and fearlessness of it. Rachel Aviv has observed that Franco's realism is born out of "profound disillusionment" with the grotesque reality he describes, a reality "absent of enchantment and magic," as in Max Weber's description of the realistic novel as reflective of "disenchantment with the world."

Gregory Rabassa tells of his apprehension over translating Franco in his memoir, *Translation and Its Dyscontents*: "When I first got *Rosario Tijeras* I wondered if I would be up to and adequate for the translation of a book from the new generation" (175). He evidently found his stride in the translation and discovered that he "wasn't all that distant from the story," given his deep familiarity with the "Latin American tale." He discovered, too, that the age difference was no bar to the translation of a contemporary work. He reflects, "In fact it might well be that a set of older eyes might see things in a more universal light and thus extract the permanence of the text better. Had I been a different age I might have used that horrid verb "to universalize" above and not thought of it, Joyce-wise, as universal eyes. The caution of age does save one from many pitfalls" (177). The translation challenges were mitigated "by the fact that Jorge's use of language is crisp and direct. There's not too much of the outlandish slang we find so much in current American movies and books, the kind that will quickly follow '23 skidoo' into the realm of the cutesy archaic" (176). The title posed an immediate problem. Since Tijeras is the character's nickname and not her surname, Rabassa explains, he chose to keep it in the original, "adding a one- or two-word definition the first time around. I've used this technique before and have found that it can be a managed as long as it's done briefly and subtly without interfering with the flow of the text" (176).

Mario Mendoza is another youthful Colombian writer, whose novel *Satanás* (Satan, 2002) received the 2002 Seix Barral Premio Biblioteca Breve, the biggest Spanish literary award, which has been given to such New World writers as Mario Vargas Llosa, Carlos Fuentes, and Guillermo Cabrera Infante. While the book is not yet in translation, it has captured the attention of reviewers in publications such as *World Literature Today* and the *Wall Street Journal*. The book is based on a chilling murder that took place in Bogotá in 1986, when a Vietnam veteran went berserk, first shooting and burning his mother and six other people and then, after finishing a meal in an Italian restaurant, opening fire and killing twenty-six people and wounding seventeen more. The police killed him a few minutes later. Mendoza had watched the report on the nightly TV news and became determined to write about it. It took him fifteen years to complete the task, but his efforts were rewarded. He states that the focus of the story is the "chaotic, self-destructive, and apocalyptic" nature of Bogotá. In the novel, evil is a real presence in the very nature of the city, which interestingly does not include drug violence in this case, and the struggle between good and evil rages with special ferocity in the character of the assassin. Apparently Campo Elias Delgado, the murderer, had in fact been writing an essay on Stevenson's novel *The Strange Case of Doctor Jekyll and Mr. Hyde.* The police found the book in his coat jacket after the murders. He was an English teacher in Bogotá who had served with the Green Berets in Vietnam. The lonely, alienated misfit character reappears in Mendoza's novel *Relato de un asesino* (Tale of a murderer, 2001). Andrés, the main character, is an artist who lives in Bogotá's seamy underworld surrounded by poverty, prostitutes, and police crime. He struggles with questions that concern many Colombian writers: "What is it with this country that seems unredeemably condemned to ruin and unhappiness? Why don't we advance? What sinister complot keeps us caught deep inside generalized chaos, corruption, and social entropy? Why do politicians and big businesses keep milking our country without giving it a break, without giving it the possibility to reorganize and obtain redemption?" (Paternostro, 29).

Brazil's Caio Fernando Abreu writes, in Fernando Arenas's words, "on the verge of the abyss—an individual abyss for the author himself, given his own personal circumstances of terminal illness, and a collective abyss, Brazil, with its socio-economic and political quagmire of the last fifteen years, still menacingly close, despite the euphoria over political and economic changes in the first years of the Fernando Henriques Cardoso era" (13). His book of short stories *Os dragões não conhecem o paraíso* (1988; tr. David Treece, *Dragons*) appeared in English in London in 1990. He is featured in such books as *Lusosex: Gender and Sexuality in the Portuguese-Speaking World*, edited by Susan Canty Quinlan and Fernando Arenas, and *Queer Issues in Contemporary Latin American Cinema*, by David William Foster. Abreu writes from the viewpoint of the bisexual man who has the modern scourge, AIDS, and who thus suffers the confusion and loss that accompany terminal illness. Abreu suggests that the illness is a metaphor for a Brazil having lost its way, and never having recovered from military rule. Like Murilo Rubião, Abreu uses dragons as a unifying symbol, but in this case they signify "those subjects that inhabit the margins of social space, beings that contest the hegemonic values of a society steeped in falsehood and artificiality. They encompass, among others, adolescents, drag queens and in general, a wide spectrum of (pluri)sexual beings that escape containment within dominant frameworks of sexuality" (Arenas, 14). One of Abreu's signature stories is "Dama da Noite" ("Queen of the Night"). It consists of a colloquial monologue by a middle-aged woman, perhaps a transvestite, who speaks to a younger male, very much in the way that the narrator of Clarice Lispector's *Água viva* speaks to an unseen lover. The Queen of the Night lives on the margins of society and observes the secure life of the upper class, which she compares repeatedly to a Ferris wheel. "Você não conhece esse gosto que é o gosto que faz com que a gente fique fora da roda que roda e roda e que se foda rodando sem parar, porque o rodar dela é o rodar de quem consegue fingir que não viu o que viu" [You don't know this pleasure that is the pleasure that makes you stay out of the wheel that goes round and round and that fucks itself going endlessly round and round because its turning is the motion of someone who gets away with pretending they didn't see what they saw] (quoted in Arenas, 15). Abreu continuously juxtaposes the personal with the political, the local with the global. Personal fears of illness and death point to the collective fear of a society not living up to its promises.

Abreu's posthumously translated novel *Onde andará Dulce Veiga?* (1990; *Whatever Happened to Dulce Veiga?*, tr. Adria Frizzi, 2000) summarizes Abreu's political and ecological concerns in the story of a disillusioned Brazilian journalist who is on a mission to find Dulce Veiga, a popular singer who has not been seen for twenty years. This quest becomes a somewhat tainted spiritual journey and is a metaphor for the unrealized dreams of a whole generation of Brazilians who grew up during the dictatorship. The book has been described as a tribute to Philip Marlowe, the Raymond Chandler character, and the protagonist goes on an elaborate search through São Paulo's dark underground, where he interacts with prostitutes, transvestites, musicians, and drug dealers. The narrative is divided into seven parts, each a day of the week, interconnected by symbolic references to Brazilian *candomblé* gods. A mix of detective story and personal memoir, the narrative is layered with a pastiche of elements from several cultures, from American pulp fiction to Afro-Brazilian song. The protagonist finally finds a sad Dulce Veiga double in drag in the urban underworld of São Paulo—the insane abandoned lover of the real Dulce Veiga, who is later found living in the remote Amazon. The fact that Dulce is inhabiting the Amazon, "at the margins of Brazil's own marginality," is seen as a symbol of "a possible new paradigm of development for self and of nation" (Arenas, 19). Adria Frizzi's "felicitous, loose-limbed translation . . . maintains a lively balance between suspense and comedy" (Giles) and is supported by her analysis of the narrative and accompanying glossary of terms.

Regina Rheda has appeared as an "irreverent new voice" (Dunn) in Brazilian letters, an acute and often very funny observer of life in the gargantuan São Paulo megalopolis. She has a degree in film from the University of São Paulo, where she gained prominence as a scriptwriter and director of films, videos, and television productions into the early 1990s. She became a well-known figure in the boom of short films, or *curta-metragens*, during that period. Her first book, *Arca sem Noé: histórias do edifício Copan* (Ark without Noah: Stories of the Copan Building, 1994), won the Jabutí Prize in 1995. The story "O mau vizinho" ("The Neighbor from Hell") was awarded the Maison de l'Amérique prize by Radio France Internationale in 1994. Regina Rheda has three more published books—a novel about a Brazilian immigrant in Europe, *Pau-de-arara classe turística* (1996; tr. Adria Frizzi, R. E. Young, David Coles, and Charles A. Perrone, *First World Third Class, and Other Tales of the Global Mix*, 2005); a collection of erotic stories, *Amor sem-vergonha* (Shameless love, 1997); and the inventive novel *Livro que vende* (Bestseller, 2003), which is a blend of thriller and postmodern narrative poem that offers a perspective on economic and cultural globalization.

Recurrent themes in Rheda's works are animal rights, the plight of immigrants in alien lands, and ecofeminism, illustrated in such stories as "Dona Carminda e o príncipe" (Dona Carminda and the prince, in the anthology *Histórias dos tempos de escola*, 2002), "O santuário" ("The Sanctuary"), and "The Front." Most of her work is published in English in *First World*.

Rheda evokes the previous generation of Brazilian women writers, which included the feminists Márcia Denzer, Edla Van Steen, and Hilda Hilst, who wrote in the 1970s and 1980s about gender issues and female sexuality. There is a marked cinematic quality to her writing that several critics have noted, with very visual and graphic scenes, varying perspectives (close-ups, pan shots, oblique camera angles), and rapid shifts of scene. Her work features small characters of the middle class, who try to patch up their flawed and somewhat unsavory lives; in this respect Rheda has been compared to Caio Fernando Abreu and Gilberto Noll (Dunn). When her 1994 collection *Arca sem Noé* (tr. Adria Frizzi and Rey Young, *Stories from the Copan Building*, in *First World Third Class*, 2005), received the Jabutí national book award in Brazil, Rheda was cited for having "created an original work of literature by pushing the boundaries between the real and the imaginary with good-hearted, keen humor and creativity. She has shaped unique characters who, although inspired by the original residence of the Copan Building, take on an existence of their own after being filtered by the magic of her narrative" (Jabutí award catalog, 1995). The Copan Building is the creation of architect Oscar Niemeyer, an S-shaped landmark in downtown São Paulo that was a symbol of the era of technocracy, of "order and progress" in the 1950s, prior to the long period of military rule that began in 1964. In the stories, the building has become run-down and decrepit, somewhat like the characters who inhabit it; building and residents are joined as a common symbol of Brazil's broken promises. The manner of storytelling, however, is not tragic but morbidly funny.

Regina Rheda's latest book, not yet in translation, *O livro que vende*, is a fable about ego and vanity in the modern metropolis. Told in shifting narrative times, the novel is about the sabotage of a science textbook by a lovelorn copy editor who has been jilted by the text's author and the subsequent tragedy as schoolchildren are blown up by the experiment that the copy editor rewrote in the course of her assignment to revise the book to comply with new government rules for school texts. The vain schoolteacher who is the catalyst of the tragedy, the puffy editor-in-chief, and the publisher all decline to take responsibility for the act:

> Meetings without small talk and not even any coffee frighten the teacher, who squirms in his chair. It was bad luck that the majority shareholder heard about it on the television news along with sixty million more pairs of eyes hypnotized by the science book, the kids with stupid faces, the girl wrapped in bandages in the hospital, the anchorwoman with the lipstick painted like a little heart. Four students in the seventh grade were injured in an experiment with explosive materials during a science class in two public schools. The experiments are from the book *The Magic of Science*, by Sandoval Cafeteira. When they followed the instructions for the experiment, the students mixed concentrated sulphuric acid with a substance that exploded on contact with the acid. The student from Porto Alegre, in the state of Rio Grande do

Sul, is at risk of losing the fingers of her right hand, and she will have to undergo reconstructive surgery on her lips. The parents and teachers of the victims intend to file a class action suit against Tornatore Publishers. The author, Sandoval Cafeteira, declines to give interviews. The teacher turns off the TV, the faces and hands of the children. In front of him, the majority shareholder's face and cigar burn bright red, the carotid arteries of the editor-in-chief expand and contract. Around the conference table, the three professionals apply their decades of experience in the design and production of textbooks to deal with the consequences of the accident responsibly and in a cooperative spirit. (tr. Elizabeth Lowe)

Regina Rheda's agile narrative technique and her liking for puns and jokes offer an attractive opportunity for the translator who enjoys wordplay. In one scene of *O livro que vende*, a group of middle-class Brazilian tourists is told by their guide, a "cute" young man: "Here on Wall Street you can see a painting by the Colombian artist Bolero. In the MoMA there are paintings by the Russian Chacal [*sic*]." The group goes to a "Woody Alien" movie.[3] Like other "new voices," Rheda's attention is no longer specifically on Brazil, Latin America, or the United States, but on a global society at risk. Her activist concerns span the rights of humans, animals, and the planet Earth. As Christopher Dunn summarizes, "This is an insurgent literature depicting a decidedly dystopian context, but with a future, however fleeting or fragile, within the global mix" (6).

Gregory Rabassa

The Translator's Translator and the Foundations of Inter-American Literary Study

Although many skilled translators were involved in bringing Latin American literature to the attention of the English-speaking audience of the United States during the 1960s, no one stands out in this endeavor more than Gregory Rabassa, whose efforts on behalf of such key writers as Gabriel García Márquez, Clarice Lispector, Julio Cortázar, Nélida Piñon, and Machado de Assis have arguably made the study of inter-American literature a viable new field, both in the United States and in the Americas generally. Rabassa has also established himself as one of our most incisive commentators on the craft of translation. His observations on the style and content of the often profoundly different Latin American texts he has re-created in English, on the nature of the act of translation itself, and on the many linguistic differences between Spanish and Portuguese are a rich resource for both readers and translators of Latin American literature. To understand why Gregory Rabassa is regarded by his peers as a great translator is to begin to understand how and why Latin American literature was received as positively as it was during the 1960s and to realize the full extent of his importance to the development of inter-American literature as a new discipline within the field of comparative literature.

Since the early 1960s, the rise of Latin American literature to a position of prominence on the world stage has been nothing short of remarkable. As Fredric Jameson avers, "Latin American literature since the *boom* has today become perhaps the principal player on the scene of world literature" (48). William Deresiewicz arrives at much the same conclusion:

> The most important development in world literature over the last half-
> century has arguably been the emergence of a new kind of writing in
> Latin America. . . . At a time when postmodernists were proclaiming
> the death of the narrative, Latin America presided over the rebirth of
> storytelling in serious fiction. . . . The achievements of Toni Morrison

and Salman Rushdie, to name just two, are unthinkable without the Latin American example.

And that example, for the English-speaking world, is unthinkable without Rabassa. (36)

Whether one agrees with such assessments or not, it cannot be disputed that a host of novelists and poets from Brazil and Spanish America have, in the past forty-odd years, established themselves as among the most imaginative and engaged writers of our time. But while names like Jorge Luis Borges, Julio Cortázar, Gabriel García Márquez, Mario Vargas Llosa, Machado de Assis, Clarice Lispector, and Jorge Amado are now well known among the world's literati, what is not nearly so acknowledged—indeed, what is conspicuously underacknowledged—is the crucial role that translation has played in the dissemination of these writers' works in the English-speaking world. And when one speaks of the importance of translation to the worldwide recognition of Latin American literature and, by extension, to the development of inter-American literature, Gregory Rabassa must be considered a central figure.

The Translator's Translator

A scholar and teacher of Latin American and comparative literature, Rabassa has, in the course of a career that now spans five decades, translated nearly sixty works of Spanish- and Portuguese-language literature, most of them major texts by major authors. Widely celebrated as "the translator's translator," and once dubbed the "pope of translation" by Alfred A. Knopf, Rabassa is now regarded as having been instrumental in establishing translation as a respected intellectual activity and academic field of study and, by dint of both the quality and the quantity of his work, bringing about the overwhelmingly positive reception of Latin American literature in the United States and Canada. As Thomas Hoeksema has written:

> In the field of contemporary Latin American prose, one of the richest sources of translation projects, Gregory Rabassa stands out as a prototype of the professional literary translator. His achievements have established a standard for all translators in the field, and the considerable quality and exposure of his translated works have facilitated the emergence of translation as an identifiable profession. (6)

Focusing more specifically on Rabassa's influence as a translator and scholar, Hoeksema then goes on to say that "his unique gift for recreative work has yielded enduring models of translation, and his critical and theoretical comments on the craft, process and art of translation offer perceptive guidelines and creative insight for translators at all levels of experience" while at the same time making "a powerful case for the necessity of including the translator as a dialogue participant in any discourse on the creative process" (6, 8).

Less obvious is that his skill as a translator has changed the course of literary relations in the Americas, making possible the exciting new field known as inter-American literary studies and breathing new life into the discipline of comparative literature, which has long considered translation an important, though not necessarily essential, aspect of its conceptual purview. Although writers like Borges, Cortázar, and García Márquez are the ones most often cited in discussions of Latin American literature's importance to American literature (see Barth, "The Literature of Exhaustion"; J. Payne; and Rostagno), it can be persuasively argued that it was actually Rabassa's superlative talents as a writer/translator that not only influenced but helped ignite a reinvigoration of American fiction during the late 1960s and 1970s, a period that John Barth and others had characterized as "exhausted" in terms of its sense of what it might accomplish and how it might do it. When our colleagues in English departments, for example, wax enthusiastic over the beauties and marvels of García Márquez's *One Hundred Years of Solitude* and contemplate its relationship to Faulkner and his fictional world, it must be remembered that, in a literal sense, they are responding not to Gabo's text, which is *Cien años de soledad,* but to another, equally beautiful text, one written/re-created (in four months' time) by Gregory Rabassa in a very different language system for a very different culture. This fact is so obviously true that it typically escapes our critical notice, but to recognize it, and to consider what it means, is to take the necessary first step toward a more discerning awareness of the translator's role in the tangled process of cross-cultural exchange that lies, often restively, at the heart of the entire inter-American initiative.

Rabassa—who has been translating continuously since his days as a faculty member at Columbia University, where in 1960 he was involved in the genesis of *Odyssey Review*—is the object of high praise not only from his colleagues but from many of the authors whose works he renders into English.[1] Referring to Rabassa's impact on the reception abroad of much modern Spanish American narrative, Alastair Reid writes: "The best of Latin American writing owes about two-thirds of its existence to Rabassa, for, single-handed, he has translated the milestone novels of Vargas Llosa, José Lezama Lima, Julio Cortázar, Miguel Angel Asturias, and many other writers" (Hoeksema, 6). Lauding his ability to re-create an author's style, Sara Blackburn observes that Rabassa's English versions of these and other Latin American authors "come so close to the sense and the atmosphere of the original Spanish that the result is almost eerie" (40). In a similar vein, Ronald Christ, an editor for *Review*—a journal that, along with *Odyssey Review*, pioneered the inter-American perspective in the United States—points out that Rabassa's "broad-minded approach as well as his generosity in dealing with texts, translations, and other translators have resulted in his becoming not only the producer of excellent translations but also the incarnation of the model translator" (Hoeksema, 6). The poet, editor, and translator Willis Barnstone speaks of Rabassa's "uninterrupted consistency . . . in which the subtlety and poetry of the original comes through magnificently," so that Rabassa becomes "invisible" in the translated version. Because his translations never call attention to themselves, argues Barnstone, "Rabassa creates the perfect counterfeit." And William Kennedy, a writer with a special interest in Latin American literature, concludes that "On the basis of *One Hundred Years of Solitude* alone, Gregory Rabassa stands as one of the best translators who ever drew breath" (Hoeksema, 6–7).

Good Translation as a Function of Good Writing

To appreciate the full extent of Rabassa's achievement, however, one must take into account two factors: the importance of the books and authors he has translated, and his skill as a creative writer—for, as Rabassa has often said, the best translations are more a function of good creative writing than of grammar books. Of the first factor, it is important to bear in mind that when Rabassa initially began to translate (sometimes under pseudonyms) material from Latin America that was to appear in *Odyssey Review*, even writers as brilliant as Borges were still largely unknown in the United States.[2] The arrival here of Latin American literature, in the literary and cultural phenomenon that would become known as "the Boom," was driven almost entirely by translation, much of it coming from the pen (an old typewriter, actually) of Gregory Rabassa himself. Impressed by his critical acumen and by the quality of his translation work on behalf of *Odyssey Review*, Sara Blackburn, then an editor at Pantheon, contacted Rabassa about the possibility of his translating a complex new novel by a talented young Argentine writer, Julio Cortázar. The novel, *Rayuela* (tr. *Hopscotch*), would immediately gain fame as the most exemplary of the great *nuevas novelas*, the "new novels" emanating from Spanish America during the 1960s. This watershed work broke new technical and thematic ground for the Spanish American novel at the same time that it internationalized Spanish American literature in ways that would henceforth allow it to be regarded as a major force in world literature. The celebrated Mexican writer and intellectual Carlos Fuentes was one of the first to recognize this aspect of Cortázar's importance and, more specifically, to praise the liberating impact *Rayuela* had on the Spanish American novel form. Combining French literary theory with a Latin American quest for identity (both cultural and personal), and wrapping both in an ironically self-conscious tale of ceaseless movement (the two poles of the novel being Paris and Buenos Aires) and in various forms of dislocation (some comic, some erotic, some philosophical), *Hopscotch* is very much a work of its time and place. It may fairly be regarded, in fact, as one of the most singular works of the early 1960s, one that had a huge influence on what Latin American novelists might write about, on the manner in which they might do it, and on what their readers might expect—of themselves and of their authors.

But *Hopscotch*, which in 1967 won the first National Book Award for translation, also proved important because of the impact it had on American critics, a group hitherto oblivious to Latin American literature. Shattering old stereotypes about what literature "south of the border" was like, *Hopscotch*, with its subversive, often absurdist humor, its international scope, its structural play, and its intellectually sophisticated content, ushered in a new age for the reception of Brazilian and Spanish American literature in the United States. For intellectual trendsetters like Edmund Wilson, who was convinced that nothing had yet been written in the Spanish language that would justify his taking the time and trouble to learn it, and Lionel Trilling, who claimed that Latin American literature had only "an anthropological value" (Rodríguez Monegal, "New Literature," 3), the appearance of *Hopscotch*, whose supple, engaging translation perfectly captured the ironies, changing registers, and wittiness of the original, was a shock, a stunning affirmation of a Latin America and of a Latin American literature long ignored and disparaged by the insular American public. "If, as many publishers agree," the United States remains today largely what it was in the 1960s, "an isolated, inward-looking country with little interest in what happens in literature beyond its borders" (White, 239), then the transformative impact of *Hopscotch* on the American critical and artistic consciousness is more easily understood and appreciated, especially in the context of what we can now see as rapidly changing patterns of inter-American literary and cultural relations. Although more artistically successful Latin American novels had already appeared—those of Machado de Assis, for example, or Guimarães Rosa's

Grande Sertão: Veredas or Juan Rulfo's *Pedro Páramo*—it was Cortázar's coolly cosmopolitan and slyly parodic *Hopscotch* that ushered in the Boom. For American readers whose image of Latin America was limited to Carmen Miranda and the Frito Bandito, the times, in the words of Bob Dylan's 1964 song, were indeed a-changin.'

The second factor, Rabassa's dexterity and inventiveness, is widely acknowledged. Alastair Reid declares that "The most essential thing for a good translator to be is a good writer, and Rabassa is a very good writer" (Tannenbaum, 1). Even more emphatically, William Kennedy writes that "Rabassa is a chameleonic stylist, a master of language, and a superb writer himself" (Kennedy, 67). Not a native speaker of Spanish—though his father was Cuban, Spanish was not much spoken at home—Rabassa learned the language at Dartmouth, where, initially a chemistry and physics major, he also began to pick up Portuguese, Russian, and German, in addition to continuing with his French.[3] At Dartmouth he learned to be a careful, discerning reader from Ramon Guthrie, whose course on Proust's *À la recherche du temps perdu* rewarded Rabassa's talent for close textual exegesis, a skill essential to his success as a translator. And he developed a taste for both Shakespeare and Joyce that continues to this day. Rabassa entered graduate school at Columbia University in 1945 after serving in the Office of Strategic Services during World War II, an experience that involved him in a unique form of translation work, in essence English-to-English since it dealt with encryptions, code breaking, double transposition ciphers, and ultimately paraphrasing. As Rabassa describes his military experience:

> In the OSS I did a lot of work with cipher to and from the field. Since many of the systems were primitive and easy to break, we used double transposition ciphers, for example, we called them DTs. The clear text had to be paraphrased before it could leave the message center. This was a kind of translation from English into a different English.[4]

A Good Translation Is the Closest Possible Reading

At Columbia, where in 1947 he completed an M.A. in Spanish, Rabassa gravitated toward Portuguese and Luso-Brazilian literature, eventually earning his Ph.D. in 1954 in this area and being asked to stay on as an instructor.[5] When Rabassa accepted the task of translating Cortázar's *Rayuela*, he had not yet read it in Spanish, though he had heard about its daunting wordplay, its many distinctive voices and levels of discourse, its "happening"-like mixture of bathos and pathos, and its notoriously open structure—one that, in a reading strategy suggested by the author himself in the preface, replicates the way the children's game hopscotch is played. Pressed for time, Rabassa translated the novel as he read it, a practice that he wryly dismisses as "an awful thing, heresy, I suppose," but that he still follows today (see *Treason*, 27) and that has led to one of his most interesting observations about translation: that the translator is really a text's best reader and that a good translation is the closest possible reading a book can have ("Gregory," 203). Earlier he put it this way: "maybe translation is nothing but close reading. Close as possible. And I think the translator is really more a reader than a writer in that sense" (Lewis).[6]

At the same time, Rabassa insists that the ideal translator is a very special kind of reader, one who is able to reformulate what he/she is interpreting—a reader, that is, whose creative efforts are "governed by" the author's imagination and yet who has the ability to "understand and follow what the latter is imagining. A translator is a reader, then, but one who writes what he reads" ("Treason," 32). When he translates a book, in fact, Rabassa feels that he is "simply reading it in English" (*Treason*, 42). Typically Rabassa moves through a text quickly, taking care to reconstruct the meaning, and then works through it again, seeking to "make it sound better" (Lewis), the translator's ear playing a crucial role in the re-creative process (see Rabassa, "Ear"). Even the transposition of an original's rhyme into an English rhyme is, Rabassa feels, "just another reading exercise." "Once the meaning is there," he says, "then I can toy with the style. Mostly word order." Finally, Rabassa himself retypes it, making "last minute" and "sometimes substantial" adjustments as he goes.

Of his efforts to translate not merely the content but the multifaceted style of *Rayuela*, Rabassa modestly observes:

> Sometimes Cortázar's a hard writer to read. That doesn't always mean difficult to translate, because the difficulty comes over in the English. . . . Difficult sentences in Spanish, difficult sentences in English, and I've done my duty. (Lewis)

The end result, of course, was felicitous, with Cortázar—whose English was quite strong and who, eventually becoming a dear friend of both Gregory and his wife, Clementine, also became something of a collaborator on the translation—impressed that "Rabassa could be so deft at handling his meaning, his wordplay, the moods that range in a line or two from murderously funny to nastily intellectual" (Blackburn, 40).[7]

Circumventing Translationese

In addition to these very formidable shifts in tone, syntax, and content, one uniquely thorny feature of *Rayuela*'s style is slang, a powerful form of language use that, like cursing and regional speech, presents a particularly difficult challenge to the translator, as, in truth, it does for the reader. For Cortázar's very talk-driven and dialogic novel, Rabassa's solution was not to attempt some sort of mid-twentieth-century English equivalency, which, for reasons that are both stylistic and cultural, would likely not ring true and which would age very rapidly into the flat "translationese" that Rabassa has always sought to eschew, but to tap his own skills as a writer to create a parallel and tonally faithful text, one that reads as if its author had originally written it in English. "What I try to do sometimes is to invent slang," Rabassa notes, "Make something that's slangy. Not slang, but slangy, and since it's not slang, it'll never be passé." For Rabassa, regionalisms fall into the same category. "You've got a gaucho. . . . You can't make him sound like a cowboy; you have to make him sound like an English-speaking gaucho. There's a difference. So you invent a little" (Lewis). "Just as words do not have real equivalents in other languages," Rabassa observes, of the problems that regional idioms present the translator, "neither do dialects or local patterns of speech" and so "it is absurd and outlandish to have a Brazilian *sertanejo* [backlands man] talking like an Appalachian mountain man. Even black English is poorly served by translation into black Spanish" ("Treason," 33).

An example of Rabassa's dexterity in solving this type of problem comes from his efforts to translate the many forms and levels of cursing that pepper the pages of *Hopscotch*. As Rabassa points out, "If any form of word can be called untranslatable, meaning having a close adherence to the word-for-word meaning of the original, it is the expletive" ("Treason," 34). To translate the standard dog-based English "insult to one's parentage," for example, Rabassa explains that "the Spanish *hijo de puta* is more direct, but the English equivalent 'whoreson' is archaic and can no longer be used. In ordinary usage *hijo de puta* must be rendered 'son of a bitch,' else we lose the emotional charge" (34). By way of contrast, Rabassa notes, contemplating the two primary languages involved in his translation work, "The Portuguese is more subtle, *filho da mãe* [son of your mother], innocent on the surface, but inviting all the vileness the imagination can bring to bear" (34). As *Hopscotch* vividly demonstrates, swearing is not only a matter of language and characterization, it is a function of culture as well. And, as Rabassa recounts it, one scene from the novel illustrates this point particularly well:

I recall an episode in Julio Cortázar's *Hopscotch* in which the hero has pounded his thumb with a hammer as he tries to straighten a nail. "*Puta que te parió*," he addresses the nail. If we leave it at that, we get a Hemingwayish "whore that bore you," but the intent is different. My solution was to have him accuse the nail of incestuous proclivities toward its dam, which is current, ripe, and even maintains a bit of the tone of the Spanish insult. The fact that insults cannot be rendered so closely as we might like means that while words can be translated directly, cultures themselves cannot be without grotesque distortion. (34)

The Silk Purse Solution

With the recognition and success that came with *Hopscotch*, Rabassa's career as a translator, a career that Rabassa himself describes as having been "serendipitous" in its origins (Morales, 116; see also Rabassa, *Treason*, 22–28), was definitively launched. Cortázar was so impressed by the quality of Rabassa's work on *Hopscotch* that he urged that another up-and-coming Spanish American author, Gabriel García Márquez, secure Rabassa's services for a novel he had just published to great acclaim, *Cien años de soledad*. Although Rabassa had read the novel and judged it "a damned good piece of writing," it would have to wait for its translation until he could finish Miguel Ángel Asturias's "Banana Trilogy," which, comprising the three novels *El viento fuerte* (1950; tr. *Strong Wind*, 1968), *El papa verde* (1954; tr. *The Green Pope*, 1971), and *Los ojos de los enterrados* (1960; tr. *The Eyes of the Interred*, 1973), "form a continuous narration and deal with the exploitation by the United Fruit Company of the lands and peoples of Central America, notably Guatemala, the home of Chiquita Banana" (Morales, 123). The recipient of the Nobel Prize for literature in 1967 and a diplomat and scholar as well as a creative writer, Asturias, like Cortázar, had an exhilarating effect on the thematic and stylistic transformation that was then taking place in the Spanish American novel, though in ways that were more indigenous and more overtly political than those of his Argentine counterpart. Of mixed-race ancestry (his family was partly Mayan), European trained (the Sorbonne), and both artistically gifted and possessed of a sharply political view of Latin America's relationship to the rest of the world, Asturias was in many respects the epitome of the twentieth-century Latin American intellectual.

Yet for all the celebrity that surrounded Asturias (born in Guatemala in

1899) and his novels during the late 1960s, and given the political unrest that marked that time, it is odd that Asturias was not as enthusiastically received in the United States as Cortázar had been. In retrospect, three factors may have played a part in this: Asturias dealt heavily with Mayan cultures and issues, at a time when Native American literature was only just beginning to be recognized in the United States; he was unrepentantly anti-American in much that he wrote, when issues of political interference and economic exploitation were still unproblematic for most Americans; and, perhaps most important, his style was quite daunting, as startling and different in its own way, perhaps, as Gertrude Stein's was in *Tender Buttons* decades earlier.

The novel that many regard as Asturias's best, *Mulata de tal* (1963, tr. Rabassa, *Mulata*, 1967), was, Rabassa suspects, "largely misread and misunderstood" (Blackburn 40), a victim of stylistic and structural complexity, cultural disconnect, and a negative reaction to a very singular variety of the Latin American exotic.[8] Exasperated at one point by a Professor Horrendo—like review in which he was "taken to task" for the alleged "excesses" of an Asturias translation he had done (as if there had been no excesses in the original Spanish text; see Kennedy, "Rabassa," 68; Green and Berreby, 6), Rabassa wrote a response in the form of a paper for the Modern Language Association convention titled "A Translator's Conflicting Responsibilities: The Silk Purse Business" (Blackburn, 42). Arguing that the translator should never "make a silk purse out of a pig's ear," Rabassa reminds us that fidelity to the original text is absolutely essential, a sine qua non of the entire translation process. If Homer nods off in the original, Rabassa has long contended, then he must do so in the translation as well. The duty of the translator, Rabassa believes, is to "reproduce the work, clone it in another tongue, so to speak, and all the warts and hairs should be there. . . . This is what I meant, in effect, when I said translators should not be in the silk purse business" (Hoeksema, 12; see also Kennedy, "Rabassa," 69; Lehman, 54).

In speaking of his struggles with nativist dialogue in Asturias's sprawling, mythopoetically inspired texts, and how he feels that "dialogue is more difficult in translation than in drama," Rabassa has said, "I have had trouble with some authors, I think Asturias in the main, who attempt to reproduce phonetically the sounds of conversation when regional or class variants of pronunciation are involved. As I said, the dramatic writer can rely on the actors to supply this. In translation such a transfer becomes awkward. I do not care much for the technique in the original and I try to get by in a translation by some other means, relying heavily on the reader's imagination" (Hoeksema, 12).[9] A function of the characters, their words, and their culture, this alien quality was not easily assimilated by American readers, who found the deeply poeticized, magical, and mythic world created by Asturias's tangled Indian novels to be fascinating but, finally, incomprehensible.[10] Reviewing *Mulata* for the *New York Times* on 25 October 1967, for example, Thomas Lask writes that Asturias is "a writer with a free-wheeling imagination in the use of words and images, a bold, surrealistic dreamer who feels compelled to follow the oblique, lurid course of his imagination rather than in keeping his characters—and his readers—within conventional bounds." Although Lask's reading of *Mulata* up to this point is basically accurate, his final response to the Asturias text is mixed and seems to highlight the yawning chasm that separates the ancient Central American world of Mayan culture from the American reading public of the late 1960s, a chasm that not even a talented Nobel laureate and a talented translator could overcome:

> The truth is, however, that for a reader not at home with these legends, tales and divinities, *Mulata* is a jungle of abstruse and noncommunicative references. The names are meaningless. The situations and quick changes will baffle and confuse the reader. Even when he is willing to let go and trust himself to the flow of Mr. Asturias's method, he'll find himself lost in the tumble of words and events. There seems to be no central concern. *Mulata* is brilliant all right, but, I think, a brilliant failure."

Although in a later review for the *Saturday Review* on 4 November 1967, Robert G. Mead Jr., a well-known and respected scholar of Latin American literature, was able to better explain both the novel's profound cultural grounding and its intensely indigenous poetic style and mythic structure, and to present these to the American reading public in ways that made them more accessible, it was *Mulata*'s fate, sadly, not to resonate with readers in the United States quite as ardently as other, perhaps less threatening Latin American novels that were appearing in translation at the time.

The Best Latin American Writer in the English Language

When Rabassa finished his extensive commitment to Asturias, he quickly turned his attention to García Márquez's *Cien años de soledad*, a work whose appearance in English was delayed by almost three years because its author, fully appreciative of what Rabassa had achieved with Cortázar's *Hopscotch*, insisted on waiting for his services. The result prompted Gabo famously to announce that he himself prefers Rabassa's translation to his own version

(Morales, 119), and that Rabassa's translation actually improved on the Spanish original (Bast).[11] As Márquez puts it:

> For me there is nothing more boring than reading the translations of my novels in the three languages in which I am capable of doing so. I don't recognize myself in any language other than Spanish. But I have read some of the books that were translated into English by Gregory Rabassa and I have to admit that I found some passages that I liked better than in the Spanish. The impression that Rabassa's translations give me is that he learns the whole book by heart in Spanish and then writes it all over again in English: his faithfulness is always more complex than simple literalness. He never inserts a footnote, which is the most lame but nevertheless most frequently exploited recourse of bad translators. ("Desire," 25)

While the exact meaning of these intriguing utterances is debatable, what is not in doubt is the inspired nature of the landmark novel's English translation, *One Hundred Years of Solitude*, which appeared to great acclaim in 1970, eventually becoming a best-seller. Of Rabassa's re-creation, John Brushwood, the celebrated scholar of Mexican and Latin American literature, would remark that it "overcomes difficulties that would sear the imagination of most translators" (Hoeksema, 6). Interestingly, Rabassa himself feels that Gabo's basic style is such that "very few queries" are required, that his vocabulary "is quite classical and universal within the Spanish context," and that "there may be only a dozen words or expressions in a book that I have to ask him about. . . . his prose simply leads the translator along" (Hoeksema, 9).

Beyond his comment about preferring the English version, García Márquez has, in tribute to Rabassa's creative skills, praised him as "the best Latin American writer in the English language." He has also said, of Rabassa's technique as a translator, "He doesn't translate phrase by phrase; I have the impression he reads the whole book and then writes it" (quoted in Morales, 124). Rabassa's response to these plaudits from the distinguished Colombian author, winner of the 1982 Nobel Prize for literature, is illuminating of his own ideas about what a successful translation should be like:

> I must say that I enjoy the first comment by García Márquez. As for the second, however, he is not very accurate. I do translate "phrase by phrase," even "word by word." I take his remark to be a compliment, however, because his description is exactly how a translation should appear to have been written. It betokens the smoothness of a good

version that might not be there in a jerky word-by-word exercise. (Morales, 124)

So closely does the translation imitate the original, Márquez feels, that Rabassa seems to have rewritten his novel in English, a contention that Rabassa denies, calling our attention instead to a subtle but crucial distinction in his approach to the translation process: "I'm reading the Spanish," he declares, "but mostly I'm reading it in English, and it comes out that way. When I talk about it, I say the English is hiding behind his Spanish. That's what a good translation is: you have to think if García Márquez had been born speaking English, that's how a translation should sound" (Bast).

Yet for all the accolades it has garnered, Rabassa's work has not escaped criticism. Gerald Martin, for example, feels that there is a problem with the title *One Hundred Years of Solitude*, and that it is "more directly linguistic and cultural than literary. Firstly, the target language, English, has two words—solitude and loneliness—whereas the source language, Spanish, has only one, 'soledad.'" Martin cautions that the "uninformed" American reader might well come away from *One Hundred Years of Solitude* with "the impression that Latin America is the home of the high-sounding and the grandiloquent"—a response that, given the poignant sense of failure that permeates the novel, is perhaps not as inappropriate as one might first think. At the same time, it is certainly true, as Martin notes, that "'soledad' is one of the most important words and concepts in Spanish and particularly Latin American Literature" (the "solitude" in which it has too long been allowed to languish) and that all three words, *soledad*, "solitude," and "loneliness," possess powerful and very "specific social meanings in their respective cultures" ("Translating," 159).

Writing of García Márquez's first novel, *La hojarasca* (1955), the title of which Rabassa rendered with an invented English term, *Leaf Storm* (1972; see also *Treason*, 100), Martin further argues that while the Spanish title speaks metaphorically to the plight of the local migrant workers depicted in the story, Rabassa's "elegant mistranslation undermines a large part of the work's subtle politics for the English-speaking reader" (158). Beyond minimizing, or obscuring, the text's economic and political underpinnings, the English title *Leaf Storm* can be said to "exoticize," and thus "distance" from the American reader, both a continent and a specific fictional locale, effects that do not pertain to the Spanish original, where in this particular case the normalcy of tropical life and the seriousness of the social conflict hold firm (Martin, 158).

What these criticisms point to, really, is the enduring difference, cultural as well as linguistic, between our reading of a text in its original language and our reading of it in translation. But the points that Martin calls to our attention also highlight the choices, like Rabassa's selection of "solitude" instead of "loneliness" for *soledad*, that the translator must inevitably make as one text—one culturally specific, immensely complicated and self-referential semiotic system—is transformed into another. In the alchemy of translation, one might say it is the *difference* of difference that comes to the fore and that must be contended with, as those readers who can handle both the original and the translation will readily attest. It goes without saying that these same choices depend on the translator's reading of the text and of his/her interpretation of it. This realization, along with the natural change of language and critical fashion through time, would seem to go a long way toward explaining why a translation, the product of a radical approach to reading—one in which a plausible interpretational choice is actually committed to paper and thus privileged over other plausible choices—has to be redone over time while the original seems eternal, a function (albeit creatively) of its cultural, stylistic, and semantic time and place but subject to endless rereadings and, thus, to endless reconstructions.

If *One Hundred Years of Solitude* contends for the title of greatest Rabassa translation—an honor the Brazilian novel *Avalovara* might also claim—then another dense and beautiful Spanish American novel, the Cuban José Lezama Lima's *Paradiso* (1966; tr. 1974), has the distinction of being the most nettlesome, the one whose syntactic complexities, subtle euphonies, and contrasting tones offered the greatest problems in its reconstruction in English. "Without a doubt," Rabassa admits, the intensely poetic and eclectically philosophical *Paradiso* has been his "most difficult book" to translate so far. As he explains his approach to the reproduction of Lezama Lima's dazzling and mesmerizing style,

> I had to be inventive with him. His admittedly baroque style was difficult to maintain in English, and then he would go about inventing or giving a new twist to words that needed sufficiently new equivalents in English to maintain the style. Part of the essence of the book was the very complexity of the style, and this had to be maintained and brought over in the language. (Morales, 124–25)

Delighted by the stylistic challenges that *Paradiso* presented, Rabassa felt that "Lezama's is a baroque prose that gave me a lot of wonderful problems" (Blackburn, 40) but that it also afforded him numerous opportunities to exercise his skills both as a careful, discerning reader and as a creative writer, the two talents, as we have seen, that he deems essential for any successful translator. Because, says Rabassa, re-creating the lyricism of the original is a matter of one's "ear," of one's ability to "hear" the music of words on paper (see "Ear"), the struggle with Lezama Lima's *Paradiso* was particularly acute, since its author enjoyed a much deserved reputation as a hermetic and challenging poet, the acknowledged leader of the neobaroque movement in modern Spanish American poetry.

And yet, ironically enough, Rabassa's initial attempt to create an English version of *Paradiso* that was "as close as you can possibly get to the novel in the original language" placed him in conflict with an editor who substantially revised Rabassa's translation, "shortening sentences and substituting simple words for baroque ones" (Tannenbaum, 31). Understandably upset with these changes, which defanged and simplified Lezama Lima's intensely baroque style and which, in the process, straightened out the "arcane labyrinth" that was the original *Paradiso* (Morales, 121), Rabassa concedes that while sections of his *Paradiso* were indeed "virtually non-English," they were carefully crafted to reflect, tangle for tangle, the author's similarly calculated "non-Spanish" (Tannenbaum, 31). What Rabassa had labored so hard to achieve, the near matching of an idiosyncratic modern English baroque of his own creation with Lezama Lima's idiosyncratic modern Spanish baroque, was subjected to a severe editorial laundering, chiefly for reasons of "readability."[12] The problem inherent in this turn of events, of course, is that aside from being "dumbed down" (Morales, 121) for the American audience, the style of the final English version of *Paradiso* simply does not, in this unique case, reflect the stylistic fireworks and semantic conundrum of the Spanish original.[13] Much to Rabassa's chagrin, one might say that not one but two silk purses—Lezama Lima's original and Rabassa's original translation of it—were turned into a sow's ear.

But to appreciate the full extent of Rabassa's importance to the dissemination of modern Latin American narrative, we must remember that he has translated a number of major Brazilian writers as well. A great enthusiast of Brazilian literature, which, as Roberto González Echevarría opines, "is, with that of the United States, the richest national literature in the New World" (*Oxford*, xii), Rabassa finds that Portuguese is more difficult to translate than Spanish "because it offers more possibilities for interpretation" (Blackburn, 42). While both languages "present specific challenges," Rabassa told Harry Morales, "Spanish is a very regular and rational tongue," though

This very regularity makes for problems in translation into English. You can't say "ain't" or "he don't" in Spanish. Solecisms are generally of an oral nature, matters of pronunciation and such. You can't say "ain't," but the most illiterate peasant quite naturally uses the imperfect subjunctive properly. Since English is a much "looser" language, grammatically, than Spanish, the translator has to find some middle ground in syntax so that the aforementioned peasant doesn't sound like an academician. (125)

Completely at ease in Spanish and Portuguese, yet declaring that he has a special "warm spot for the Portuguese language because it is so widespread and yet so unknown outside its open borders," with "half the population of South America" speaking it (126), Rabassa contrasts Portuguese to both Spanish and English:

Portuguese is just the opposite. The Brazilian version, grammatically, is even looser than English, so it runs the risk of looking too untidy if it's not policed up in translation. Portuguese does have expressions comparable to "ain't" and "he don't." Working in both tongues makes me aware of the extreme differences in sound between the two, something that is tragically lost in translation. We can read the meaning of the original language, but we can't get the unique sound of it. (125)

Rabassa, we have seen, has translated a number of landmark Brazilian novels, works that vividly demonstrate how strong Brazil's narrative tradition is, as indeed it has been since the nineteenth century, when "Brazilian fiction was unequaled in the rest of Latin America in terms of production and quality" (González Echevarría, *Oxford*, 15). However, a delicious novel by his close friend Nélida Piñon, *Fundador*, enjoys a special status with Rabassa in that, even after two drafts, it continues to resist his best efforts to reproduce it in English. Aware that he still has not fully penetrated, in the ebb and flow of her elusive, fluid Brazilian, "what she's really up to" (Blackburn, 42), Rabassa says of Piñon: "Her style is so personal and so Portuguese that it simply will not come over in English. She has milked the native secrets of Portuguese stylistic possibilities more than any writer ever has in that language and, indeed, I can think of no writer in any other language who has achieved so much from the unique native pith of his tongue except perhaps James Joyce," though, Rabassa hastens to add, Piñon "is not at all what we would call 'Joycean'" (Hoeksema, 11).

A seminal Brazilian author who has yielded to Rabassa's efforts is Clarice Lispector, one of twentieth-century literature's most neglected figures and a very distinctive writer whose work, discovered in French translation, provided the model for Hélène Cixous's well-known concept of *l'écriture féminine.*[14] *A maçã no escuro* (1961; tr. Gregory Rabassa, *The Apple in the Dark*, 1967) was Lispector's fourth novel but her first to be transformed into English, and it actually became the second book that Rabassa translated, coming between *Hopscotch* and *Mulata*. An unusual feature of this translation, published by Knopf, is that Rabassa provides a short but very concise critical introduction to Lispector's work, situating it in the broad context of Brazilian literature. In addition, Rabassa comments briefly on the particular translation problems that Lispector's text presented: "The invention is not as obvious as in Guimarães Rosa because it is less a matter of neologisms and re-creation than of certain radical departures in the use of syntactical structure, the rhythm of the phrase being created in defiance of norms, making her style more difficult to translate at times than many of Rosa's inventions" (xii). Continuing with the stylistic comparison, Rabassa concludes:

> Nor is the traditional vocabulary here anywhere as rich as in the works of Nélida Piñon. It is precisely in their styles of presentation that the three writers diverge: Guimarães Rosa using the primitive resources of the language for the creation of new words in which to encase his vast and until then amorphous sensations; Piñon extracting every bit of richness from the lexicon of a very rich language without falling into archaisms or other such absurdities; and Lispector marshaling the syntax in a new way that is closer perhaps to original thought patterns than the language had ever managed to approach before. These three elements are the stylistic basis of all good contemporary Brazilian literature. (xii)

What is perhaps most beguiling about this reference to the essential problem that had to be solved in translating Lispector's novel is that Rabassa does not elaborate upon how he dealt with it, how he went about handling her unorthodox syntax in modern English, a language whose grammar rules do not lend themselves to the re-creation of the Brazilian writer's signature style, an entrancing amalgam of philosophical ambiguity, intense sensuality, and poetic nuance, all leavened by a wry humor. It is possible, as César Braga-Pinto suggests, that Rabassa "draws the reader's attention to a space to which the reader has no access (the foreign language)" and that "he wished to share the problem with the reader," a tactic that, if true, would seem to run contrary to the idea that translators should always remain "invisible" (62; see Venuti, *Invisibility*; see also Rabassa, *Treason*, 3–9, 40–46; Morales, 120). At the same time, it is also possible that the intent here is not only to educate and inveigle the reader about the stylistic peculiarities of Lispector's text, which stand out as a defining feature of her writing, but also to call attention to the fact that in the work we read as *The Apple in the Dark* a deliberate attempt has been made to reconstruct Lispector's novel, replete with all its many stylistic idiosyncracies, in modern American English. In other words, Rabassa may be alerting readers here that what they will encounter, stylistically speaking, in *The Apple in the Dark* faithfully reproduces what is encountered by a reader of *A maçã no escuro*. The short passage quoted above, coming as it does in the midst of the introduction to *The Apple in the Dark*, thus not only presages the stylistic struggle characterizing the conflicted English reinvention of both *Mulata* and *Paradiso* but constitutes a highly distilled declaration of the translator's art, the goal as well as the duty.

Finally, a word needs to be said about the less than avid reception of *The Apple in the Dark* in the United States. Although it was praised in the *Saturday Review* by Richard Franko Goldman,[15] its sales never matched those of its Spanish American counterparts, perhaps because "it was presented as part of a movement," the Latin American Boom, "with which the book has little in common" (Braga-Pinto, 63). A densely lyrical and introspective tale more about the vagaries of language, desire, being, and human relationships than about exotic landscapes or locales, *The Apple in the Dark* was nevertheless

> fascinating simply because Miss Lispector is a superb writer, an artist of vivid imagination and sensitivity, with a glorious feeling for language and its uses. She employs words playfully, meaningfully, deceptively, and of course seriously, not necessarily as a poet does but as few novelists do. . . . [The novel is] a delight to read. (Goldman, 48)

What strikes one about this positive and entirely accurate review, however, is that the author's comments relate most directly not to a text written by Clarice Lispector but to one written by Gregory Rabassa, a point that, though often lost in translation criticism, must be kept in mind. The key question, of course, is really this: How faithfully does the translator reproduce the original, the style and tone as well as the content, the slips and moments of awkwardness as well as the moments of transcendent beauty and grace? On this question Goldman, noting the difficulty of Lispector's text, stresses that Rabassa "has succeeded remarkably well" in its translation, adding that he "has consistently found the right words, not always an easy job, and also preserved a flexible and compelling prose rhythm" (48), one that, it should be noted, corresponds very closely to the rhythm of the original. In the case of *The Apple in the Dark* and its critical introduction, then, it can be argued that Rabassa, acutely aware both of the stylistic challenges that had to be dealt with and of the reader's need to know this, alerts the reader to a little-appreciated but decisive aspect of the translation process—its inherent, if circumscribed, creativity.[16]

Following the Writer's Lead

Although Rabassa has achieved success with many other Brazilian texts, most notably his version of Osman Lins's *Avalovara*,[17] perhaps his best work so far has come with his efforts on behalf of Brazil's greatest author, Machado de Assis. Machado, as he is known in Brazil, was a great ironist and social critic. Critics are increasingly realizing that he was also a revolutionary with respect to the evolution of the novel genre in the Western tradition. Though born poor and of mixed-race parentage in 1839 in Rio de Janeiro, Machado eventually learned French, English, and German well enough to read deeply in these languages and to translate some of the texts he most enjoyed. Influenced by a number of European writers, including Shakespeare, Dante, and Flaubert, Machado slowly evolved in his own literary career away from poetry and theater and toward narrative, particularly the short story and the novel. After 1880 he began, in dramatic fashion, to experiment with the novel's form, style, and content and to examine what the concept of verisimilitude meant with respect to the relationship between language and reality and therefore to the art of the novel (as his contemporary Henry James would phrase it) itself. Though still not as widely appreciated outside the Luso-Brazilian ken as he should be—a situation being slowly rectified by the various translations of his poems, stories, and novels that now exist—Machado was, according to the prominent critic Roberto González Echevarría,

> the premier nineteenth-century Latin American writer and one of the best of all time anywhere. Had he been born French or English, there is little doubt that his works would be prominently featured in the Western canon. In the Americas he is certainly on the level of Melville, Hawthorne, and Poe. No one in Spanish comes close to his polish and originality. . . . A master of subtle psychological intrigues and of dramas involving the great questions vexing humankind, Machado was devoted to Shakespeare, who, he said "wrote in the language of the soul." (*Oxford*, 95)

Hailed by Harold Bloom as one of the "exemplary geniuses" (*Genius*, 673), Machado numbers among those rare writers in whose work form and content meld perfectly, a seamless web of thought and form, yet one enriched, in Machado's case, by radical experimentation in point of view, irony, allegory, unreliable narrators, metafiction, and, above all, the new, more actively engaged role Machado felt the reader had to play in the creation of a text's various meanings. Long a favorite of Rabassa, who has taught his major texts in Portuguese for many years (thereby doing for his students what Ramon Guthrie did for him at Dartmouth), Machado has existed in English since the 1950s, which is when John Barth, who would later designate Machado the "proto-post-modernist" (Fitz, *Machado*, 45) and whose first novel, *The Floating Opera*, was directly influenced by him, first discovered the acerbic and iconoclastic Brazilian master (see Barth, *Fridays*, 44–45, 257–58). As part of Oxford University Press's Library of Latin America series, Rabassa retranslated two of Machado's three best-known novels, *The Posthumous Memoirs of Brás Cubas* and *Quincas Borba*. Of his new English renditions of these two fascinating works, Rabassa notes that, highly unusual for him, he actually enjoyed reading the proofs. "As I translated Machado," he says, "I was carried along by his prose, and I sensed that the translation was going well and would be good because Machado was such a master that only a cretin could screw him up," a feeling, he says, that was akin to how he felt about his translation of *Hopscotch* and his work with García Márquez (Morales, 124). "As I discovered translating Machado de Assis and García Márquez," affirms Rabassa, "the masters will enable you to render their prose into the best possible translation if you only let yourself be led by their expression, following the only possible way to go. If you ponder you will have lost the path" (*Treason*, 17).

One element in Rabassa's confidence that his translations of Machado were succeeding is that he trusted his own close readings of the texts, his own interpretations of them. As Rabassa explains it, "I know that a translation is going well when I get the feeling that the English is sounding just the way the author sounded in the original. This is completely instinctive, and I cannot explain it in any rational way, but it's there" (Morales, 120–21). This response is not unlike the way creative writers gauge the progress of their own work. After taking into account his years of experience teaching and writing about Machado and his narratives, it becomes clear that Rabassa's translations of Machado's texts are as successful as they are largely because Rabassa has become a discerning and incisive reader of Machado, a reader able to identify and appreciate not only the stylistic and structural fireworks but the disenchanted tone that make Machado seem more modern than, chronologically speaking, he was. Crucially, however, Rabassa is himself an experienced poet and fiction writer, one able to reconstruct Machado's charming yet chilling narratives in another language and for an audience in another time and place. Speaking of the translator's responsibility to the text, an issue that, given the importance of Machado de Assis, bears special significance in his case, Rabassa declares:

> The translator must respect the text on two levels: meaning and tone. Since these two things come together naturally in the original language in the hands of a true artist, the translator is hard put to reproduce them entirely in his version. There will always be some little bit of baggage added to the meaning, and there will always be a little bit left behind. Tone is the impossible part; it can only be approached, as languages sound so different. This process can only be compared to the transposition of a melody from one instrument to another. (Morales, 120)

A good example of Rabassa's approach to the problems posed by tone and meaning appears in *The Posthumous Memoirs of Brás Cubas,* a Machado novel that changed forever the way narrative would be written and read in Brazil and that, in translation, is steadily gaining a worldwide audience. When viewed from a comparative perspective, this startling text also proves that a stunningly original "new narrative" had been established in Latin America as early as 1880 and that it merits inclusion in any serious study of the modern novel's evolution, in the Americas and beyond. Indeed, one can easily make the case that *Memórias Póstumas de Brás Cubas* is, in many ways, the missing link that, in terms of technique and subject matter, completes the genre's progression from Flaubert to Proust, that anticipates Kafka, and that becomes, in the process, the first great novel of our alienated modern age. The sardonic voice of the novel's skeptical, gimlet-eyed narrator is absolutely fundamental to it, an integral part of its originality, and it comes across pitch-perfect in Rabassa's 1998 translation. The wry tone of this deceased but still very voluble bourgeois is conveyed to the reader early in chapter 1 of Machado's first great novel when he declares "eu não sou pròpriamente um autor defunto, mas um defunto autor" (511), a crucial line that, in Rabassa's hands, delivers to the English-speaking reader the same wit and verve that it delivers in Portuguese: "I am not exactly a writer who is dead but a dead man who is a writer" (7). The key to the original line lies in its syntax, in the way the meaning of the adjective "defunto" changes in relation to its placement either before or after its noun, "autor," and Rabassa's version faithfully reproduces this semantic wordplay, the original's drolly antirealistic tone being completely reconstructed at the same time that the original sentence's structure is being rebuilt, replete with its pivotal inversion of the normal semantic function, in English. The reader of Rabassa's translation is thus able to savor not only the playful tone of Machado's Portuguese text but the play of its complicating syntax as well.

Whether working with Spanish or Portuguese, Rabassa's basic approach to a text remains the same: imagine how the original writer would write it if (s)he were working in late-twentieth- and early-twenty-first-century American English. Reflecting on the extraordinary variety of writers and styles he has translated since his initial efforts with *Odyssey Review* in the early 1960s, Rabassa feels he has been successful precisely because he does not have, or seek, "a translation style." Instead, Rabassa's success as a translator resides in his own creative skills and his own innate sense, honed by years of experience as a teacher and scholar, of what good fiction and poetry should be like. In discussing his own efforts as a writer who translates (as opposed to a translator who writes, a distinction of which Machado might well have approved), and the many works he has translated, and the connections between them, Rabassa opined recently: "They're all so different, the ones I did. I think it works because I don't think I have a translation style. It's a positive feeling I have about them. I find a lot of instinct in what I do. You have to hit it just right. I'm never sure whether something is right, but I know damn well when something is wrong" (Bast).

In his eighties, Rabassa is still going strong in the classroom and at his work desk and, indeed, completed his long-awaited treatise on translation and on his years as the leading practitioner of this neglected art form.[18] *If This Be Treason: Translation and Its Dyscontents*, published by New Directions in the Spring of 2005, consists of three parts: the first a memoir of Rabassa's career and of what he describes as his "serendipitous" evolution as a translator ("Gregory," 191; see also *Treason*, 10, 22–28), the second a personal reflection on the many authors and texts he has dealt with, and the third a brief and enigmatic statement on the inherently incomplete nature of translation, even, as with so many of Rabassa's own efforts, in its moments of greatest achievement. "It focuses on my life and the many voyages through the lives and times of great Latin American authors and how I see their work" (Rivera, 2). The book's epilogue, Rabassa says, will appear unfinished since "translation is never finished" (Bast).

No Translation Is Ever Final

This latter contention, gleaned from a lifetime of translation experience and scholarship, is one of Rabassa's most famous pronouncements about his work, one that he elaborates in his new study. "My thesis in the book," he declares, "is that translation is impossible. People expect reproduction, but you can't turn a baby chick into a duckling. The best you can do is get close to it" (Bast). Echoing Walter Benjamin's belief that "no translation would be possible if in its ultimate essence it strove for likeness to the original" and that "While a poet's words endure in his own language, even the greatest translation is destined to become part of the growth of its own language and eventually to be absorbed by its renewal" (Benjamin, 74, 75), Rabassa's point is one that he has been developing for many years. In 1975, explaining why he has never been satisfied with the "final" versions of translations he has done, Rabassa concluded that "while a novel may have a final form, such is not possible with translation, even when it is the work of a single translator." This is so, he believes, because

> Translation is hard put to extend its life beyond its time. A transla-
> tion, no matter how good, is apt to be too contemporary and rarely
> endures. An exception, the King James Version, has become institu-
> tionalized to the degree that it is almost another book in itself. . . . It
> is known that every age must have its own translation of a classic and
> for reasons that go beyond accuracy, while the classic itself is usually
> as "modern" . . . as when it was written. Cervantes' *Quijote* read today
> is much more modern than Motteux's version, and a century from
> now the Putnam and Cohen translations will no doubt sound old-fash-
> ioned. The reason is hard to explain, for these are good translations.
> It must have something to do with the fact that no translation is ever
> final. ("Treason," 32; see also "Snowflakes")

Even when considering his own many successes, Rabassa remains adamant: "I do not think that any translation can really be called either definitive or final. Ambivalence and ambiguity come to the fore; words change subtly over the years . . . so that both translation and original will present a different meaning now from what they did a hundred years ago" (Morales, 120; see also Rabassa, "Snowflakes," 8–9).

The Paredros Puzzle

In advancing this argument, Rabassa engages a concept, that of the Other, near and dear to much late-twentieth-century literary theory. Rabassa, as we shall see, does not see literary theory as bearing very directly on his practice of the art of translation. As he explains it, apropos of translation's otherness:

> Otherness is the foundation of translation in almost every sense of the word. The translator must become the author's other, his Doppelgänger, what Julio Cortázar called his *paredros*, using a Greek term for an old Egyptian concept of otherness. At the same time the translator must turn the author into another possibility of his own existence. The writer stays himself but is now writing in another language and therefore at least partially in another culture. ("Gregory," 191)

The point Rabassa makes here concerning translation's inescapable otherness is similar to one advanced by Maurice Blanchot, who has written (via translation) that "Translation is the sheer play of difference: it constantly makes allusion to difference, dissimulates difference, but by occasionally revealing and often accentuating it, translation becomes the very life of this difference" (83). Blanchot's point is particularly germane to Rabassa's career as a translator when one considers the tremendous impact his translations of so many, and so many very different, Spanish American and Brazilian writers have had on the reception of Latin American literature in the United States, a culture traditionally indifferent, if not outright hostile, to its hemispheric neighbors beyond the Rio Grande. Thanks to Rabassa's tenacity, the cultural differences between Latin America and the United States, and—much less often appreciated—between the various nations of Spanish America (the differences between Cortázar's cosmopolitan Buenos Aires–Paris axis, for example, and Asturias's ancient Mayan cosmology are vast) and between Spanish America and Brazil, are slowly being overcome. And, as even a cursory review of Rabassa's record as a translator/cultural ambassador clearly shows, this has been achieved without any imposition whatsoever of the cultural imperialism, "cultural elitism," or "grossly unequal" and "hegemonic" cultural exchanges about which Lawrence Venuti warns us and which he feels are bound up in what he terms "fluent translation strategies" (*Rethinking*, 2, 5, 4), a kind of bland, homogenizing, and culturally denatured English that, with the possible exception of *Paradiso*, in no way pertains to Rabassa's work. Indeed, in Rabassa's case the opposite is true, for one can easily argue that his insistence on maintaining in his translations the very real linguistic and cultural differences that exist between his Latin American works and authors and their American readers embodies the very goal that Venuti claims for his ideal translator, a writer (as Rabassa might say) whose "resistant strategies can help to preserve the linguistic and cultural difference of the foreign text by producing translations which are strange and estranging, which mark the limits of dominant values in the target-language culture and hinder those values from enacting an imperialist domestication of a cultural other" (*Rethinking*, 13).

As Patai declares, "Rabassa's reflections on translation focus on the translator making *decisions*, not the *translator* making decisions in an overdetermined environment, as is the current theoretical penchant" (102). By attacking Rabassa's contention that a translation can approach the original but never equal it, Venuti advances his argument that relegating translation to a status somewhere below the "original" work amounts to the creation of a "hierarchy of cultural practices" (*Rethinking*, 3), a conclusion that seems of dubious applicability to Rabassa's work and his efforts to promote the study of Brazilian and Spanish American literature, culture, and history in the United States.

Although Venuti criticizes Rabassa for believing that the original text lives on "in all its glory" while its translations need to be periodically updated and redone (3; see also Rabassa, "Snowflakes," 8),[19] he backs away from arguing that a translation is truly the same as the original. This position, however, has been explored by Jacques Derrida (see *Tours*) and Paul de Man (see "Conclusions") and, as Venuti correctly contends, the theoretical stance taken by Derrida and de Man calls into question the traditional distinctions between the original text and its translation(s). Yet not even the mystically inclined Walter Benjamin could fully endorse this conclusion, though for Benjamin the original text sometimes endures in its "Überleben," an interpretational "afterlife" granted some books that often manifests itself through the act of translation. Instead Venuti elects to argue, not without reason, that too many English-language publishers prefer translations that "efface" the "foreign" nature of the text being translated and that this strategy "produces the effect of transparency," which, for Venuti, neuters "the linguistic and cultural difference of the foreign text" and thus makes the translator an accomplice in the creation or maintenance of a variety of cultural hegemonies and hierarchies (4, 5, 6).

The basic problem with this argument is that none of it applies to Rabassa, a scholar and translator fluent in several languages (and competent in others), politically aware, and culturally sensitive in ways that have long defined him as the proto-comparatist and cultural agent. Indeed, it might well be asserted that the esteem in which Rabassa is held not only by his peers but by his Latin American authors as well stems precisely from the fact that he avoids the very pitfalls enumerated by Venuti. By remaining cognizant of the political, economic, and historical particularities of the original texts, he builds these elements into his translations and, in the process, makes the textual and cultural difference of Latin American literature an essential part of the lesson learned by the American reader.[20]

When we take into consideration Rabassa's long professional history as an advocate of Latin American literature and culture, it is simply not credible to view his translation work as in any way "appropriative" or "imperialist" (Venuti, *Rethinking*, jacket). At the same time, as Gerald Martin suggests, we know that there are cases where a word in the original Portuguese or Spanish, such as *hojarasca*, conjures up a host of meanings and associations that are simply not present in the English term *leaf storm*. But this essentially sociolinguistic problem is of a different type than the more theoretical issue Venuti is discussing here, one that is based on power relations between dissimilar and unequal cultures. This issue may look quite different when viewed from the perspective of an English department faculty member as opposed to a teacher, scholar, and translator laboring in a department of Spanish and Portuguese to increase awareness of Latin American literature and to develop it as the basis of a more comprehensive approach to the literature of the Americas.

The many translations we have of Homer, to cite a parallel case, differ considerably among themselves—exhibiting, in fact, a great deal of Blanchot's "play of difference"—while also differing, undoubtedly, from Homer's original language use (whatever it was). And much the same can be said of the many translations of *Don Quixote* that we now have. Or, now, thanks to some of Rabassa's latest efforts, of Machado de Assis. A comparatist knows that one of the most rewarding exercises one can undertake is to contrast different translations of the same original text and to observe the different reading strategies, aesthetic standards, and interpretive approaches that mark different eras, even those circumscribed by a common language—which, of course, is itself evolving through time. For all our recognition of the fundamental importance of Saussurean linguistics and the welter of theoretical progeny it has spawned, who would assert that Cervantes's *Don Quixote* is the same as Edith Grossman's 2003 *Don Quixote*? Or that Grossman's version is not different from Putnam's version?[21] Or from Cohen's? It is not "marginalizing" of either the translation or the translator to argue that the text Cervantes produced does not need to be rewritten but that its translations, its endless rereadings, do; though closely related, and therefore comparable, the original and its translations are nevertheless different and distinct from each other, even as the concept of "originality" can be debated in a variety of ways. Elaborating his point, and again recalling Benjamin, Rabassa continues:

> there will be more than one translation of a classic, meaning that even in its otherness the classic has other possibilities. Mandelbaum, Singleton, Sayers, and Ciardi are all partially Dante in that they are his others, yet they are not clones, not even identical twins, and usually not even close enough to be fraternal ones. Theirs is an otherness within the same language, different variations on the same theme as it were. ("Gregory," 191)

There Are No Theories to Be Had about Translation

As a corollary to this view of the translator as the author's Other, and of the translation's basic otherness or "difference," Rabassa's position on translation theory (a point of contention for Venuti; see *Rethinking*, 2) is both succinct and instructive, the product of a lifetime of professional experience and critical thought:

> I am very cautious about theories that lie outside the natural sciences, where there are fewer unknowns. Having started out in physics in college, I learned to be skeptical of quick solutions and observations. I don't think there are any theories to be had about translation, or about anything artistic and literary, for that matter. Most of what is called theory nowadays in those fields is a developed notion or sometimes even wishful thinking. (Morales, 119)

"Although I am rather amused," Rabassa demurs, "at the idea of a theory concerning something I do in a completely untheoretical way, I am nonetheless pleased at the attention it is getting from these serious minds" (*Treason*, 45). Reverting to military parlance, Rabassa says in summation: "translation is essentially a tactical operation, and strategists, who tend to be academic theorists, inevitably fail in the field" (Morales, 121).

With specific reference to the status of translation within the world of letters, Rabassa has this to say:

> I have always maintained that the proof that translation is an art is that it cannot be taught; you can teach a craft, but you cannot teach an art. I have given courses in the making of translation, but most of what we did was to examine the work of translators and that of each other.

I found that I could tell the students what *not* to do but could not tell them *what* to do. (Morales, 119)

This too is a point that Rabassa has been making for decades. In 1981, for example, he told William Kennedy: "Heaven-sent or hell-bent, according to the critic, translation is really something apart from the other arts. But it is, indisputably, an art. Too many people have defined it in terms that only partially apply, for it has never received the massive attention given to other aspects of literature. It follows, it serves, it is the squire of the arts, but it was Sancho Panza who made Don Quixote possible" (Kennedy, "Rabassa," 67).

Finally, and with respect to the once again contentious issue of the translator's "invisibility" (see Venuti, *Invisibility*; *Scandals*), Rabassa declares that "if one tries to be invisible or inconspicuous, he will end up being just the opposite. This so-called invisibility of the translator should come about in a completely unconscious way. It should be the natural result of a good translation if the translator has done his proper duty" (Morales, 120). For Rabassa, then, translation, in addition to being the closest and most discerning reading a text can have ("Snowflakes," 6), "is natural writing and not an analysis," because "too much thought about technique might dull and stultify the results. What has really moved me along these lines, however, is the natural reader's suspense at going along and being kept moving by wanting to see what happens next. As simple as that, just like reading a book" ("Gregory," 203).

Conclusion

The issues of influence and reception rank among the most intriguing and complex in all of literary study. Ranging from the closely textual to the broadly psychological, and from the work of individual authors to the attitudes and stereotypes one culture has about another, questions about how a certain author or text is received, or interpreted, by someone else inevitably involve the scholar in a multitude of compelling, if elusive, topics. Though very real and often of critical importance, the interplay of influence and reception is complex and difficult to evaluate even when limited to writers and readers within the same linguistic community, as José Donoso demonstrates with respect to Spanish America in *The Boom in Spanish American Literature: A Personal History*, or to those working within the same national tradition, as is the case with Clarice Lispector and her literary progeny in Brazil or with Faulkner and his legacy in the United States. But when the dynamic exchange that characterizes this process involves writers and translated texts from a different and little-known culture—particularly one judged to be inferior or inconsequential by the receiving culture—the chances for misinterpretation become much greater. This, as we have seen, has long been the basic problem plaguing the reception of Latin American literature in the United States, a superpower whose culture has, with very few exceptions, tended to disparage or dismiss the work of writers and intellectuals from Brazil and Spanish America. As Richard Nixon once expressed it, in a comment directed at a then very callow Donald Rumsfeld, "Latin America doesn't matter. . . . People don't give one damn about Latin America" (*Economist*).[1]

Flying in the face of such chauvinism, gifted translators led by Gregory Rabassa became the intermediaries whose work would, in the 1960s, begin to illuminate English-speaking North America about its Spanish- and Portuguese-speaking cousins to the south. Long ignored or repressed but still volatile questions of political self-determination and intervention, economic exploitation, race, class, gender, identity, and respect were suddenly being exposed, via authors like Borges, Neruda, Paz, Amado, and Lispector, for comparative consideration as the three Americas, North (including Canada), Central, and South, found themselves forced to deal with one another in new and unsettling ways. Thanks to the efforts of these translators, an extraordinary process of New World cultural exchange was begun, one that epitomizes what scholars now refer to as "transculturation" (see Pratt, *Eyes*; Spivak), a very fluid and, ineluctably, destabilizing arrangement in which both the dominant culture and the nondominant culture find their own sense of identity transformed, along with their attitudes and stereotypes of the other. Although, as Waïl Hassan points out, Pratt uses the term *transculturation* to examine the power structures that bind the colonizer to the colonized and that dictate the terms of their relationship, it also interrogates those "modes of active agency that seek to transform the stereotyped identities of hegemonic discourse" (756). Both of these issues speak directly to the heart of the entire inter-American project, which most definitely calls into question the nature of the existing New World power structures and the various discourses that have sustained them. A prototypical form of comparative literary study, inter-American literature grows, as a field, out of this restive and contentious transcultural matrix, one characterized by profound linguistic and cultural differences and defined to an exceptional degree by the issues of influence and reception. It has been the purpose of this book to emphasize the crucial role that translation has played in its conception and development.

As several scholars have shown, the reception of Latin American literature in the United States of the 1960s was aided and abetted (and sometimes complicated) by a number of disparate events and situations, one of which, of course, was the Cuban Revolution of 1959. It is quite reasonable to argue, as Ilan Stavans, Johnny Payne, Deborah Cohn, Sophia McClennen, and others have, that the state of American literature in the late 1950s and early 1960s was so tepid that the introduction, via some marvelous translations, of Latin American literature to readers in the United States of that time actually served as a catalyst, a transforming force. In the very influential view of John Barth, whose love affair with Latin American literature spans roughly fifty years, it began to show American writers new ways to think about old topics, topics some felt had lost their potency and vitality. Given the excellence of the Latin American literature that was being translated, it seems certain that its influence on American letters would have eventually taken place anyway, though it also seems likely that the speed of its dissemination and acceptance was accelerated by the doldrums that these commentators felt afflicted creative writing in the United States at the time. As Payne writes, assessing Barth's exuberant praise (in "Replenishment") of *One Hundred Years of Solitude* and the Spanish language, for most Americans the emergence of Spanish American literature in the United States during this tumultuous period "marks the 'discovery' of a new literary continent" (17), one whose inhabitants could boast of powerful and imaginative literary traditions that dated from 1492 (Spanish America) and 1500 (Brazil) and that were thus considerably more evolved than the United States itself was. Moreover, Payne adds, "García Márquez's novel," the beneficiary of a well-intended but ultimately misguided "cultural myth" promulgated by its American readership, quickly comes to be seen as an effective antidote to what many writers and critics feared was "North America's exhausted possibility," an end the Colombian writer's extraordinary narrative will achieve, thanks to Rabassa's celebrated translation, because of its singular ability to "'magically' recover the conventions and artifices of the past, while at the same time cross-fertilizing U.S. writing with its organic originality" (17). In a sense, then, it is entirely plausible to contend that the Spanish American "new narrative"—Borges, Fuentes, Asturias, Rulfo, Cortázar, García Márquez, Vargas Llosa—was exerting an invigorating and renovating influence on American letters, even as it was frequently being misinterpreted by readers in the United States who too often erroneously concluded that Latin American literature had somehow "begun" in the 1960s and who, especially in the case of *One Hundred Years of Solitude*, allowed themselves to be "uncritically" enthralled by what, for them (and for Barth; see "Replenishment"), was its exhilarating postmodernism and its intoxicating "exoticism" (Payne, 17). At the same time, we must not forget that Barth, so closely identified with the Spanish American tradition, was also an early enthusiast of Brazil's Machado de Assis, whose darkly comic metafictions had been successfully translated into English in the early 1950s and who, through these, exerted a decisive influence on Barth's early development as a writer, though by the early 1960s he would be supplanted first by Borges and then, a few years later, by García Márquez (see *Fridays*). The full story of the reception of Brazilian literature in the United States during the Boom period, especially as it compares to the reception given to texts and writers from Spanish America, still awaits a thorough investigation. In general, however, one can easily conclude that the influence of Latin American writing on the literature of the United States during the 1960s and 1970s ranks as the most significant event in American literature of the period, one whose many effects are only now beginning to be understood in their full social, cultural, and political contexts.

While this process is nearly always a positive experience for the influenced author (or culture), affording a source of energy, renewal, and vision, there is another, less commodious dimension to it, one that involves a decentering of the status quo and a serious reconsideration of hoary assumptions about writers, artists, and thinkers from cultures long judged to be deeply alien and not worthy of consideration. Placing the argument that Bloom makes in *The Anxiety of Influence* in an international context, and bearing in mind the

myriad problems involved in trying to reconcile cultures that have been profoundly different (and, at times, antagonistic) in their historical experiences,
one can cite any number of instances from inter-American literary relations
where the influenced author must reject some, if not all, of her/his literary
and cultural heritage in order to fully embrace the new creative forces that
are presenting themselves. Perhaps the most famous and successful example
of this process, as we have seen, is Barth's unabashed declaration of support,
in the 1950s, for the innovative and iconoclastic work of the Brazilian master Machado de Assis and, in the 1960s, for the new writing coming out of
Spanish America. But there are other examples as well, including the transforming reception of *One Hundred Years of Solitude* by a host of English Canadian narrativists who saw in the murky concept of "magical realism" (perhaps conveyed more precisely by Alejo Carpentier's original term, the *real
maravilloso*) the means by which they could break free of the old strictures
of rote realism and create alternative forms of narrative expression, infused
with fantasy and renewed by "the conventions of an oral story-telling tradition" (Hutcheon, 89). Clearly evident in many of the works of such writers
as Jack Hodgins (*The Invention of the World*, 1977, and *The Resurrection of
Joseph Bourne*, 1979), Robert Kroetsch (*What the Crow Said*, 1978), Michael
Ondaatje (*Running in the Family*, 1982), Susan Swan (*The Biggest Modern
Woman of the World*, 1983), and Rudy Wiebe (*My Lovely Enemy*, 1983), the
influence of García Márquez and *One Hundred Years of Solitude* has proved
to be "especially congenial to the Canadian novel, itself working within, but
questioning and pushing realism's limits" (Hutcheon, 89; see also Stratford,
107). As David Hayne has suggested,[2] however, no discussion of "magical realism's" influence, or presence, in Canadian letters would be complete without
a consideration of Jacques Ferron, whose plays and narratives, dating back
to the 1950s, have been extensively translated into English and, in some respects, seem to anticipate the techniques of García Márquez. "Magical realism" in the Americas, then, clearly represents a marvelous opportunity for
a scholar interested in lacing together the literatures of Canada, the United
States, Spanish America, and Brazil, where even the existence of this kind
of writing as a viable literary mode remains very much a contested point.
Indeed, the entire question of literary relations between both Anglophone
and Francophone Canada and Latin America has tremendous potential for
the comparatist, most especially the inter-Americanist, who could easily expand and strengthen the critical perspective by integrating these and other
Canadian texts into it (see Stratford; Souza; Bernd; Bernd and Campos).

   Another, more tangled example concerns the Peruvian poet César Vallejo,
whose idiosyncratic and profoundly autochthonous voice was reconstructed

in his early English translations in the 1960s and 1970s to the point that, in the hands of such poets as Clayton Eshleman, Thomas Merton, James Wright, and Robert Bly, he became, for readers who knew him only in English, much more of a standard European modernist than was really warranted. He also became, à la Bloom, something of an inspiration for the poet/translators themselves, leading them to create some English versions of his poems that had more to do with their as yet unrealized creative desires, and with the Western poetic traditions in which they worked, than with Vallejo in his original Spanish (Seiferle, xii–xiv). Eshleman, for example, has written candidly that, for him, translating Vallejo was a matter of "becoming or failing to become a poet," a way of "giving birth" to himself, as a creative artist and as a sentient, socially conscious human being (xxix, xxx). While this experience is not uncommon among translators, it can lead to distortions of the original text and, consequently, to unanticipated and unjustified variations in the ways a translated author is received by readers in a different culture. As impressive as Vallejo is in these early, Boom-period translations, he is quite different than he is in his native idiom, where he indulges in neologisms involving both Spanish and Quechua,[3] in striking and culturally unique indigenous images, and in the promulgation of a worldview that, as he outlined it in a 1927 article in the journal *Variedades*, called for Latin American writers to reject the then prevailing notion that, in order to be "successful," they had to embrace the norms, tenets, and standards of the Western tradition. Ironically, this was exactly what Vallejo's early translators turned him into, "a poet of modern angst, like Eliot or Verlaine" (Seiferle, xiv), and it has only been with new translations done by Rebecca Seiferle (*The Black Heralds*, 2003) that Vallejo's distinctive voice, his iconoclasm, and his "aboriginal sensibility" (Vallejo, quoted in Seiferle, xv) were at last restored to him, allowing his later English-speaking audience to get closer than ever before to the true César Vallejo. As cases like this remind us, if we read only in translation, and as a substitute for the source text rather than as a linguistically sensitive interpretation of it, we run the risk of getting something other than what the author originally intended, although the translator who writes a careful and detailed critical preface that explains the problems and solutions involved in the translation can, to an extraordinary degree, elucidate both the original text, in all its linguistic and cultural complexity, and the translated text. As we have also tried to show, the importance of translation as the ultimate interpretive act should never be underestimated. Historically speaking, the nature of the relationship between the United States and Latin America has, from the beginning, been beset by animosity, mistrust, and inconsistency, and this unfortunate reality has made any sort of positive cultural exchange very challenging. Even now, in the early twenty-first century, when the need for hemispheric solidarity and cooperation has never been more urgent, the antagonisms, abuses, and misapprehensions of our shared past continue to undermine our efforts to work together for the common good. For the inter-American project to succeed, American readers in particular need to be aware of the nature and extent of their country's involvement in the events of 1898 in Cuba, of 1954 in Guatemala, of 1964 in Brazil, and of 1972–1973 in Chile, to cite just four of the more egregious cases of American intervention in Latin American affairs. A new and more egalitarian sense of New World rapprochement can and must be achieved, one that takes an unflinchingly honest look at the ways relations between the Americas have evolved, how they are at the present time, and, most important, how they might be improved in the future. The weight of cultural disdain that still, to some degree, emanates from one side of the relationship—a situation exacerbated by still unresolved issues of economic exploitation, racism, and political interference that date back to the nineteenth century and even earlier—has made it difficult, though not impossible, for the Americas to join together in new projects that, for the first time, could be beneficial to everyone involved. America's struggle today with the explosive issue of illegal immigration serves as a case in point.

Freighted with traces of racism, xenophobia, and historical ignorance, the bitter and divisive debate over Hispanic immigration into the United States is also deeply ironic since, as Tony Horwitz has shown, this nation's cultural and political past is profoundly Spanish in nature, a fact that seems to be lost on the great majority of Americans, whose most essential sense of identity dates only from the arrival of the English Puritans in 1620 (or, thinking of the Jamestown settlement, in 1607). But, Horwitz writes, if Americans studied their own history with a bit more diligence, they would discover that "The early history of what is now the United States was Spanish, not English, and our denial of this heritage is rooted in age-old stereotypes that still entangle today's immigration debate" (13). Holding in abeyance for a moment the fact that millions of Native Americans inhabited the hemisphere for thousands of years before any Europeans arrived, history shows that, in addition to their explorations in South and Central America,

> Spaniards pioneered the present-day United States. . . . Within three decades of Ponce de León's landing, the Spanish became the first Europeans to reach the Appalachians, the Mississippi, the Grand Canyon and the Great Plains. Spanish ships sailed along the East Coast, penetrating to present-day Bangor, Me., and up the Pacific Coast as far

as Oregon. . . . In all, Spaniards probed half of today's lower 48 states before the first English tried to colonize, at Roanoke Island, N.C.

The Spanish didn't just explore, they settled, creating the first permanent European settlement in the continental United States at St. Augustine, Florida, in 1565. Santa Fe, N.M., also predates Plymouth: later came Spanish settlements in San Antonio, Tucson, San Diego and San Francisco. The Spanish even established a Jesuit mission in Virginia's Chesapeake Bay 37 years before the founding of Jamestown in 1607. As late as 1783, at the end of the Revolutionary War, Spain held claim to roughly half of today's continental United States (in 1775, Spanish ships even reached Alaska). (13)

As Americans pushed westward, however, they found it convenient, Horwitz and others contend, to seize Spanish lands, an act they often justified by invoking the Black Legend, that sixteenth-century retelling of history done by northern European nations jealous of Spain's New World power and wealth, in which the Spanish were depicted as rapacious, greedy, cruel, treacherous, driven by "papist depravity," and engaging in the "mongrelization" of the white race by permitting sexual relations between themselves and both Indians and African slaves (13). By thus demonizing the Spanish, it was a simple matter to displace them and feel sanctimonious doing so—a point not lost on today's Mexican immigrants, who not infrequently invoke precisely this Hispanic past to justify their presence in an America they see as rightfully theirs. In the light of this more complete view of American history, its "ancient Hispanophobia" and its sad story of "Anglo encroachment," it is much easier to appreciate the wry humor in Carlos Fuentes's observation that "The Hispanic world did not come to the United States; the United States came to the Hispanic world" (quoted in Horwitz, 13). The Portuguese, occupied from 1500 on with the colonization of Brazil, did not experience the same sort of head-to-head conflict with Anglo America and, indeed, came to have a historical experience with the United States that differed considerably from that of Spanish America.

These old animosities continue to haunt us, unfortunately, as we try to move ahead with a variety of inter-American ventures. In the summer of 2006, for example, when the MERCOSUR trading block, made up of South American nations, admitted oil-rich Venezuela into its organization, many observers saw it, in symbolic terms, as a declaration of independence from the control of the United States, whose economic policies in the region were widely viewed as a failure and as the cause of undue distress to poor and middle-class Latin Americans. In challenging the economic and political hegemony of Washington and of NAFTA—which, in its current form, integrates the markets of Canada, the United States, and Mexico—a suddenly more powerful MERCOSUR with a "combined market of 250 million people and a combined output of $1 trillion in goods and services annually" (Cormier) may be gaining a position that one day will enable it to chart its own future, not only in Latin America and the hemisphere but the world. As Brazil's president, Luis Ignácio Lula da Silva, observes, "No one's talking anymore" about the Free Trade of the Americas proposal, pushed by the United States and blocked by the MERCOSUR nations in 2005. "Who knows?" Lula says, thinking perhaps of a new economic paradigm for the New World. "We could come to have a Merco-America and not just a Mercosur!" (Cormier). Agreeing with this assessment of MERCOSUR's future, the president of Argentina, Néstor Kirchner, stressed his group's commitment to fighting inequality in the region and to helping its member nations to participate more successfully in the global economy. "Democracy, human rights, liberty and the fight against poverty," Kirchner declared, form the foundation of "a new world order" in Latin America, one endowed with a new and more progressive identity based on cooperation and a unified desire to eliminate poverty, hunger, and joblessness for its citizens (Cormier). It would be a shame, and perhaps a geopolitical disaster, if the nations of the Americas were to grow closer together economically and commercially at the same time that they allowed themselves to become alienated from each other and to drift apart politically and culturally. While the basic motivation behind MERCOSUR is undoubtedly economic self-determination, and the political respect that comes with it, anyone familiar with the political and economic history of the Americas would not be surprised to discover more than a bit of payback in it as well, a clear sense that we have entered a new age of inter-American relations, one in which the United States must reembrace, on all fronts, the ennobling liberal principles of its founding and forge new and more mutually beneficial relationships with its hemispheric neighbors.

As a part of this process, the emergence of inter-American literature as a new discipline proves both that a balanced and productive dialogue between North and South America can be attained and that this dialogue needs to be understood in the context of these larger social, political, and economic issues, for they provide us with the background necessary to read each other's literature accurately. As we have seen, Latin American writers, from de Assis to Neruda, Paz, Fuentes, Vargas Llosa, Ribeiro, and Fuguet, have traditionally been acutely aware of these issues, often building them into the very warp and woof of their texts. And, if inter-American literature is to develop as evenly and felicitously as it should, North American readers will have to learn to do the same—just as Brazilians and Spanish Americans, like Borges, Paz, and Ribeiro, have long done, as evidenced by their very informed readings of American literature and culture. Linguistically, culturally, and historically, Americans have to learn more about the other nations of the New World, for, as the architects of MERCOSUR indicate, our future may well depend on our ability to work together on a variety of issues that concern us all. Although literary study may not rise to the same level of importance as international diplomacy, economics, and statecraft, it is not difficult to see how the development of inter-American literature figures into the natural evolution of hemispheric solidarity—a concept first explored in a systematic sense by the historian Herbert Bolton at the beginning of the twentieth century but actually stretching back at least to the nineteenth century and such figures as the educator John Melish (whose 1818 textbook *Universal School Geography* called for the term *America* to be understood as a single intercontinental entity), the politician Henry Clay, who already in 1820 was advocating that the Americas unify themselves economically and politically, and Walt Whitman, whose influence on generations of Latin American writers has been well documented and whose 1856 letter to Ralph Waldo Emerson evinces a distinctly inter-American ethos. Seen from the perspective of 2007, it would seem imperative that, to check the growing influence of India and, especially, China in Latin America, the United States must abandon the dismissive attitude so eloquently expressed by Richard Nixon (and embraced by so many) and engage Brazil and the nations of Spanish America in ways that will strengthen them and improve living conditions for their people. The United States must become a Good Neighbor in fact and not merely in theory, and it must do so quickly, before it is too late. Since part of this effort will perforce involve the nurturing of a new sense of cultural respect for Latin America and Canada, the study of the literatures of the Americas will have an important role to play, and as this field evolves, the translator will remain a key figure in it. Eventually the Americas, from the northernmost reaches of the Canadian arctic to the windswept barrens of Argentina's Tierra del Fuego, and from the sun-splashed beaches of Ipanema to the fabulous Incan ruins at Macchu Picchu, will benefit most from a strong, proactive alliance, one based on principles of justice, mutual respect, understanding, and support. The development of inter-American literature, arising out of its common historical experience and unified by its innumerable examples of influence and reception, will play a positive, constructive role in bringing this very laudable goal to its full fruition.

There are problems to be overcome, however. The stubborn monolingualism of the United States, coupled with its traditional disdain of foreign language study and its cultural arrogance, has produced a kind of warped and enervating insularity, leading to increased isolation within the world community and a diminution of respect in the eyes of our hemispheric neighbors. A serious imbalance, or disconnect, has resulted from this lamentable situation. Educated Latin Americans tend to know not only English but French as well, and (like their Canadian counterparts) they typically know a great deal about the United States, its literature, history, and culture, while we in the United States know very little about them. This level of ignorance about the interconnectedness of New World history poses a serious complication for the reception of Latin American (or Canadian) literature in the United States, because a truly productive cultural exchange cannot develop if only one side of the discussion knows enough to comment intelligently on the other. As we have sought to demonstrate, this lack of understanding about our common and deeply intertwined American past, a problem exacerbated by our cultural biases, may well have handicapped the initial reception of Latin American literature in the United States of the 1960s. And the same conditions, albeit to a lesser degree, may still be working against us even now, on a variety of fronts.

In the absence of intensive and required foreign language instruction in our schools and colleges (and the cultural, political, and historical instruction that would accompany it), only translation finds itself in a position to help offset our deeply rooted provincialism and connect us with our sister states in the New World and, indeed, with the rest of the world. "Without translators," as David Remnick observes of this problem's literary ramifications, "we are left adrift on our various linguistic ice floes, only faintly hearing rumors of masterpieces elsewhere at sea. So most English-speaking readers glimpse Homer through the filter of Fitzgerald or Fagles, Dante through Sinclair or Singleton or the Hollanders, Proust through Moncrieff or Davis, García Márquez through Gregory Rabassa" (98). With only a few exceptions, one concludes that Latin American literature has, on the whole, been very well served by its English-language translators, and that this felicitous trend is continuing. It is, moreover, no exaggeration to argue that just as Russian and French translations exerted a major influence on the reading and writing of American literature in the first half of the twentieth century, translations of Latin American literature have, from the 1950s to the present, dominated and, in the process, effectively reshaped the American literary landscape. In purely literary terms, then, it is our belief that the growing influence of Spanish American and Brazilian literature in the United States today is a direct function of the work already done, and being done now, by Gregory Rabassa and his many disciples and colleagues.

Interestingly, many of these same points are increasingly being made by progressive-minded English department faculty. J. Hillis Miller, for example, has called for a new focus on what he terms the "literatures of the Americas," a project that will rely heavily on translation, while in a 2005 *PMLA* article Robert Scholes argues for a reconceptualization of the humanities by emphasizing our need to regain our sensitivity to language, grammar, and style and their importance to both the generation of meaning and the act of interpretation, to study more foreign languages (if only to better understand our own native tongue and the ways it shapes our view of reality), and, citing arguments made in *Death of a Discipline* by the eminent comparatist Gayatri Spivak, to learn "how other people think and how they see us" (732). But to do this in any serious fashion, Scholes rightly warns, "we need to know how their languages represent the world" (732), a statement that, if taken at face value, would seem to call for a radical reappraisal of how we educate our students, and particularly with respect to the importance we place on foreign language instruction. If the language in question is not one's native language but an idiom learned in the classroom, then this indisputable good can only be achieved by intense and sustained foreign language study in school, beginning, ideally, in grade school and continuing unabated throughout one's formal education. Reading foreign literature in translation is the second best option, although, as we have sought to demonstrate in the preceding pages, it is important to bear in mind that no matter how meticulously done a translation may be, it simply does not offer the same range of experiences that reading a text in its original language offers. It is one thing to read the text known as *One Hundred Years of Solitude*, but it is quite another thing to read the one known as *Cien años de soledad*, and it is yet another thing to read the two together, comparing and contrasting the linguistically driven Weltanschauung that each projects (Rabassa's English versus García Márquez's Spanish) and contemplating the similar yet different ways these worldviews are developed, transmitted, and, above all, interpreted. The serious reader of inter-American literature needs to be aware of the historical and sociopolitical consciousness that the language of each generates (see Zamora) as well as the manner in which it manifests itself, the mysterious ways the style of each text works upon the reader and manipulates a response to it, as cultural document and as semiotic system. It would seem to be incontrovertible, therefore, that the newly language-sensitive educational process championed by both Scholes—who, terming it "textuality," advocates it as forming "the base or center of our enterprise" (732)—and Spivak inevitably involves the translator's rhetorical skills at least as much as those of the original author, whose work, in all its stylistic and semantic complexity, the translator is seeking both to interpret and re-create in the most complete and accurate manner possible.

Although he does not mention it specifically, Scholes's recommendation that we need to know how the languages of other people represent the world, how they shape reality and imbue it with both ontological and epistemological significance, comes very close to reaffirming the sine qua non of comparative literature as academic discipline and intellectual pursuit—its insistence, at the graduate level, that its practitioners possess fluency in at least two languages other than their native tongue and that their doctoral programs involve a full slate of grammar and literature classes in these languages. By requiring this same level of language expertise, scholars of inter-American literature, whether trained in comparative literature programs or in forward-looking departments of Spanish and Portuguese (whose training and unique perspective on the larger American experience make them ideal bases from which to develop a specialization in inter-American literature), will typically prepare themselves to work *in* English on both American and Anglophone Canadian literature, *in* Spanish on Spanish American literature, and *in* Portuguese on Brazilian literature. And since, as we have noted, most Latin Americanists have typically studied French, they are also prepared to at least read Québécois literature as well, thus gaining a niche for a rich and vital artistic culture that, along with that of Brazil, is too often ignored or given short shrift in the inter-American pantheon. Native American languages can at any time be substituted for these European-based languages, and indeed, when they are, they remind us, as with Vallejo, both of the foundational importance of the New World's vast and varied indigenous heritage and of its continuing relevance to the entire inter-American project. When coupled with proper methodological training and a solid grounding in theory, this strong foundation in foreign language study and in the study of literary texts in their original language prepares the doctoral student of inter-American literature to chart the healthy development of the field well into the future and to teach and conduct research as a comparatist par excellence.

For doctoral students, translations may be used to round out or expand a reading list, they might serve as the focus of an influence and reception study (much as we have sought to do in this book), or they might facilitate a close comparative reading of a translation and its original text to ascertain what was gained and what was lost, linguistically, aesthetically, and culturally, in the process of translation itself. This latter form of translation scholarship, when amplified with notes and full analytical discussions of the myriad decisions that the translator makes when interpreting the original text, can often be very successfully developed as a doctoral dissertation, as can a close comparative study of the various translations that may exist of a single source work, such as Borges, Neruda, or Machado in their various English versions. For the graduate student, translations should not be used as a substitute for working in the original language, though for the undergraduate major, who must also take upper-level literature courses in at least one foreign language, a course or two involving literature in translation (particularly if one deals with non-Western literature) is not only permissible but desirable. While the place of translation in the undergraduate curriculum is thus somewhat expanded and more flexible, for the doctoral student who intends to work in inter-American literature professionally, the issue is different since, with the exceptions of the situations noted above, the ability to work with texts in their original language must be regarded as an absolute requirement, just as it is for all translators and scholars of translation.

In reflecting on our own experience of studying and translating Clarice Lispector, a process that began in our classes with Gregory Rabassa and continued into our careers as scholars and teachers of inter-American literature, we can now appreciate what a daunting task we took on and how much we grew in the process of doing it. As cotranslators of *Água viva* (*The Stream of Life*, 1989) we learned firsthand how highly complex and exacting the task of the translator is. Clarice Lispector is a demanding mistress not only linguistically but psychologically and culturally. She challenged our ability to think creatively while also expanding our knowledge of the Portuguese language and Brazilian culture as we learned to "ride" her text (in a fashion akin to Cixous' writing over her reading of Clarice) and to guide it into an English-language equivalent of her very unique prose style. Cixous elucidates in her preface to our translation: "One cannot talk about *Água viva*. One has to take a leap at the very moment at which what could be called 'a now-instant' or 'an instant-already' is about to reveal itself. The only thing to do is to delve into the luminous arch. One has to give oneself to that which gives itself" (x)—that is to say, to language. Lispector's syntax and punctuation do not come easily in English, a language system that demands more clarity and precision than her very fluid Brazilian Portuguese. Indeed, syntax, we came to believe, provides the key to understanding not merely Lispector's intensely poetic universe but her often visceral sense of the connection between language and being, between language and the vagaries of human existence. We like to think of Clarice Lispector as a writer who cultivates the ineffable, an ongoing tension between what we are feeling and thinking and the actual saying (or writing) of it. This is, after all, why language is such a powerful issue for Clarice Lispector, thematically as well as stylistically. We recall that

Água viva has a lot of both unexpected and very subtle tone changes in it, and we had to pick up on these, for tone is so hard to get right. We learned to listen to each other as we worked, reading out loud and revising until we felt we had captured Clarice's verbal music. And in general, we remember struggling not so much with what Clarice was saying, which was characteristically lyrical and philosophical, but how she was saying and writing it. The issue of gender perspective looms large in Clarice's themes and style. In fact, one could argue that Lispector writes androgynously, incorporating the male and the female into her characters and her prose. Rabassa remarks in his memoir that he was continually asked if he had trouble translating a female author declaring finally that "I was always more concerned with the style than with the sex of the writer" (*Treason*, 73). The fact that both of us brought our own gender perspectives to the task of "writing in Lispector" we believe enriched our work and made it better. That we were able mostly to reproduce that evanescent, flowing style in English was one of our greatest successes in translating this complex and mysterious work. The project gave us much more than an intense experience in translation; it was an excursion into the heart and soul of a brilliant and rigorous literary figure, one whom we will always remember as a bright star of twentieth-century Brazilian letters.

This shared experience in inter-American literary translation has reinforced our view that the study of inter-American literature works to overcome cultural prejudice, ignorance, and provincialism and replaces these with the kind of knowledge and understanding that enable the people of the New World to see each other, and perhaps themselves, in a new light. This refreshed point of view emphasizes the commonality of the American experience while also recognizing and celebrating the innumerable differences that make us unique, as individuals and as cultures (see Pérez Firmat). The driving force behind this entire enterprise is the work of the translator, the person (fated to be ignored except when being maligned) whose interpretive skill and expertise as a creative writer will introduce to each other not only different and hitherto unknown writers but entire cultures as well. From the perspective of readers in the United States, for example, the Spanish American and Brazilian literature that was being translated into English in the 1960s, from Asturias to Cortázar, took us both back in time to an ancient world of Mayan myth and legend and forward to a sophisticated and cosmopolitan world of art, philosophy, and aesthetic theory. With the early translations of Borges, Americans saw how the intellectual complexities of structuralism might be made manifest in a provocative new kind of fiction, while with the poetically and philosophically charged narratives of Clarice

Lispector those same readers could also see how even an arcane system of thought like poststructuralism actually spoke to the deepest anxieties and desires of the human condition. In short, the astonishing variety of Latin American fiction, poetry, and drama that was being rendered into modern, American English was opening new vistas to American writers and intellectuals at the same time that it began to engage both Latin and Anglo culture to an extent hitherto unknown by either side (see Stavans, *Mirror*; Cohn, *History*; McClennen, "Literature"; Larsen; Wood). This extraordinary movement would be the genesis of inter-American literature as an emergent—and very challenging—new field for comparative literary studies. Although the systematic study of the literature of the Americas did not yet possess an official name or programmatic delineation, the writers leading the way in this revolutionary project were coming together at international symposia and meetings to learn more about each other and to find the common ground that, as inhabitants of the New World, they all knew existed beneath the layers of rancor, disdain, and misinformation that had obscured it for so long. Crucially, a small cadre of visionary teachers and scholars, many of whom, like Gregory Rabassa, were themselves active, committed translators, also attended these groundbreaking meetings, preparing themselves to return to their colleges and universities to educate their students about these exciting new developments. Armed with the requisite knowledge of both Latin American and American culture, and often fluent in both Spanish and Portuguese as well as French (again, Rabassa is the prototype), these teacher-scholar-translators became, in the 1960s, the pioneers whose work would prepare the ground for the development of a new literary discipline, one that is profoundly comparative in nature and that, as we are seeing today, is rapidly transforming our old notions about what it means to be "American" and to study "American" literature.

Notes

Preface and Acknowledgments

1. Stavans's essay, in *Prospero's Mirror*, aptly captures the irony of what is "lost in translation" in Latin America, a region that "has been perceived as a colossal misunderstanding" (xxiv).

2. Gregory Rabassa addresses the history of the publication of translations from Latin America in the English language from 1960 to 2000 in his 2005 book *Translation and Its Dyscontents*. He discusses the importance of backing by key publishers as well as the critical role of the Center for Inter-American Relations in New York, supported by the Rockefeller Foundation, which actually paid for the translation of major works, including his own translation of Gabriel García Márquez's *Cien Años de Soledad*.

3. Translation studies programs in universities such as the University of Texas at Dallas address the techniques for critical review of literary translations in their curriculum.

4. Other statistics of note: In 1980, 198 translations from the Portuguese were translated worldwide, and in 1996 this number reached 217. The principal languages into which these works were translated were Spanish and French in 1980 and French, English, and German in 1996. Similarly, in 1980, 851 translations from Spanish appeared, and in 1996 this number increased to 1,240. The major languages into which the Spanish works were translated were French and German in 1980 and French, English, and German in 1996. Gabriel García Márquez and Jorge Amado were included on the list of most translated authors worldwide (UNESCO, 1998).

5. *The New York Times Book Review*, April 2007, featured fiction in translation, with a summary of translation data. (Jascha Hoffman, "Comparative Literature."

6. Weinberger's remarks are drawn from a review of his talk to the Inter-American Bank in 2003, which appeared in the bank's only journal, *America* (Alexandra Russell-Bitting, "The Joys and Vexations of the Translator's Craft: Eliot Weinberger Speaks on that Problematic Necessity" <www.iaelb.org/idbamerica>, accessed August 24, 2003).

7. See note 24 to chapter 4.

Chapter 1. An Inter-American Approach to Translation and Its Implications for the Study of Latin American Literature, Reception Theory, and the Development of Comparative Literature as a Discipline

1. As regular readers of the *Economist* know, for example, their magazine now features a separate section titled "The Americas" that reports on political and economic issues relating to New World nations from Canada to Cuba and from Brazil to Mexico.

2. It is not clear from Mr. Shapiro's screed whether he believed he was competent to judge when a translation was "garish" or whether he was merely reacting to an English-language text that he knew was a translation and that he pronounced garish. For a less strident discussion of the impact that translations of Spanish American poetry may have had on English-language poetry in the late twentieth century, see Heaney.

3. Cortázar's *Hopscotch* has often been thought of as an "antinovel" as well, suggesting yet another possible affinity between the literary cultures of North and South America in the 1960s. The "antipoetry" of Nicanor Parra is also of this type.

4. In an odd way, this argument is not entirely dissimilar to the one then being used to justify or explain the phenomenon of "magical realism," namely, that Latin American reality was so strange and different that only this technique could account for it.

5. The novel was a favorite of President Bill Clinton, who declared it to be "the greatest novel written in any language since William Faulkner" (186).

6. It is important to remember here that if American reviewers knew precious little about Spanish America during this period, they knew even less about Brazil and its quite distinct literary traditions. The greatest narrativist of the late nineteenth and early twentieth century, Brazil's Machado de Assis, affords a telling example of this problem. In a 1953 review of Helen Caldwell's version of Machado's masterpiece, *Dom Casmurro*, Jean Holzhauer speculates that the narrator's guilt may be a product of "the rigid Castilian-like framework of his social milieu," even though Machado lived his entire life in Brazil, his birthplace, and never spent any time in Castile, a region in Spain. In a similar vein, Elizabeth Hardwick, who clearly "knows little of her subject or of Brazilian history," writes in another review of *Dom Casmurro* that Machado's mother was "Spanish, from the Azores," when in fact she was born and bred in Brazil (see Patai, 109).

7. The first of his novels to be translated was *Epitaph of a Small Winner*, which was rendered into English by William L. Grossman. In 1921 Machado had three translated stories, "The Attendant's Confession" ("O Enfermeiro"), "Life" ("Viver"), and "The Fortune-Teller" ("A Cartomante"), appear in Isaac Goldberg's *Brazilian Tales*.

8. Much the same argument can be made with respect to the politically volatile literature that was coming out of Québec during the 1960s.

9. For some later critics, notably Judith Fetterley, Jane Tompkins, and Mary Louise Pratt, this key issue was directly challenged. Tompkins, especially, argued that reader-response criticism did not, in fact, break from formalism and that, in practice, it really only reoriented formalism's basic principles, placing them in a new key, as it were.

10. It is interesting to note, in this regard, that it was a prominent Latin Americanist, Mary Louise Pratt, who in 1982 pointed out this weakness in the reader-response approach. Merging feminist and Marxian arguments, both of which are crucial to properly understanding even such supposedly fanciful "magical realist" texts as *One Hundred Years of Solitude*, Pratt calls for an expansion of reader-response criticism so as to include issues of history, politics, economics, and sociology in its discus-

sions. See her "Interpretive Strategies/Strategic Interpretations: On Anglo-American Reader-Response Criticism."

11. An inter-American study that needs to be undertaken involves a comparison of the "new novel" as it was being cultivated in the Québec and the Latin America of the 1960s. This core focus might be expanded to include similar experimentations with the novel form in English-speaking Canada, where the influence of García Márquez's *One Hundred Years of Solitude* appears to have touched an entire generation of writers (Robert Kroetsch, to name just one), and in the United States, where the influence of several Spanish American writers, especially Borges, Cortázar, Fuentes, and García Márquez, was also being felt.

12. In 2003 a new organization, the International American Studies Association, was formed. Its goal was to free the United States from its hemispheric isolation and integrate it into the more comprehensive framework advocated by inter-Americanists.

Chapter 2. Translation and the Liberation of Brazilian and Spanish American Literature from the Solitude of Cultural Ignorance and Prejudice

Note: Material in chapters 2 and 4 has been previously published as "Translation, Reception Theory and the Rise of Inter-American Literature," by Elizabeth Lowe and Earl E. Fitz. ATA 46th Annual Conference Proceedings, 111–35. Reprinted with permission from the American Translators Association.

1. A Parisian lawyer by trade until, apparently disgusted with the intrigues of European legal and court life, he decamped to Acadia in 1606, Marc Lescarbot wrote a poem around this same time, "Adieu à la France," which describes his quest to find an edenic paradise in the New World, a place he hopes will be less corrupt than the Old World. His 1606 play *Le théâtre de Neptune* amusingly integrates Native American diction and characterizations with European types and theatrical conventions while at the same time subtly celebrating France's overseas ambitions. Its initial staging may well represent the first European-based theatrical production in North America.

2. The Incan citadel, never captured by the Spanish, was discovered by the Yale anthropologist Hiram Bingham in 1911.

3. In addition to employing the Indian heritage as a central focus, both Neruda and Tarn cultivate images of the sea and nature, and the sterility of both the modern city and modern life.

4. Although Latin American scholars had long been publishing works that compared the nations of Spanish America and Brazil with the United States (see, for example, José Enrique Rodó's 1900 treatise *Ariel*, which argued that the United States had allowed its great gift of liberty to be corroded by a crude and unchecked materialism, Manuel de Oliveira Lima's century-old study *The Evolution of Brazil Compared with That of Spanish America and Anglo-Saxon America,* or Vianna Moog's thoughtful 1954 comparative consideration *Bandeirantes and Pioneers*), Paz's study was different in that it elicited a significant response in the United States.

5. Harvard, where Paz taught on and off for many years, awarded him an honorary degree in 1980.

6. Paz himself cultivated this indigenous theme in much of his work. In *Piedra de sol* (1957; tr. Muriel Rukeyser, *Sun Stone*, 1963), perhaps his greatest long poem, Paz structures his 584 unpunctuated hendecasyllabic lines around the famous Aztec calendar stone.

7. The novel is dedicated to William Styron, a writer long interested in Spanish American literature and a close friend of Fuentes. Styron was a board member of IAFA, the Inter-American Foundation for the Arts, which had been established in 1962 by a New York City group led by Rodman Rockefeller, the eldest son of Nelson Rockefeller, who had worked during the Roosevelt administration to strengthen relations between the United States and Latin America. This inter-American dialogue, so important and productive during the war years, came to an abrupt end in the 1950s, when the U.S. turned its attention to Europe and Asia. Possibly to offset a growing Cuban influence in the hemisphere in the early 1960s, the IAFA group was committed to improving intellectual and cultural relations between the United States and Latin America and, in a sense, reigniting the inter-American dialogue initiated during the 1930s and 1940s. After a merger of the two organizations in 1967, the very successful work of the IAFA would be taken up and carried on by the Center for Inter-American Relations, now the Americas Society, whose energetic promotion of Latin American literature and arts as well as relations between the United States and Latin America still includes the publication of the very influential journal *Review*. In addition to Styron, IAFA board members from the United States included Edward Albee, Lillian Hellman, Gore Vidal, and Alfred A. Knopf. Styron and Fuentes might have met for the first time at IAFA's 1964 conference in Chichen Itzá, Mexico, which was also attended by such other luminaries as Hellman, Knopf, Oscar Lewis, Rodríguez Monegal, Juan Rulfo, Nicanor Parra, Marta Traba, and José Donoso—who, after earning his B.A. in English at Princeton in 1951, would teach creative writing at the University of Iowa between 1965 and 1967, becoming the first active Latin American writer to give classes on this subject in the United States.

8. Another of Fuentes's novels, *Aura* (1962; tr. Lysander Kemp, 1965), also experimented with the use of second-person narration.

9. Although a narrator who calls himself Freddy Lambert actually brings the narrative to an end by signing his name to it on page 462, the true narrator of the novel, the critical consciousness that recalls Ixca Cienfuegos of *Where the Air Is Clear*, may really be an Aztec deity, Xipe Totec, who, first introduced on page 371, then serves as the living tradition that links the world of the conquest and the Aztecs to the world of the Nazis and the characters of the novel, who are, in a sense, traveling between Mexico's modern present and its ancient indigenous past. In Aztec cosmology, "Xipe Totec is the Mexican god of newly planted seed and of penitential torture. Like the maize seed that loses its husk as it begins to sprout, Xipe Totec gave food to mankind by having himself skinned alive. In short, Xipe is an Aztec Christ-figure. Message: someone always has to be sacrificed before man can move to another level of awareness" (*Time*, 76–77).

10. This comment seems to reflect West's belief that Fuentes's real concern here is

not so much over the murder of a former Nazi guard, a character who serves an almost motiflike role in the novel, "as over mankind's astonishing capacity for rationalizing blood sacrifices at every level of cultural development and under every form of social organization. . . . The feeling is that the earth itself is a blood-soaked pyramid, and the book as a whole reads—at least in the Spanish version—like a nightmare warning that man is at his most dangerous when saying 'I love you,' on the one hand, or when professing his loathing of evil, on the other" (74–75). This interpretational line casts light upon the various forms of violence and oppression that permeate the book and shows clearly that the violence of the Aztec past is not all that distant—that, indeed, it is very closely linked to that of our own times.

11. Although the word *jagunço* originally meant a hired thug, assassin, or backlands bandit (many of whom swelled the rebel ranks), da Cunha uses the term more or less interchangeably with *sertanejo*.

12. The reaction of the victorious side once again invites a comparison between what happened in Brazil at the end of the Canudos conflict and what President Lincoln ordered with respect to the defeated South and its soldiers at the end of the Civil War.

13. Da Cunha, acutely aware of how words failed to capture the essence of what happened at the end, dramatically describes the insurrection's final moment in this fashion: "Canudos did not surrender. The only case of its kind in history, it held out to the last man. Conquered inch by inch, in the literal meaning of the words, it fell on October 5, toward dusk—when its last defenders fell, dying, every man of them. There were only four of them left: an old man, two other full-grown men, and a child, facing a furiously raging army of five thousand soldiers" (475).

14. In a verse couplet, da Cunha once described himself as being partly Indian (Putnam, *Rebellion in the Backlands*, xviii).

15. As in the medieval romance, the hero's faithful companion, the lethal Diadorim, turns out in the end to be a beautiful young woman.

16. One of these, "The Slaughter of the Ponies," appears in Rodríguez Monegal and Colchie, *Borzoi Anthology*, 2:683–86.

Chapter 3. Urbanization and the Evolution of Contemporary Latin American Literature into a Hemispheric Context

1. Fonseca and his late wife, Théa Maud Fonseca, maintained years-long relationships with his translators, corresponding with them, visiting them in their home countries, and receiving them at the Fonseca home in Leblon in Rio de Janeiro. Otherwise reclusive and reluctant to give interviews, Fonseca has taken great interest in the translations of his work and in the people doing them.

2. The title story of the collection has appeared in English translation by Peter Schoenbach in the *Literary Review* (see expanded bibliography of translations), reprinted in *Review: Latin American Literature and Arts*, no. 53 (Fall 1996).

3. This was true in Brazilian song composition as well, as evidenced by the work of

Gilberto Gil, Caetano Veloso, and other great poet songwriters of the era. See Charles Perrone, *Masters of Brazilian Song.*

4. Giudice was the keynote speaker at La Semana de la Literatura Brasileña, hosted in 1979 by the Universidad Javeriana in Bogotá, where he was celebrated by Colombian academics and writers.

5. Giudice wrote numerous sonnets during his lifetime, a fact little known by his friends and translators. In the 1990s he participated with friends in a literary society that required correspondence to be done in sonnets with verses of ten syllables. His pseudonym was Judicis Marinus.

6. Giudice's own life was stranger than fiction. He lived with his first wife and sister-in-law in an old house in Lapa, the north district of the city of Rio de Janeiro. His wife, who gradually slipped into mental illness, would spend most of her days in the bathtub. Victor maintained marital relations with his sister-in-law for some time until he left his house to live with his mistress, with whom he had a relationship for many years and who later became his second wife.

7. Giudice was a gourmand, bon vivant, musician, and excellent host. He used to entertain his guests, and his translators, at the famed Lamas Restaurant in Rio's northern district (Zona Norte), where samba lyrics are memorialized in mosaics on the sidewalks.

8. Rubem Fonseca also uses rotten teeth as a metaphor for poverty.

9. *Reading Lolita in Teheran,* by Azar Nafisi, speaks to the power of literature, and by extension myth, in rescuing young women's lives from the oppression of the Iranian theocracy.

Chapter 4. Translation and the Ontologies of Cultural Identity and Aesthetic Integrity in Modern Brazilian and Spanish American Narrative

1. Originally published in 1944, Borges's *Ficciones* appeared in English in 1962, one year after he won the prestigious international publishing prize, the Prix Formentor, which he shared that year with Samuel Beckett. Painfully aware that he had been largely invisible outside the confines of certain parts of the Spanish-speaking world until, from 1944 to the early 1950s, he began to be translated into French, Borges generously credited his French translators for bringing him the fame, in Europe, that would allow him to be considered for the Prix Formentor and that would eventually lead to his being translated into English. Because of translation, then, one can surely conclude, as Rodríguez Monegal does, that Borges was "the first Latin American writer to be recognized worldwide" (*Borges*, 444).

2. In a widely read and influential study, Genette, focusing on the celebrated Borges *ficción* "Pierre Menard, Author of the *Quixote*," argues (in accordance with Borges himself) that the reading of a text is always more important than its writing because the meanings of a book are always ahead of it, produced by the reader's experience of it, and not behind it, which is the terrain of the author. See Genette, 323–27.

3. It is interesting to note that, although he elected to translate it, Borges did not believe *The Wild Palms* to be of the same quality as *Light in August, Absalom, Absalom!*, and *The Sound and the Fury*. For an elaboration of his opinion of *The Wild Palms*, see his 5 May 1939 review of it in *El Hogar*.

4. Given his popularity in the France of the 1950s and early 1960s, it is easy to see Borges as the quintessential structuralist writer, as the writer who actually put the abstruse theories of structuralism into fiction, or, more precisely, into *ficciones*. John Sturrock, for example, describes "The Library of Babel," one of Borges's most anthologized texts, as "the bad dream of a Structuralist, not of a bored Buenos Aires librarian" (xviii).

5. Andrew Hurley reports that while the "first known English translation of a work of fiction" by Borges "appeared in the August 1948 issue of *Ellery Queen's Mystery Magazine*," it was "not until 1962, fourteen years after that first appearance, that a book-length collection of fiction appeared in English" (81).

6. It is, for example, interesting to compare the Irby and the di Giovanni versions of "Borges y yo" ("Borges and I"), or the Irby and the Anthony Bonner re-creations of "Pierre Menard, Author of the *Quixote*," and to consider the different interpretive acts that underlay these significantly distinct English translations.

7. The theoretical roots of Borges's invention of a "new narrative" can be seen in two difficult but important essays he wrote in 1932 for *Discusión*: "La postulación de la realidad" ("The Postulation of Reality"), in which he takes up the problem of verisimilitude, and "El arte narrativo y la magia" ("Narrative Art and Magic"), which focuses more on the issue of narrative techniques and their relative advantages and disadvantages and which discusses as an example of the successful use of "magic" in this nonrealistic, nonmimetic sense Poe's short novel *The Narrative of Arthur Gordon Pym*. For more information on these articles and their importance to Borges's new theory of narrative, see Rodríguez Monegal, *Borges*, 247–49.

8. To understand the many historical and cultural differences between Spanish America and Brazil, González Echevarría, Pupo-Walker, and Haberly offer this summary: (1) during the colonization of Brazil, the Portuguese settlers tended to remain in the coastal areas rather than penetrating the hinterland, a development that would come in the seventeenth century, and "were not confronted by populous and complex indigenous cultures"; (2) in comparison to the wealthy Spanish viceroyalties, "Brazilian colonial society seems less developed institutionally. The economic growth of the colony was sustained mainly by a feudal agricultural economy which depended on slave labor imported from Africa"; (3) "Centers of higher learning were not established in Brazil until 1927, and the first university was authorized only in 1920. In Spanish America, on the other hand, the Dominican college of Santo Domingo was elevated to the rank of a university (called St Thomas) in 1538, and Mexico City and Lima had printing presses by 1535"; (4) "Much to its advantage, colonial Brazil was a society receptive to the foreign intellectual currents that often came with trade. French, British, and US ships frequently anchored in Brazilian ports. Though the Portuguese crown sought a strict administrative control of its vast American colony,

it never developed the paranoid fear of foreigners displayed by Spanish authorities"; and (5) in spite of repeated attempts by such European powers as France, Spain, and Holland to take control of various parts of Brazil, such "adverse developments . . . did not lead to the kind of political fragmentation that eventually took place in Spanish America after Independence." Such a breakup did not happen in part because in 1808 "the cohesion of Brazilian society was enhanced when . . . this colony became the center of the Portuguese Empire. After fleeing Napoleonic troops with a British naval escort, the Prince Regent (later King João VI) settled his court in Rio de Janeiro, and remained there until 1821. On December 16, 1815, Brazil became a kingdom and as such an equal of Portugal. Obviously, such an extraordinary turn of events has no equivalent in the history of Spanish America," which suffered an extreme form of balkanization after its numerous wars for independence were played out (3:2–3).

9. Machado's publisher, H. Garnier of Paris, had completed the printing of *Dom Casmurro* by 5 December 1899, but the finished copies did not arrive in Rio de Janeiro until sometime after 12 February 1900, with the result that the date of publication is sometimes given as 1899 and sometimes as 1900.

10. John Gledson has persuasively argued this position; see his *Machado de Assis: Ficção e História* and *The Deceptive Realism of Machado de Assis* (1984).

11. Of all the "misplaced ideas" in play, it was the continuing existence of slavery in Brazil (where abolition did not come until 1888, one year before the republic was established) that perhaps more than any other showed how ill-prepared Brazil was to embrace and benefit from the ideas of politically liberal and progressive nations. In metaphoric terms, this point is made in chapter 3, in which Rubião's black slave is forced to hide behind the kitchen door while white, European servants are hired to do the work.

12. Other technical and theoretical parallels between Machado and Borges include these: both writers know but elect to ignore or alter the standard modes of European realism in the creation of their "new narratives"; both employ narrators who sometimes allude correctly to historically accurate authors and texts but who also, mixing fact with fiction in the creation of a new hybrid genre, sometimes invert, distort, or deliberately misquote these same authors and texts in order to develop their own narratives; and both comment constantly, typically by means of their (often unreliable) narrators, on the inadequacies of their readers, on the need to read more carefully and thoughtfully, or, more generally, on the problem of reading, interpretation, and the gleaning of meaning from texts.

13. It must be remembered that, since Borges never wrote a novel but only short fictions and essays, his influence on the formal development of that particular genre was less direct. This explains why Cortázar is regarded as such a decisive figure in the historical evolution of the *nueva novela hispanoamericana*.

14. In the tradition of Machado's Brás Cubas, Cortázar's slightly sardonic narrator informs the reader in *Hopscotch*'s "Table of Instructions" that

In its own way, this book consists of many books, but two books above all.

The first can be read in a normal fashion and it ends with Chapter 56, at the close of which there are three garish little stars that stand for the words *The End.* Consequently, the reader may ignore what follows with a clean conscience.

The second should be read by beginning with Chapter 73 and then following the sequence indicated at the end of each chapter. In case of confusion or forgetfulness, one need only consult the following list:

73-1-2-116-3-84- . . .

Each chapter has its number at the top of every right-hand page to facilitate the search.

15. In the *Ficciones*, for example, women are hardly mentioned, whereas in *Near to the Wild Heart* the protagonist is a woman and women are featured in the text. Another key difference is that Lispector's text exemplifies much more the concepts of poststructuralism—the inherent instability of language, the fluid nature of meaning—while the Borges *Ficciones*, as Sturrock suggests, have much more in common with French structuralism of the 1950s. Finally, Lispector's novel, as dramatically innovative as it is, nevertheless comes out of a Brazilian tradition of narrative experimentation that dates back at least as far as Machado de Assis; the Borges *Ficciones*, for all that Borges was part of Spanish America's native tradition, are much more *sui generis.*

16. We know only that she is an upper-class woman, whose initials, G. H., are embossed on a set of luggage.

17. This problem of possession, particularly as it relates to human relationships, is endemic to Lispector's fictive world. Specifically, Lispector's characters ask, in a variety of ways: how can one be in love without possessing the loved one? In her first novel, *Near to the Wild Heart*, for example, the protagonist, an unconventional married woman named Joana, asks herself: "how was she to tie herself to a man without permitting him to imprison her? How was she to prevent him from enclosing her body and soul within his four walls? And was there some means of acquiring things without those things possessing her?" (29).

18. At another point, the text tells us: "Although for pleasure your edges are sufficient—Lacan explained to him one day—little does the king of bouquets enjoy his" (*Cobra*, 15).

19. For a more detailed explanation of this entire process, the "transformation" of one form of *Cobra* into another, see Levine, *The Subversive Scribe*, 36–45, "Opio into Coca (Cobra)."

20. In this regard, Cunha's debt to Clarice Lispector, and her influence on Hélène Cixous, is clear.

21. Epitomized in its 1928 Antropofagia, or Cannibalist, movement—one that, initiated by Oswald de Andrade, must be regarded as among the most influential forces in all of modern Brazilian culture—this ability to assimilate foreign influences, blend them into national trends, and then create something new and different even today serves as a defining force in Brazilian identity.

22. As they figure into the narrative, some of the most important of these are:

Candomblé, an Afro-Brazilian religious ceremony; Xangô, the god of storms and lightning, represented in the text by the black boy and the black man; Yansan, the warrior queen and mistress of the winds; Oxum, the goddess of water, including streams and rivers; mirrors; the wind; water; thunder and lightning (associated with Xangô); lavender; basil; seashells; mango trees; beads of different colors; dance; drumming; medals and medallions.

23. For readers familiar with the work of Lispector, and especially with her 1944 novel *Near to the Wild Heart*, this issue of "possession," understood as a problem of human identity and being as well as a political question, will be quickly perceived to be a basic motif of modern Brazilian literature.

24. The issue of what constitutes a truly "American" identity has a long and complex history in the New World. As early as 1891, the Cuban patriot José Martí could write the essay "Nuestra América" (Our America), which for many years served as a kind of model for inter-American scholarship, while in 1929 the Canadian writer and critic Frederick Philip Grove argued in *It Needs to Be Said* that the term *America* was more appropriate as a reference to an entire continent than to a single country within it. Even Walt Whitman, in his 1856 letter to Ralph Waldo Emerson, could consider both Montreal and Havana as being "American" and as one day forming part of the "Hundred States" that would make up its greater hemispheric scope.

25. An exception to this rule was, to a degree, Edmund Wilson's 1965 study *O Canada: An American's Notes on Canadian Culture*, a work that, though interesting, did not inspire a surge in Canadian-related scholarship in the United States. In that sense, it stands in contrast to Paz's *The Labyrinth of Solitude*.

26. The importance of *joual* to the new writers of Quebec in a way parallels the importance of language to the new novelists of Spanish America, though there is a key difference involving the issue of cultural and political identity.

Chapter 5. Translating the Voices of a Globalized Latin American Literature

1. The term *Third Culture Kid* (TCK) was coined by sociologist Ruth Hill Useem in the 1960s to refer to someone who spent a significant period of time in a culture other than his/her own while growing up, and integrated elements of those cultures into a third culture. TCKs include children of military, missionary, government, business, and diplomatic families. The phenomenon is worldwide. TCKs are known to have a particular psychological profile. While they become sophisticated, multilingual global citizens, they have difficulty identifying with and taking ownership of any one culture. They are often perceived as aloof or snobbish. Their sense of belonging is confined to relationships with others who share the same background.

2. Danny Anderson provides an in-depth analysis of the philosophical dimensions of Volpi's prose in his excellent article "The Novels of Jorge Volpi and the Possibility of Knowledge."

3. Ms. Rheda suggested that Chacal be translated as Marc Jackal to connote the

wild animal. Her original misspelling of Chagall seemed equally effective and so was left that way.

Chapter 6. Gregory Rabassa

1. For more details, see Hoeksema, 7; Morales, 116–18; Rabassa, *Treason*, 22–24.

2. The June 1963 issue of *Odyssey Review* contains a story, "The Iriarte Family," by the Uruguayan writer Mario Benedetti. The translator of the story, in truth Gregory Rabassa, is listed as one George Rothenberg; the initials GR provide the clue. See Morales, 116–18, for a more complete explanation.

3. "The old man didn't speak much Spanish around the house," reports Rabassa, who had already studied French and Latin in high school in Hanover, New Hampshire, and who also "dabbled in Italian" at Dartmouth (Bast).

4. Morales, 118; see also Rabassa, *Treason*, 37–39. Rabassa was mustered out of the army with a rank of staff sergeant of infantry.

5. His M.A. thesis was titled "The Poetry of Miguel de Unamuno." Rabassa's doctoral dissertation, later published as a book, was *The Negro in Brazilian Fiction since 1888*.

6. In a 1978 interview he put this same thought somewhat more forcefully: "I translated *Hopscotch* as I read it. I did have to go back and change some things, but only a snippet here and there, nothing important. I think that this bears out my contention that a translation is nothing but a close reading, perhaps the closest reading possible" (Hoeksema, 10).

7. Of his working relationship with Cortázar, Rabassa in 1978 had this to say: "Of all the authors I have done the best by far to work with was Julio Cortázar. His English is quite good and he is a conscientious reader. He also has great respect for what the translator must do (being one himself) and therefore never asks the impossible. Many times Julio has even suggested a slightly better turn of phrase in English, sometimes one that is quite slangy. He also has a good eye for spotting slips in meaning. Sometimes a seemingly innocent word or phrase is really something else quite different because the context is Argentine slang" (Hoeksema, 8–9). Rabassa also said that he and Cortázar shared many interests, such as a love of jazz, and that they were "on the same wavelength." He also reported that his "greatest honor" was being dubbed *cronopio* by Cortázar himself, the inventor of the term, which basically designates someone who is "a creative and exemplary being" (Morales, 119).

8. This same issue, the impact of the exotic on American readers of the time, came up in Rabassa's translation of another canonical Spanish American writer, Peru's Mario Vargas Llosa. As Rabassa writes, "The problem . . . is that what is commonplace in, say, Peru is exotic for the outsider. Mario Vargas Llosa was concerned when I was translating *The Green House* that it might seem more exotic to the foreigner than he wanted it to be; that is, he wanted it to be read as if by a Peruvian. I told him that even in the starkest and most banal language the Amazonian region would still be exotic to the northern reader" (Morales, 122–23).

9. It is interesting to note that Rabassa judges Asturias more difficult to have translated than Cortázar, whose texts, especially *Hopscotch*, were "fun" for Rabassa (Morales, 124). "People keep marveling at my translations of Cortázar, such a difficult writer, and yet, I think that he has been substantially 'easier' than Asturias, especially when the 'gran' old 'lengua' was at his worst" (Hoeksema, 11).

10. Of the prolix nature of Asturias's novels, and especially his "Banana Trilogy," Rabassa once declared, "God save us, he needed Maxwell Perkins. . . . I was tempted to improve upon it, but I couldn't because the improvements would have been more cutting than anything else" (Green and Berreby, 6).

11. According to Rabassa, García Márquez also said that "American reviewers, on the whole, have understood *One Hundred Years of Solitude* much better than critics in his own language." This comment suggests to Rabassa that, since many of these American reviewers likely did not know Spanish and were thus unable to compare the translation to the original, "it is almost possible for an astute reader to judge the merits of a translation without recourse to the original language" ("Treason," 35, 36).

12. The editor, who is said to have been bilingual, counters that Rabassa himself was less than perfectly satisfied with his original efforts to capture the full measure of Lezama Lima's baroque divagations (Tannenbaum).

13. There are two other stories connected with the translation of *Paradiso* that deserve retelling. First of all, Rabassa enjoyed with Lezama Lima, as he had with Cortázar and a few others, a certain kind of collaborative working relationship, one complicated, however, by political issues between Cuba and the United States. As Rabassa relates it, "I would send Julio Cortázar, Lezama's dear friend and admirer, finished pages. Julio would pass them on to a Cuban friend in Paris who was returning home, who would give them to Lezama. After Lezama made his comments, the route would be reversed. In spite of all, this was a quicker method than direct mail which was well nigh impossible given the U.S. boycott of Cuba. The Padilla episode put an end to the triangular system, which had been quite helpful" (Hoeksema, 9). The second story, which highlights Rabassa's modesty, his creativity, and his knowledge of American poetry, is recounted by Sara Blackburn: In a conversation with her, Rabassa recalled that "during his early work on *Paradiso*, he came to passages quoted, in Lezama Lima's own translation, from Whitman and Hart Crane. Not having the proper references at hand, he went ahead and translated them back into English, intending to substitute the exact English texts later. When he checked, he found that he'd been two words off on the Whitman, and one word off on the Crane, a phenomenon he attributes not to his skill, but to Lezama Lima's" (42).

14. Although some scholars feel that the French version of *A paixão segundo G. H.* (1964; tr. Clelia Pisa, *La Passion selon G. H.*, 1978) was the first Lispector text to inspire Cixous, with the immediate result being Cixous's *Vivre l'orange* (1979), it was a later Lispector text, *Água viva* (1973; tr. Lowe and Fitz, *The Stream of Life*, 1989), that Cixous praises as the prototype of *l'écriture feminine*, feminine writing, and that may well have provided the initial point of contact between the two writers.

15. A translator familiar with the grammatical and phonetic peculiarities of Portuguese—he translated the Portuguese writer Eça de Queiroz's *The Mandarin, and Other Stories*—Goldman is thus writing this review from the perspective of both linguistic expertise and professional experience.

16. In characteristically self-effacing fashion, Rabassa has termed translation "a very narrow act," and modestly likens it to the work done by paint-by-the-numbers artists: "Such painters don't have much choice as to what to paint, but some will come closer than others in duplicating the original because of a better sense of color and tones" (Tannenbaum, 31), the latter clause clearly suggesting what he feels is the true importance of the translator's interpretive skills and creativity.

17. *Avalovara* can in many ways be profitably compared with Cortázar's *Hopscotch*, as well as with Thomas Pynchon's *V.*

18. Rabassa, a Distinguished Professor of Romance Languages and Comparative Literature, who regards teaching as a "good, youthful operation" (Bast), still offers his very popular freshman lecture course, "Hispanic Literature in Translation," at Queens College of the City University of New York.

19. For a more detailed defense of Rabassa against this charge, see Patai, esp. 101–11.

20. Rabassa's concerns over the style of the final published version of *Paradiso* is a case in point.

21. As Rabassa himself notes in "Snowflakes," 8, both George Steiner in *After Babel* and Borges in his well-known *ficción* "Pierre Menard, Author of the *Quijote*" discuss this same issue, the fact that translations of certain texts seem to proliferate through the ages while the original text remains the same.

Conclusion

1. Also indicative of how little Americans know about Latin America is a 1982 comment by President Ronald Reagan, who, upon returning from a trip there, said, "You'd be surprised. They're all individual countries" (qtd. by Carolyn Curiel, in "Hello, Neighbor," a 3 February 2008, New York Times Book Review of *Forgotten Continent: The Battle for Latin America's Soul*, by Michael Reid).

2. David Hayne to Earl Fitz, e-mail, 6 December 2004.

3. For Latin Americanists, the question of Quechua also recalls the Peruvian poet, anthropologist, and novelist José María Arguedas, whose extraordinary narrative, Los ríos profundos (1958; Deep Rivers, 1978), was translated into English by Frances Horning Barraclough and published by the University of Texas Press. Although Arguedas wrote a great deal of poetry in Quechua, a language that is still spoken by millions of people in five Andean nations, his fame rests chiefly on Los ríos profundos, a novel that sought to translate the grammar, syntax, poetic devices, and Weltanschauung of Quechua into modern Spanish. The result was a dauntingly hybrid text, one that presented unique and all but insurmountable problems for its English language translator who won the 1978 Columbia University Translation Center Award for her sensitive and faithful re-creation of this Latin American classic.

Bibliography

Adams, Robert M. *Proteus, His Lies, His Truth: Discussions of Literary Translation.* New York: W. W. Norton, 1973.

Anderson, Danny J. "The Novels of Jorge Volpi and the Possibility of Knowledge." *Studies in the Literary Imagination* 33, no. 1 (2000): 1–20.

Arenas, Fernando. "Writing After Paradise and Before a Possible Dream: Brazil's Caio Fernando Abreu." *Luso-Brazilian Review* 36, no. 2 (Winter 1999): 13–22.

Atwood, Margaret. *Survival: A Thematic Guide to Canadian Literature.* Toronto: Anansi, 1972.

Aviv, Rachel. "One Hundred Years of Solitude—on Crack." *Salon*, 21 January 2004. <www.salon.com/books/feature/2004/01/21/mcondo>.

Babel Guides. Review of *Zero*, by Ignácio de Loyola Brandão, translated by Ellen Watson. <babelguides.com/view/work/54674>.

Balderston, Daniel, and Marcy E. Schwartz, eds. *Voice-Overs: Translation and Latin American Literature.* Albany: State University of New York Press, 2002.

Barth, John. *Further Fridays.* Boston: Little, Brown, 1995.

———. "The Literature of Exhaustion." *Atlantic*, August 1967, 29–34.

———. "The Literature of Replenishment." *Atlantic*, January 1980, 65–71.

Bassnett, Susan. *Comparative Literature: A Critical Introduction.* Oxford: Blackwell, 1993.

Bast, Andrew. "A Translator's Long Journey, Page by Page." *New York Times*, 25 May 2004.

Bellow, Saul. "Some Notes on Recent American Fiction." In Klein, *American Novel*, 159–74.

Benjamin, Walter. "The Task of the Translator." Translated by Harry Zohn. In Schulte and Biguenet, *Theories of Translation*, 71–82.

Bernd, Zilá, ed. *Americanidade e transferências culturais.* Porto Alegre: Movimento, 2003.

Bernd, Zilá, and Maria do Carmo Campos, eds. *Literatura e americanidade.* Porto Alegre: Editora da Universidade, 1995.

Biguenet, John, and Rainer Schulte, eds. *The Craft of Translation.* Chicago: University of Chicago Press, 1989.

Blackburn, Sara. "Translator Supreme." *New York Times Book Review*, 15 September 1974, 40–42.

Blanchot, Maurice. "Translating." Translated by Richard Sieburth. *Sulfur* (Ypsilanti, Michigan) 26 (1990): 82–86.

Bloom, Harold. *The Anxiety of Influence: A Theory of Poetry.* New York: Oxford University Press, 1973.

———. *Genius: A Mosaic of One Hundred Exemplary Creative Minds.* New York: Warner, 2002.

Bolton, Herbert E. "The Epic of Greater America." *American Historical Review* 38, no. 3 (April 1933): 448–74.

Boullosa, Carmen. "Dead Souls." *Nation,* 5 June 2006. <www.thenation.com/doc/20060605/boullosa>.

Braga-Pinto, César A. *An Other of One's Own: Clarice Lispector, Hélène Cixous, and American Audiences.* Master's thesis, San Francisco State University, May 1993.

Brower, Keith H., Earl E. Fitz, and Enrique Martínez-Vidal, eds. *Jorge Amado: New Critical Essays.* New York: Routledge, 2001.

Brushwood, John. "Two Views of the Boom: North and South." In Miller and Williams, "The Boom in Retrospect," 13–31.

Caldwell, Helen. *The Brazilian Othello of Machado de Assis.* Berkeley and Los Angeles: University of California Press, 1960.

Castro-Klarén, Sarah, and Héctor Campos. "Traducciones, tirajes, ventas, y estrellas: El 'boom.'" *Ideologies and Literature* 4, no. 17 (September–October 1983): 319–38.

Chamberlain, Bobby J. "Striking a Balance: Amado and the Critics." In Brower, Fitz, and Martínez-Vidal, *Jorge Amado,* 31–41.

Cixous, Hélène. Foreword to the translation by Elizabeth Lowe and Earl Fitz of *The Stream of Life,* by Clarice Lispector. Translated by Verena Conley. Minneapolis: University of Minnesota Press, 1989.

Clinton, Bill. *My Life.* New York: Alfred A. Knopf, 2004.

Cohn, Deborah N. *History and Memory in the Two Souths: Recent Southern and Spanish American Fiction.* Nashville: Vanderbilt University Press, 1999.

———. "Tale of Two Translation Programs." *Latin American Research Review* 41, no. 2 (June 2006): 139–64.

Coleman, Alexander. "A Hero of Enormous Appetites." Review of *Macunaíma,* by Mário de Andrade, translated by E. A. Goodland. *New York Times Book Review,* 3 March 1985.

Cormier, Bill. "Mercosur Trade Bloc Admits Venezuela." *Tennessean,* 22 July 2006.

Cortázar, Julio. *Rayuela.* 18th ed. 104–5. Buenos Aires: Sudamericana, 1975.

Courteau, Joanna. "*Gabriela, Clove and Cinnamon*: Rewriting the Discourse of the Native." In Brower, Fitz, and Martínez-Vidal, *Jorge Amado,* 43–56.

Crichton, Sarah. "El boom de la novela latinoamericana." *Publisher's Weekly,* 24 December 1982, 26–30.

Damrosch, David. "Comparative Literature?" *PMLA* 118, no. 2 (March 2003): 326–30.

Davidson, Arnold E., ed. *Studies on Canadian Literature: Introductory and Critical Essays.* New York: Modern Language Association of America, 1990.

de Man, Paul. "Conclusions: Walter Benjamin's 'The Task of the Translator.'" In *The Resistance to Theory,* 73–105. Minneapolis: University of Minnesota Press, 1986.

Dende Collective. "The Piranha Lounge." <www.dendecollective.org/plays/piranha/index.html>.

Deresiewicz, William. "The Interpreter." Review of *If This Be Treason*, by Gregory Rabassa. *New York Times Book Review*, 15 May 2005, 36.

Derrida, Jacques. Excerpt from "Des Tours de Babel." Translated by Joseph F. Graham. In Schulte and Biguenet, *Theories of Translation*, 218–27.

Dirda, Michael. "A Chilean American's Coming of Age." Review of *The Movies of My Life*, by Alberto Fuguet, translated by Ezra E. Fitz. *Washington Post*, 19 October 2003.

Donoso, José. *The Boom in Spanish American Literature: A Personal History*. Translated by Gregory Kolovakos. New York: Columbia University Press; Center for Inter-American Relations, 1977.

Donoso, José, and William Henkin, eds. *The TriQuarterly Anthology of Contemporary Latin American Literature*. New York: Dutton, 1969.

Douglass, Ellen H. "'Dressing Down' the Warrior Maiden: Plot, Perspective, and Gender Ideology in *Tereza Batista cansada de guerra*." In Brower, Fitz, and Martínez-Vidal, *Jorge Amado*, 83–109.

Dunn, Christopher. Introduction to Rheda, *First World Third Class*. <www.utexas.edu/utpress/excerpts/exrhefir.html#ex1>.

Economist. "The Battle for Latin America's Soul." 20–26 May 2006, 11.

Edinger, Catarina. "Dona Flor in Two Cultures." *Literature and Film Quarterly* 19, no. 4 (1991): 235–41.

Eshleman, Clayton. Introduction to *César Vallejo: The Complete Posthumous Poetry*, translated by Clayton Eshleman and José Rubia Barcia, xix–xxxvii. Berkeley and Los Angeles: University of California Press, 1978.

Feal, Rosemary G. "'All Languages Are Up': A Look at Foreign Language Enrollments Today." *MLA Newsletter* 36, no. 1 (Spring 2004): 4.

Fernández Retamar, Roberto. *Caliban and Other Essays*. Translated by Edward Baker. Minneapolis: University of Minnesota Press, 1989.

Fish, Stanley. "Literature in the Reader: Affective Stylistics." *New Literary History* 2, no. 1 (1970): 123–63. Reprinted in *Is There a Text in This Class?* (Cambridge, Mass.: Harvard University Press, 1980).

———. *Self-Consuming Artifacts: The Experience of Seventeenth-Century Literature*. Berkeley and Los Angeles: University of California Press, 1972.

———. *Surprised by Sin: The Reader in "Paradise Lost."* New York: St. Martin's Press, 1967.

Fitts, Dudley. Review of *The Heights of Macchu Picchu*, by Pablo Neruda, translated by Nathaniel Tarn. *New York Times Book Review*, 21 May 1967. Reprinted in *Review '68*, 25–27.

Fitz, Earl E. "In Quest of Nuestras Américas." *AmeriQuests* 1, no. 1 (2004).

———. *Machado de Assis*. Boston: Twayne, 1989.

———. *Rediscovering the New World: Inter-American Literature in a Comparative Context*. Iowa City: University of Iowa Press, 1991.

———. "Spanish American and Brazilian Literature in an Inter-American Perspective: The Comparative Approach." In McClennen and Fitz, *Comparative Cultural Studies*, 69–88.

———. "Translation and Poststructural Theory: The Unexpected Convergence." *Exchanges: A Journal of Translation*, no. 3 (1991): 63–65.

———. "Translation as Political Act: The Creation and Exportation of Canada Through Its Literature." *Mid-Atlantic Journal of Canadian Studies* 1, no. 1 (Spring 1986): 31–39.

Foster, David William. *Queer Issues in Contemporary Latin American Cinema*. Austin, Tex.: University of Texas Press, 2003.

Frenz, Horst. "The Art of Translation." In *Comparative Literature: Method and Perspective*, rev. ed., edited by Newton P. Stallknecht and Horst Frenz, 98–121. Carbondale: Southern Illinois University Press, 1971.

Frizzi, Adria. "Osman Lins: An Introduction." *Review of Contemporary Fiction* 15, no. 3 (1995): 150–55.

Fuentes, Carlos. *La nueva novela hispanoamericana*. Mexico City: Joaquín Mortiz, 1969.

Fuguet, Alberto. "Estados Unidos es un país latinoamericano." Interview with Ernesto Escobar Ulloa. *Barcelona Review*, May 2004. <www.barcelonareview.com/42/ s_af_int.htm>.

———. "Magical Neoliberalism." *Foreign Policy*, no. 125 (July–August 2001): 66–73.

Fuguet, Alberto, and Sergio Gómez, eds. *McOndo*. Barcelona: Grijalbo Mondadori, 1996.

Gabara, Esther. "Facing Brazil: The Problem of Portraiture and a Modernist Sublime." *New Centennial Review* 4, no. 2 (2004): 33–76.

Galantière, Lewis, ed. *The World of Translation*. New York: PEN American Center, 1971.

García Márquez, Gabriel. "The Desire to Translate." Translated by Daniel Balderston and Marcy Schwartz. In Balderston and Schwartz, *Voice-Overs*, 23–25.

———. "Latin America's Impossible Reality." *Harper's*, January 1985, 13–16.

Gardner, John. *On Moral Fiction*. New York: Basic Books, 1978.

Gass, William H. *Fiction and the Figures of Life*. New York: Knopf, 1970.

———. "The First Seven Pages of the Boom." In Miller and Williams, "The Boom in Retrospect," 33–56.

Genette, Gerard. "La littérature selon Borges." *L'Herne* 4 (1964): 323–27.

Giles, Jana. "Last Samba in São Paulo." Review of *Whatever Happened to Dulce Veiga?* by Caio Fernando Abreu, translated by Adria Frizzi. *New York Times*, 18 February 2001.

Gitlin, Todd. *The Sixties: Years of Hope, Days of Rage*. New York: Bantam, 1987.

Gledson, John. *The Deceptive Realism of Machado de Assis: A Dissenting Interpretation of Dom Casmurro*. Liverpool: F. Cairns, 1984.

———. *Machado de Assis: Ficcao e Historia*. Rio de Janeiro: Paz e Terra, 1986.

Giudice, Victor. *Necrológio*. Rio de Janeiro: O Cruzeiro, 1972.

Goldberg, Isaac, ed. and trans. *Brazilian Tales*. Boston: Four Seas, 1921.

Goldman, Francisco. Introduction to *The Adventures and Misadventures of Maqroll*, by Álvaro Mutis, translated by Edith Grossman, vii–xvi. New York: *New York Review of Books*, 2002.

Goldman, Richard Franko. "Deeds in the Mind." *Saturday Review*, 19 August 1967, 33, 48.

González Echevarría, Roberto. "Latin American and Comparative Literatures." In McClennen and Fitz, *Comparative Cultural Studies*, 89–104.

———, ed. *The Oxford Book of Latin American Short Stories*. Oxford: Oxford University Press, 1997.

———. "Severo Sarduy, the Boom, and the Post-Boom." Translated by Caroline A. Mansfield and Antonio Vera León. In Miller and Williams, "The Boom in Retrospect," 57–72.

González Echevarría, Roberto, Enrique Pupo-Walker, and David Haberly. Introduction to vol. 3, *The Cambridge History of Latin American Literature*, edited by Roberto González Echevarría and Enrique Pupo-Walker, 1–10. Cambridge: Cambridge University Press, 1996.

Gordus, Andrew M. "The Vampiric and the Urban Space in Dalton Trevisan's 'O Vampiro de Curitiba.'" <rmmla.wsu.edu/ereview/52.1/articles/gordus.asp>.

Gould, Karen. "Writing and Reading 'Otherwise': Quebec Women Writers and the Exploration of Difference." In Davidson, *Studies on Canadian Literature*, 207–25.

Gowland de Gallo, María. "Latin American Literature: A Rising Star: The Novel." *Américas* 28, no. 2 (February 1976): 37–41.

Green, Amy, and David Berreby. "Translating: A Conversation on the Craft." *Thesis* (Graduate School and University Center, CUNY) 1, no. 2 (Spring 1987): 5–9.

Grossman, Edith. Review of Suzanne Jill Levine, *The Subversive Scribe*. <www.amazon.com/SubversiveScribe-Translation Latin American Fiction/dp/1555971466>.

Grossman, William L. "Outlaw with a Problem." Review of *The Devil to Pay in the Backlands*, by João Guimarães Rosa, translated by James L. Taylor and Harriet de Onís. *New York Times Book Review*, 21 April 1963, 4, 27.

Haberly, David T. Introduction to *Quincas Borba*, by Machado de Assis, translated by Gregory Rabassa, xi–xxvi. New York: Oxford University Press, 1999.

Hassan, Waïl. "Agency and Translational Literature: Ahaf Soueif's *The Map of Love*." *PMLA* 121, no. 3 (May 2006): 753–68.

Heaney, Seamus. "The Impact of Translation." *Yale Review* 76, no. 1 (Autumn 1986): 1–14.

Hochman, Sandra. Review of *The Heights of Macchu Picchu*, by Pablo Neruda, translated by Nathaniel Tarn. *Book Week*, 28 May 1967, 19–20. Reprinted in *Review '68*, 18–23.

Hoeksema, Thomas. "The Translator's Voice: An Interview with Gregory Rabassa." *Translation Review*, no. 1 (Spring 1978): 5–18.

Hoffman, Jascha. "Data: Comparative Literature." *The New York Times Book Review*, 15 April 2007, 27.

Holzhauer, Jean. Review of *Dom Casmurro*, by Machado de Assis. *Commonweal*, June 1953, 254–55.

Horwitz, Tony. "Immigration—and the Curse of the Black Legend." *New York Times,* "Op Ed," 9 July 2006, 13.

Howe, Irving. "Mass Society and Post-Modern Fiction." In Klein, *American Novel,* 124–41.

Hurley, Andrew, trans. *A Universal History of Iniquity,* by Jorge Luis Borges. New York: Penguin, 2004.

Hutcheon, Linda. "The Novel." In New, *Literary History of Canada,* 73–96.

Huyssen, Andreas. *After the Great Divide: Modernism, Mass Culture, Postmodernism.* Bloomington: Indiana University Press, 1986.

Irvine, Lorna, and Paula Gilbert Lewis. "Altering the Principles of Mapping: Teaching Canadian and Québec Literature outside Canada." In Davidson, *Studies on Canadian Literature,* 323–37.

Iyer, Pico. "Virtual Unrest." Review of *Turing's Delirium,* by Edmundo Paz Soldán, translated by Lisa Carter. *New York Times Book Review,* 16 July 2006, 9.

Jackson, K. David. "Madness in a Tropical Manner." *New York Times Book Review,* 22 February 1998, 14–15.

———, ed. *Oxford Anthology of the Brazilian Short Story.* Oxford: Oxford University Press, 2006.

Jameson, Fredric. "Modernism and Imperialism." In *Nationalism, Colonialism, and Literature,* edited by Terry Eagleton, Fredric Jameson, and Edward W. Said, 43–66. Minneapolis: University of Minnesota Press, 1990.

Jefferson, Margo. "The Fortress of Monoglot Nation." *New York Times Book Review,* 26 October 2003, 31.

Johnson, Harvey L. Review of *Seraphim Grosse Pointe,* by Oswald de Andrade, translated by Kenneth D. Jackson and Albert Bork. *South Central Bulletin,* Spring/Summer 1983, 24–25.

Kaup, Monika, and Debra J. Rosenthal, eds. *Inter-American Literary Dialogues: Mixing Race, Mixing Culture.* Austin: University of Texas Press, 2002.

Kazin, Alfred. "The Alone Generation: A Comment on the Fiction of the Fifties." In Klein, *American Novel,* 114–23.

Kennedy, William. "Gregory Rabassa and the Art of Translation." *Quest* 5, no. 7 (September 1981): 67–69.

———. Review of *A Change of Skin,* by Carlos Fuentes, translated by Sam Hileman. *National Observer,* 26 February 1968. Reprinted in *Review '68,* 71–73.

Klein, Marcus, ed. *The American Novel since World War II.* Greenwich, Conn.: Fawcett, 1969.

Koch, Stephen. "Premature Speculations on the Perpetual Renaissance." *TriQuarterly* 10 (Fall 1967): 4–19.

Kristal, Efraín. *Invisible Work: Borges and Translation.* Nashville: Vanderbilt University Press, 2002.

La Bossière, Camille R. "Past and Present: The Neobaroque Novel in French Canada." In *Studies in Canadian Literature,* edited by Arnold E. Davidson. New York: The Modern Language Association of America, 1990: 193–206.

LaPorte, Nicole. "New Era Succeeds Years of Solitude." *New York Times*, 4 January 2003.

Larsen, Neil. *Reading North by South: On Latin American Literature, Culture, and Politics*. Minneapolis: University of Minnesota Press, 1995.

Lask, Thomas. "Nobel Laureate Corruption of a Dictatorship Jungle of the Abstruse." Review of *Mulata*, by Miguel Ángel Asturias, translated by Gregory Rabassa. *New York Times*, 25 October 1967.

Lefevere, André, ed. *Translation/History/Culture: A Sourcebook*. London: Routledge, 1992.

Lehman, David, with Theodore Stanger and Barbara Rosen. "Ambassadors of the World: Best-Selling Authors You Probably Never Heard Of." *Newsweek*, 3 November 1986, 53–55.

Levine, Suzanne Jill. *Manuel Puig and the Spider Woman: His Life and Fictions*. New York: Farrar, Straus and Giroux, 2000.

———. *The Subversive Scribe: Translating Latin American Fiction*. Saint Paul, Minn.: Graywolf Press, 1991.

Lewis, Maggie. "Enchanting Translations: Gregory Rabassa Puts Latin America on Our Literary Map." *Christian Science Monitor*, 24 November 1982.

Lowe, Elizabeth. "A Character in Spite of Her Author: Dona Flor Liberates Herself from Jorge Amado." In Brower, Fitz, and Martínez-Vidal, *Jorge Amado*, 125–31.

———. *The City in Brazilian Literature*. Madison, N.J.: Fairleigh Dickinson University Press, 1982.

———. Foreword to *The Brazilian People*, by Darcy Ribeiro, translated by Gregory Rabassa, ix–xii. Gainesville: University Press of Florida, 2000.

———. "The 'New' Jorge Amado." *Luso-Brazilian Review* 6, no. 2 (December 1969): 73–82.

———. Preface to *Os Banheiros*, by Victor Giudice, 7–8. Rio de Janeiro: Codecri, 1979.

Lucas, Fábio. Introduction to *Antes do baile verde*, by Lygia Fagundes Telles. Rio de Janeiro: Nova Fronteira, 1986.

Machado de Assis. *Obra Completa*. Edited by Afrânio Coutinho. Rio de Janeiro: José Aguilar, 1962.

Manguel, Alberto. "The Young and the Restless." Review of *Shorts: Stories*, by Alberto Fuguet, translated by Ezra E. Fitz. *Washington Post*, 9 February 2006.

Martin, Gerald. "Maqroll versus Macondo: The Exceptionality of Álvaro Mutis." *World Literature Today* 77, no. 2 (July–September 2003): 23–27. <www.ou.edu/worldlit/onlinemagazine/SA2003/_05-July-Sept03-Martin.pdf>.

———. "Translating Garcia Marquez, or, The Impossible Dream." In Balderston and Schwartz, *Voice-Overs*, 156–63.

McCaffery, Larry. *The Metafictional Muse: The Works of Robert Coover, Donald Barthelme, and William H. Gass*. Pittsburgh: University of Pittsburgh Press, 1982.

———, ed. *Postmodern Fiction: A Bio-Bibliographical Guide*. New York: Greenwood, 1986.

McClennen, Sophia A. "Comparative Literature and Latin American Studies: From

Disarticulation to Dialogue." In McClennen and Fitz, *Comparative Cultural Studies*, 105–30.

———. "Inter-American Studies or Imperial American Studies?" *Comparative American Studies* 3, no. 4: 393–413.

McClennen, Sophia A., and Earl E. Fitz, eds. *Comparative Cultural Studies and Latin America*. West Lafayette, Ind.: Purdue University Press, 2004.

Mead, Robert G., Jr. "After the Boom: The Fate of Latin American Literature in English Translation." *Américas* 30, no. 4 (April 1978): 2–8.

———. "Latin America's Changing Image of the United States." *Américas* 32, no. 1 (January 1980): 3–8.

———. Review of *Mulata*, by Miguel Ángel Asturias, translated by Gregory Rabassa. *Saturday Review*, 4 November 1967. Reprinted in *Review '68*, 49–51.

Mendoza, Mario. "Novela Negra." Interview by Luis García. Literaturas.com. <www.literaturas.com/mariomendoza.htm>.

Miller, J. Hillis. Contribution to "Looking Backward, Looking Forward: MLA Members Speak." In Special Millennium Issue, *PMLA* 115 (December 2000): 2062.

Miller, Yvette E., and Raymond Leslie Williams, eds. "The Boom in Retrospect: A Reconsideration." Special issue, *Latin American Literary Review* 15, no. 29 (January–June 1987).

Moog, Clodomir Vianna. *Bandeirantes and Pioneers*. Translated by L. L. Barrett. New York: George Braziller, 1964.

Morales, Harry. "You Can't Say 'Ain't' in Spanish—Or Can You? A Conversation with Gregory Rabassa." *Hopscotch: A Cultural Review* 2, no. 4 (2001): 116–27.

Mutis, Álvaro. "Álvaro Mutis on Himself." *World Literature Today* 77, no. 2 (July–September 2003): 9–11. <www.ou.edu/worldlit/onlinemagazine/SA2003/_03-July-Sep03-Mutis.pdf>.

New, W. H., ed. *A Literary History of Canada: Canadian Literature in English, Volume IV*. Toronto: University of Toronto Press, 1990.

Nida, Eugene A. *Toward a Science of Translating*. Leiden: E. J. Brill, 1964.

Oliveira Lima, Manuel de. *The Evolution of Brazil Compared with That of Spanish America and Anglo-Saxon America*. Edited by Percy Alvin Martin. 1914. Westport, Conn.: Greenwood, 1975.

Patai, Daphne. "Machado in English." In *Machado de Assis: Reflections on a Brazilian Master Writer*, edited by Richard Graham, 85–116. Austin: University of Texas Press, 1999.

Paternostro, Silvana. "Colombia's New Urban Realists." *Críticas*, 1 December 2003. <www.criticasmagazine.com/article/CA337352.html>.

Payne, Johnny. *Conquest of the New Word: Experimental Fiction and Translation in the Americas*. Austin: University of Texas Press, 1993.

Payne, Judith A., and Earl E. Fitz. *Ambiguity and Gender in the New Novel of Brazil and Spanish America: A Comparative Assessment*. Iowa City: University of Iowa Press, 1993.

Paz, Octavio. *Corriente Alterna*. Mexico: Siglo XXI, 1967. For quote on Rulfo, see <www.letraslibres.com/pdf.php?id=1906>.

———. "A Literature of Foundations." Translated by Lysander Kemp. In Donoso and Henkin, *TriQuarterly Anthology*, 3–8.

———. "Translation: Literature and Letters." Translated by Irene del Corral. In Schulte and Biguenet, *Theories of Translation*, 152–62. Chicago: University of Chicago Press, 1992.

Peden, Margaret Sayers. "Translating the Boom: The Apple Theory of Translation." In Miller and Williams, "The Boom in Retrospect," 159–72.

Pérez Firmat, Gustavo, ed. *Do the Americas Have a Common Literature?* Durham, N.C.: Duke University Press, 1990.

Perrone, Charles A. *Masters of Contemporary Brazilian Song: MPB 1965–1985*. Austin: University of Texas Press, 1989.

Phillips, William. "Notes on the New Style." In Klein, *American Novel*, 252–61.

Pratt, Mary Louise. *Imperial Eyes: Travel Writing and Transculturation*. New York: Routledge, 1992.

———. "Interpretive Strategies/Strategic Interpretations: On Anglo-American Reader-Response Criticism." *Boundary* 2 11 (Fall–Winter 1982–83): 201–31.

———. "Presidential Address 2003: Language, Liberties, Waves, and Webs—Engaging the Present." *PMLA* 119, no. 3 (May 2004): 417–28.

Pring-Mill, Robert. Preface to *The Heights of Macchu Picchu*, by Pablo Neruda, translated by Nathaniel Tarn, vii–xix. New York: Farrar, Straus and Giroux, 1966.

Publishers Weekly. Review of *Rosario Tijeras*, by Jorge Franco, translated by Gregory Rabassa. 19 January 2004, 54.

Quinlan, Susan Canty, and Fernando Arenas, eds. *Lusosex: Gender and Sexuality in the Portuguese-Speaking World*. Minneapolis: University of Minnesota Press, 2002.

Rabassa, Gregory. "The Ear in Translation." In Galantière, *The World of Translation*, 81–85.

———. "From Lima Barreto to Osman Lins: Reinventing the Novel to Invent Brazil." *Review '64: Latin American Literature and Arts* (Spring 2002): 6–9.

———. "Gregory Rabassa." In *Contemporary Authors Autobiography Series*, 9:191–206. Detroit: Gale Research, 1989.

———. *If This Be Treason: Translation and Its Dyscontents*. New York: New Directions, 2005.

———. "If This Be Treason: Translation and Its Possibilities." *American Scholar* 44, no. 1 (Winter 1974–75): 29–39.

———. Interview by authors. Tape recording. New York, 25 September 2003.

———. "No Two Snowflakes Are Alike: Translation as Metaphor." In Biguenet and Schulte, *The Craft of Translation*, 1–12.

———. "Osman Lins and *Avalovara*: The Shape and Shaping of the Novel." *World Literature Today* 53, no. 1 (1979): 30–35.

———. "Words Cannot Express . . .: The Translation of Cultures." In Balderston and Schwartz, *Voice-Overs*, 84–91.

Rama, Ángel. *La novela en América Latina.* Veracruz: Fundación Ángel Rama, 1986.

Ramos, Jorge. *The Latino Wave.* Translated by Ezra E. Fitz. New York: Rayo/HarperCollins, 2004.

Reid, Alistair. "The Latin American Lottery." *New Yorker,* 26 January 1981, 106–11.

Reid, John T. *Spanish American Images of the United States, 1790–1960.* Gainesville: University Presses of Florida, 1977.

Remnick, David. "The Translation Wars." *New Yorker,* 7 November 2005, 98–109.

Review '68. New York: Center for Inter-American Relations, 1969.

Rivera, Lucas. "The Translator in His Solitude." *OP Magazine,* July–August 2003. <www.opmagazine.com4-rabassa.htm>, accessed August 31, 2005.

Robinson, Douglas. *The Translator's Turn.* Baltimore: Johns Hopkins University Press, 1991.

Rodó, José Enrique. *Ariel.* Translated by Margaret Sayers Peden. Austin: University of Texas Press, 1988.

Rodríguez Monegal, Emir. *El boom de la novela latinoamericana.* Caracas: Tiempo Nuevo, 1972.

———. *Jorge Luis Borges: A Literary Biography.* New York: Dutton, 1978.

———. "The New Latin American Literature in the USA." In *Review '68,* 3–13.

———. "The New Latin American Novelists." In Donoso and Henkin, *TriQuarterly Anthology,* 9–28.

Rodríguez Monegal, Emir, and Thomas Colchie, eds. *The Borzoi Anthology of Latin American Literature.* 2 vols. New York: Knopf, 1977.

Rosenthal, M. L. Review of *The Heights of Macchu Picchu,* by Pablo Neruda, translated by Nathaniel Tarn. *Saturday Review,* 2 September 1967. Reprinted in *Review '68,* 23–26.

Rossberg, Susana. "Introspecção e imobilidade em *As meninas* de Lygia Fagundes Telles." <ccat.sas.upenn.edu/romance/gra/WPs1999/telles.html>.

Rostagno, Irene. *Searching for Recognition: The Promotion of Latin American Literature in the United States.* Westport, Conn.: Greenwood Press, 1997.

Roth, Philip. "Writing American Fiction." In Klein, *American Novel,* 142–58.

Ruffato, Luiz, ed. *Mais 30 Mulheres que Estão Fazendo a Nova Literatura Brasileira.* Rio de Janeiro: Record, 2005.

Ryan, Alan. "Another Brazilian Bombshell." Review of *Bufo & Spallanzani,* by Rubem Fonseca, translated by Clifford E. Landers. *Washington Post,* 21 October 1990.

Scholes, Robert. "Presidential Address 2004: The Humanities in a Posthumanist World." *PMLA* 120, no. 3 (May 2005): 724–33.

Schulte, Rainer, and John Biguenet, eds. *Theories of Translation: An Anthology of Essays from Dryden to Derrida.* Chicago: University of Chicago Press, 1992.

Schwarz, Roberto. *Misplaced Ideas: Essays on Brazilian Culture.* Edited and translated by John Gledson. London: Verso, 1992.

Seiferle, Rebecca. "César Vallejo: The Thread of Indigenous Blood." Introduction to *The Black Heralds*, by César Vallejo, translated by Rebecca Seiferle, xiii–xxxv. Port Townsend, Wash.: Copper Canyon Press, 2003.

Shapiro, Karl. "The Critic Outside." *American Scholar* 50 (Spring 1981): 197–210.

Sharpe, Peggy. "Fragmented Identities and the Process of Metamorphosis in Works by Lygia Fagundes Telles." In *International Women's Writing: New Landscapes of Identity*, edited by Anne E. Brown and Marjanne E. Goozé, 78–85. Westport, Conn.: Greenwood, 1995.

Shaw, Donald L. *The Post-Boom in Spanish American Fiction*. Albany: State University of New York Press, 1998.

Shek, Ben-Z. *French-Canadian and Québécois Novels*. Toronto: Oxford University Press, 1991.

Sheppard, R. Z. "Where the Fiction is *Fantástica*." *Time*, 7 March 1983, 78–82.

Siemens, William L. "Creativity in Mutis: The Role of Maqroll." *World Literature Today* 77, no. 2 (July–September 2003): 31–35. <www.ou.edu/worldlit/onlinemagazine/SA2003/_07-July-Sept03-Siemans.pdf>.

Sontag, Susan. "The Aesthetics of Silence." In *A Susan Sontag Reader*, 181–204. New York: Farrar, Straus and Giroux, 1982.

Sousa, Ronald W. Introduction to *The Passion According to G. H.*, by Clarice Lispector, vii–ix. Minneapolis: University of Minnesota Press, 1988.

Souza, Lúcia Soares de. *Utopies américaines au Québec et au Brésil*. Québec: Presses de l'Université Laval, 2004.

Spillman, Rob. "I Am Not a Magic Realist: A Young Latin American Novelist Says No More Flying Grannies." <www.salon.com/june97/magicalintro970611.html>.

Spivak, Gayatri Chakravorty. *Death of a Discipline*. New York: Columbia University Press, 2003.

Stavans, Ilan. "A Brief (Happy) Talk with Paco Ignacio Taibo II." *Literary Review* 38, no. 1 (Fall 1994): 34–37. <www.findarticles.com/p/articles/mi_m2078/is_nl_v38/ai_15896332>.

———, ed. *Prospero's Mirror: A Translators' Portfolio of Latin American Short Fiction*. Willimantic, Conn.: Curbstone Press, 1998.

Steiner, George. *After Babel: Aspects of Language and Translation*. London: Oxford University Press, 1975.

Stratford, Philip. "Translation." In New, *Literary History of Canada*, 97–107.

Sturrock, John. Introduction to *Ficciones*, by Jorge Luis Borges, edited by Anthony Kerrigan, xi–xxiv. New York: Knopf, Everyman's Library, 1993.

Tannenbaum, Jeffrey A. "The Translator's Role Is Crucial and Delicate, and Widely Unnoticed." *Wall Street Journal*, 15 September 1977.

Time. "Volkswagen of Fools." Review of *A Change of Skin*, by Carlos Fuentes, translated by Sam Hileman. 26 January 1968. Reprinted in *Review '68*, 76–77.

Trevisan, Dalton. "Vampiro de Almas." Interview. *Veja*, September 1975, 8.

Unruh, Vicky. *Latin American Vanguards: The Art of Contentious Encounters*. Berkeley and Los Angeles: University of California Press, 1994.

UNESCO World Culture Report. Paris: UNESCO, 1998. <www.unesco.org/culture/ worldreport/html_eng/tables2.shtml(tables 21,22,23)>

Updike, John. "The Lone Sailor: Tales of a Colorful Voyage to Nowhere." *New Yorker*, 13 January 2003, 81–84.

Van Steen, Edla. "An Interview with Osman Lins." *Review of Contemporary Fiction* 15, no. 3 (1995): 155–65.

Vargas Llosa, Mario. *La guerra del fin del mundo*. Barcelona: Seix Barral, Biblioteca de Bolsillo, 1987.

———. "Literature Is Fire." Translated by Maureen Ahern de Maurer. In *Doors and Mirrors: Fiction and Poetry from Spanish America, 1920–1970*, edited by Hortense Carpentier and Janet Brof, 430–35. New York: Grossman, 1972.

———. "Saved by Rita Hayworth." Review of *Manuel Puig and the Spider Woman*, by Suzanne Jill Levine. *New York Times Book Review*, 13 August 2000.

———. "Thugs Who Know Their Greek." Review of *High Art*, by Rubem Fonseca. *New York Times Book Review*, 9 July 1986.

Venuti, Lawrence, ed. *Rethinking Translation: Discourse, Subjectivity, Ideology*. London: Routledge, 1992.

———. *The Scandals of Translation: Towards an Ethics of Difference*. London: Routledge, 1998.

———. *The Translator's Invisibility: A History of Translation*. London: Routledge, 1995.

Vinarov, Kseniya A. "La novela detectivesca posmoderna de metaficción: cuatro ejemplos mexicanos." Ph.D. diss., University of California, Riverside, 2004.

Warren, Rosanna, ed. *The Art of Translation: Voices from the Field*. Boston: Northeastern University Press, 1989.

Wasserman, Renata R. Mautner. "The Guerrilla in the Bathtub: Telles's *As Meninas* and the Irruption of Politics." *Modern Language Studies* 19, no. 1 (1989): 50–65.

West, Anthony. Review of *A Change of Skin*, by Carlos Fuentes, translated by Sam Hileman. *New Yorker*, 8 June 1968. Reprinted in *Review '68*, 73–75.

White, Steven F. "Translation and Teaching: The Dangers of Representing Latin America for Students in the United States." In Balderston and Schwartz, *Voice-Overs*, 235–44.

Williams, Raymond Leslie. "The Boom Twenty Years Later: An Interview with Mario Vargas Llosa." In Miller and Williams, "The Boom in Retrospect," 201–6.

———. Review of *The Post-Boom in Spanish American Fiction*, by Donald L. Shaw. *Hispania* 74 (March 2000): 74–75.

Wilson, Jason. Review of *In Search of Klingsor*, by Jorge Volpi, translated by Kristina Cordero. *Independent*, 24 May 2003.

Wood, Michael. "Master Among the Ruins." In "The Author as Plagiarist: The Case of Machado de Assis," edited by João Cezar de Castro Rocha, 293–303. Special issue, *Portuguese Literary and Cultural Series* (Massachusetts Center for Portuguese Studies and Culture, University of Dartmouth), no. 13/14 (2006).

Wright, James. Review of *The Heights of Macchu Picchu*, by Pablo Neruda, translated by Nathaniel Tarn. *Poetry*, June 1968. Reprinted in *Review '68*, 27–30.

Zamora, Lois Parkinson. *Writing the Apocalypse: Historical Vision in Contemporary U.S. and Latin American Fiction*. Cambridge: Cambridge University Press, 1989.

Expanded Bibliography of Translations

Abreu, Caio Fernando. *Dragons*. Translated by David Treece. London: Boulevard, 1990.

———. *Whatever Happened to Dulce Veiga? A B-Novel*. Translated by Adria Frizzi. Austin: University of Texas Press, 2000.

Amado, Jorge. *Captains of the Sands*. Translated by Gregory Rabassa. New York: Avon, 1988.

———. *Dona Flor and Her Two Husbands*. Translated by Harriet de Onís. New York: Knopf, 1969.

———. *Gabriela, Clove and Cinnamon*. Translated by James L. Taylor and William L. Grossman. New York: Knopf, 1962.

———. *Home Is the Sailor*. 1979. Translated by Harriet de Onís. New York: Knopf, 1964.

———. *Jubiabá*. Translated by Margaret A. Neves. New York: Avon, 1984.

———. *Sea of Death*. Translated by Gregory Rabassa. New York: Avon, 1984.

———. *Tent of Miracles*. Translated by Barbara Shelby. New York: Knopf, 1971.

———. *Tereza Batista: Home from the Wars*. Translated by Barbara Shelby. New York: Knopf, 1975.

———. *Tietá, the Goat Girl*. Translated by Barbara Shelby Merello. New York: Knopf, 1979.

———. *The Two Deaths of Quincas Wateryell*. Translated by Barbara Shelby. New York: Knopf, 1985.

Andrade, Mário de. *Hallucinated City*. Translated by Jack E. Tomlins. Nashville: Vanderbilt University Press, 1968.

———. *Macunaíma*. Translated by E. A. Goodland. New York: Random House, 1984.

Andrade, Oswald de. "Sentimental Memoirs of John Seaborn." Translated by Ralph Niebuhr and Albert Bork. *Texas Quarterly* 15, no. 4 (1972): 112–60. New York: Delacorte, 1973.

———. *Seraphim Grosse Pointe*. Translated by Kenneth D. Jackson and Albert Bork. Austin, Tex.: New Latin Quarter, 1979.

Asturias, Miguel Ángel. *The Eyes of the Interred*. Translated by Gregory Rabassa. New York: Delacorte, 1973.

———. *The Green Pope*. Translated by Gregory Rabassa. New York: Delacorte, 1971.

———. *Mulata*. Translated by Gregory Rabassa. New York: Delacorte, 1967.

———. *Strong Wind*. Translated by Gregory Rabassa. New York: Delacorte, 1968.

Borges, Jorge Luis. *Ficciones*. Edited by Anthony Kerrigan. Translated by Anthony Bonner. New York: Grove Press, 1962.

———. "Pierre Menard, Author of the *Quixote.*" Translated by James E. Irby. In *Labyrinths: Selected Writings and Other Stories by Jorge Luis Borges*, edited by Donald A. Yates and James E. Irby. New York: New Directions, 1962: 36–44.

Brandão, Ignácio de Loyola. *Zero.* Translated by Ellen Watson. New York: Avon, 1983.

Brossard, Nicole. *These Our Mothers; or, The Disintegrating Chapter.* Translated by Barbara Godard. Toronto: Coach House Press, 1983.

Cortázar, Julio. *Hopscotch.* Translated by Gregory Rabassa. New York: Pantheon, 1966.

Cunha, Euclides da. *Rebellion in the Backlands.* Translated by Samuel Putnam. Chicago: University of Chicago Press, 1944.

Cunha, Helena Parente. *Woman Between Mirrors.* Translated by Fred P. Ellison and Naomi Lindstrom. Austin: University of Texas Press, 1990.

Eco, Umberto. *The Name of the Rose.* Translated by William Weaver. London: Secker and Warburg, 1983.

Fagundes Telles, Lygia. *See* Telles, Lygia Fagundes.

Fonseca, Rubem. *Bufo & Spallanzani.* Translated by Clifford E. Landers. New York: Dutton, 1990.

———. "Happy New Year." Translated by Peter J. Schoenbach. *Literary Review* 27, no. 4 (Summer 1984): 430–36.

———. *High Art.* Translated by Ellen Watson. New York: Harper and Row, 1986.

———. "Large Intestine." Translated by Elizabeth Lowe. *Review* 76, no. 8 (Fall 1976): 69–75.

———. *The Lost Manuscript.* Translated by Clifford E. Landers. London: Bloomsbury, 1997.

Franco, Jorge. *Rosario Tijeras.* Translated by Gregory Rabassa. New York: Seven Stories Press, 2004.

Fuentes, Carlos. *A Change of Skin.* Translated by Sam Hileman. New York: Farrar, Straus and Giroux, 1968.

———. *The Death of Artemio Cruz.* Translated by Sam Hileman. New York: Farrar, Straus, 1964.

———. *The Death of Artemio Cruz.* Translated by Alfred Mac Adam. New York: Noonday Press / Farrar, Straus and Giroux, 1991.

———. *The Hydra Head.* Translated by Margaret Sayers Peden. New York: Farrar, Straus and Giroux, 1978.

———. *The Old Gringo.* Translated by Margaret Sayers Peden. New York: Farrar, Straus and Giroux, 1985.

———. *Where the Air Is Clear.* Translated by Sam Hileman. New York: I. Obolensky, 1960.

Fuguet, Alberto. *Bad Vibes.* Translated by Kristina Cordero. New York: St. Martin's Press, 1997.

———. *The Movies of My Life.* Translated by Ezra E. Fitz. New York: HarperCollins, 2003.

————. *Shorts: Stories.* Translated by Ezra E. Fitz. New York: HarperCollins, 2005.

García Márquez, Gabriel. *Leaf Storm, and Other Stories.* Translated by Gregory Rabassa. New York: Harper and Row, 1972.

————. *One Hundred Years of Solitude.* Translated by Gregory Rabassa. New York: Knopf, 1970.

Giudice, Victor. "The File Cabinet." Translated by Elizabeth Lowe. *Translation* 5 (Spring 1978): 84–86.

Guimarães Rosa, João. *See* Rosa, João Guimarães.

Lezama Lima, José. *Paradiso.* Translated by Gregory Rabassa. New York: Farrar, Straus and Giroux, 1974.

Lins, Osman. *Avalovara.* Translated by Gregory Rabassa. New York: Random House, 1979.

————. *The Queen of the Prisons of Greece.* Translated by Adria Frizzi. Normal, Ill.: Dalkey Archive Press, 1995.

Lispector, Clarice. *The Apple in the Dark.* Translated by Gregory Rabassa. New York: Knopf, 1967.

————. *Near to the Wild Heart.* Translated by Giovanni Pontiero. New York: New Directions, 1990.

————. *The Passion according to G. H.* Translated by Ronald W. Sousa. Minneapolis: University of Minnesota Press, 1988.

————. *The Stream of Life.* Translated by Elizabeth Lowe and Earl Fitz. Foreword by Hélène Cixous. Minneapolis: University of Minnesota Press, 1989.

Machado de Assis, Joaquim Maria. *Dom Casmurro.* Translated by John Gledson. New York: Oxford University Press, 1997.

————. *Epitaph of a Small Winner.* Translated by William L. Grossman. New York: Farrar, Straus and Giroux, 1952.

————. *The Posthumous Memoirs of Brás Cubas.* Translated by Gregory Rabassa. New York: Oxford University Press, 1997.

————. *Quincas Borba.* Translated by Gregory Rabassa. New York: Oxford University Press, 1998.

Molloy, Sylvia. *Certificate of Absence.* Translated by Daniel Balderston. Austin: University of Texas Press, 1989.

Mutis, Álvaro. *The Adventures and Misadventures of Maqroll.* Translated by Edith Grossman. New York: New York Review of Books, 2002.

Neruda, Pablo. *Canto General.* Translated by Jack Schmitt. Berkeley and Los Angeles: University of California Press, 1991.

————. *The Heights of Macchu Picchu.* Translated by Nathaniel Tarn. New York: Farrar, Straus and Giroux, 1967.

Paz, Octavio. *The Labyrinth of Solitude.* Translated by Lysander Kemp. New York: Grove Press, 1961.

Paz Soldán, Edmundo. *Turing's Delirium.* Translated by Lisa Carter. Boston: Houghton Mifflin, 2006.

Piñon, Nélida. *The Republic of Dreams*. Translated by Helen Lane. New York: Knopf, 1989.

Puig, Manuel. *Betrayed by Rita Hayworth*. Translated by Suzanne Jill Levine. New York: Dutton, 1971.

———. *Heartbreak Tango*. Translated by Suzanne Jill Levine. New York: Dutton, 1973.

———. *Kiss of the Spider Woman*. Translated by Thomas Colchie. New York: Knopf, 1979.

Rheda, Regina. *First World Third Class, and Other Tales of the Global Mix*. Translated by Adria Frizzi, R. E. Young, David Coles, and Charles A. Perrone. Austin: University of Texas Press, 2005.

Ribeiro, Darcy. *The Brazilian People: The Formation and Meaning of Brazil*. Translated by Gregory Rabassa. Foreword by Elizabeth Lowe. Gainesville: University Press of Florida, 2000.

———. *Maíra*. Translated by E. H. Goodland and Thomas Colchie. New York: Vintage, 1984.

Rosa, João Guimarães. *The Devil to Pay in the Backlands*. Translated by James L. Taylor and Harriet de Onís. New York: Knopf, 1963.

Rubião, Murilo. *The Ex-Magician, and Other Stories*. Translated by Thomas Colchie. New York: Harper and Row, 1979.

Rulfo, Juan. *Pedro Páramo*. Translated by Margaret Sayers Peden. New York: Grove Press, 1994.

Sarduy, Severo. *Cobra*. Translated by Suzanne Jill Levine. New York: Dutton, 1975.

Sclair, Moacyr. *The Carnival of the Animals*. Translated by Eloah F. Giacomelli. New York: Ballantine, 1985.

———. *The Centaur in the Garden*. Translated by Margaret A. Neves. New York: Avon, 1985.

———. *The Collected Stories of Moacyr Scliar*. Translated by Eloah F. Giacomelli. Albuquerque: University of New Mexico Press, 1999.

———. *Max and the Cats*. Translated by Eloah F. Giacomelli. New York: Ballantine, 1990.

Telles, Lygia Fagundes. "Before the Green Dance." Translated by Leland Guyer. *Literary Review* 38, no. 4 (Summer 1995): 634–41.

———. *The Girl in the Photograph*. Translated by Margaret A. Neves. New York: Avon, 1982.

———. "Just a Saxophone." Translated by Eloah F. Giacomelli. *Literary Review* 21, no. 2 (Winter 1978): 225–33.

———. *The Marble Dance*. Translated by Margaret A. Neves. New York: Avon, 1986.

———. *Tigrela, and Other Stories*. Translated by Margaret A. Neves. New York: Avon, 1986.

Trevisan, Dalton. *The Vampire of Curitiba, and Other Stories*. Translated by Gregory Rabassa. New York: Knopf, 1972.

Valenzuela, Luisa. *The Lizard's Tail*. Translated by Gregory Rabassa. New York: Farrar, Straus and Giroux, 1983.

Vallejo, César. *The Black Heralds*. Translated by Rebecca Seiferle. Port Townsend, Wash.: Copper Canyon Press, 2003.

Vargas Llosa, Mario. *Conversation in The Cathedral*. Translated by Gregory Rabassa. New York: Harper and Row, 1975.

———. *The Green House*. Translated by Gregory Rabassa. New York: Harper and Row, 1968.

———. *The War of the End of the World*. Translated by Helen R. Lane. New York: Farrar, Straus and Giroux, 1984.

Volpi, Jorge. *In Search of Klingsor*. Translated by Kristina Cordero. New York: Scribner, 2002.

Index

Elizabeth Lowe is associate director and associate scholar in the Center for Latin American Studies at the University of Florida, were she was also the founder and director of the Translation Studies Certificate Program. Author of *The City in Brazilian Literature* (1982) and numerous publications on Latin American literature and culture, Lowe has translated Clarice Lispector, Machado de Assis, Darcy Ribeiro, Rubem Fonseca, and others.

Earl E. Fitz is professor of Portuguese, Spanish, and comparative literature at Vanderbilt University, where he was also the director of the Program in Comparative Literature. Author of *Rediscovering the New World: Inter-American Literature in a Comparative Context* (1991) and numerous other works on inter-American literature, Fitz has translated Lispector and has written widely on Latin American literature, comparative literature, and inter-American literary relations.

Lowe and Fitz are cotranslators of Lispector's *Água viva* (*The Stream of Life*, 1989).

Ilan Stavans is Lewis-Sebring Professor in Latin American and Latino Culture and Five College 40th Anniversary Professor at Amherst College. His books include *The Hispanic Condition* (1995), *The Riddle of Cantinflas* (1997), *On Borrowed Words* (2001), *Spanglish* (2003), *Dictionary Days* (2005), and *The Disappearance* (2006). His oeuvre has been translated into a dozen languages.